The London & North Eastern Railway

THE
LONDON & NORTH
EASTERN
RAILWAY

Cecil J. Allen

F.R.S.A., M.Inst.T., A.I.Loco.E.

LONDON

IAN ALLAN

Published by Ian Allan Ltd., Shepperton, Surrey
and printed in the United Kingdom by
The Press at Coombelands Ltd., Addlestone, Weybridge, Surrey

CONTENTS

Chapter		Page
I	The Aftermath of War	9
II	The Constituent Companies:	
	1 The Great Northern	16
	2 The Great Central	17
	3 The Great Eastern	19
	4 The North Eastern	21
	5 The Hull and Barnsley	23
	6 The North British	25
	7 The Great North of Scotland	27
	8 The Joint Railways	28
III	The East Coast Joint Service	34
IV	The New Company—Its Formation	38
V	The New Company—Its Chairman	48
VI	The New Company—Its Chief General Manager ...	54
VII	The New Company—Its Name	62
VIII	The New Company—Its Organisation	65
IX	The Way Ahead—1923–1925	69
X	1926 and the General Strike	75
XI	The Years of Depression—1927–1933	77
XII	The Years of Fulfilment—1934–1939	83
XIII	War and the Last Phase—1940–1947	89
XIV	The "Way and Works"	93
XV	Pre-Grouping Locomotives	103
XVI	The First Locomotive Years—1923–1924	113
XVII	Locomotive Developments under Gresley—1924–1934	119
XVIII	Gresley's Final Years—1935–1941	131
XIX	Thompson and Peppercorn Locomotives—1941–1947	139
XX	L.N.E.R. Locomotives at Work	150
XXI	Electrification	175
XXII	The Evolution of Coaching Stock — 1923–1947 ...	178
XXIII	The Evolution of Wagon Stock — 1923–1947 ...	190
XXIV	Passenger Train Services — 1923–1947	195
XXV	Maritime Interests	205
XXVI	The Chief Officers—1923–1947	214

Tables

No.   *Page*

1. Capital Issued by L.N.E.R. Constituent Cos. to 1922 ... 31
2. Dividends Paid by L.N.E.R. Constituent Cos., 1900–1922 31
3. Gross Receipts & Expenditure in 1922 32
4. Number of Passengers Conveyed & Season Tickets, 1922 32
5. Freight Tonnage & Live Stock Carried, 1922 32
6. Mileage, Rolling Stock & Staff, 1922 33
7. Capital Structure, L.N.E.R., January, 1923 42
8. Whitelaw's Proposals for Proportions of L.N.E.R. Directorate 46
9. Reduction in L.N.E.R. Mileage & Rolling Stock, 1923–1947 91
10. Steam Locomotives Brought into L.N.E.R. Stock, 1923 ... 110
11. Reduction in L.N.E.R. Steam Locomotive Stock, 1923–1947 147
12. Locomotives of L.N.E.R. & Constituent Cos., being Preserved 148

Locomotive Performances

13. N.E.R. Class R 4–4–0, Darlington—York 151
14. G.E.R. "Claud Hamilton" 4–4–0, North Walsham—Liverpool St. 152
15. G.E.R. "1500" (Cl. B12) 4–6–0, Liverpool St.—Parkeston Quay 153
16. G.C.R. Robinson 4–4–2 (Cl. C4), Marylebone—Leicester 154
17. G.C.R. "Director" 4–4–0 (Cl. D11), Marylebone—Leicester 155
18. N.B.R. Reid 4–4–2, Aberdeen—Dundee 157
19. N.E.R. Raven Class Z (Cl. C7), Grantham—Darlington ... 158
20. G.N.R. Ivatt Atlantic (Cl. C1), King's Cross—Peterborough 159
21. G.N.R. Ivatt Atlantic (Cl. C1), Grantham—York ... 160
22. L.N.E.R. Gresley (Cl. A1) 4–6–2, King's Cross—York ... 162
23. L.N.E.R. Gresley (Cl. A3) 4–6–2, Doncaster—King's Cross 164
24. L.N.E.R. Gresley (Cl. A4) 4–6–2, King's Cross—York ... 166
25. L.N.E.R. Gresley (Cl. V2) 2–6–2, Doncaster—King's Cross 168
26. L.N.E.R. Gresley (Cl. B17) 4–6–0, Leicester—Marylebone 170
27. L.N.E.R. Thompson (Cl. B1) 4–6–0, Leicester—Marylebone 171
28. L.N.E.R. Peppercorn (Cl. A2) 4–6–2, Aberdeen—Dundee 172
29. L.N.E.R. Peppercorn (Cl. A1) 4–6–2, York—King's Cross 173
30. L.N.E.R. Ocean-going Steamers 212

AUTHOR'S PREFACE

It was with a certain feeling of apprehension that many of us who were in the service of the lesser railways of the London & North Eastern group faced what seemed to us might be a doubtful future after we had been swallowed up by the larger company. By that date I myself had served the Great Eastern Railway for 14 years; the G.E.R. was not a wealthy concern, particularly as compared with the North Eastern, but it had developed a personality of which Great Eastern men were proud, and our happy family was now to lose its identity. Moreover, under the General Managership of Sir Henry Thornton, the American, we had had better financial treatment than ever previously.

But there need not have been any fears. We of the rank-and-file knew little of the complicated negotiations, not entirely free from jealousy and intrigue in the higher administrative circles, which, as related in this book, preceded the fusion of six railways and the difficult settling-down period that followed; in the lower echelons of the service things went on much as before. And then, as gradually we accustomed ourselves to the new title, London & North Eastern Railway, to seeing the letters "L.N.E.R." broadcast over rolling stock, stations, posters and everything else, and to the appearance of all our locomotives and coaches in the new standard colours, the fact began to dawn that we were now part and parcel of something big, indeed, of a company that was beginning to establish a reputation greater than anything we had known before.

To that reputation, needless to say, the chief rival, as in the days long past of the East and West Coast Routes, was the London Midland & Scottish Railway, and every new record that left the L.M.S.R. behind was something to stir the pulses. In 1928, for example, there was the 393-mile non-stop run of the "Flying Scotsman" that beat by 92 miles the longest daily L.M.S.R. break; in 1937 there followed the regular 6-hour flight of the "Coronation" streamliner over the same course that had the advantage by no less than 30 minutes over the competing L.M.S.R. "Coronation Scot" between Euston and Glasgow; in 1938 the immortal 126 m.p.h. feat of the Gresley locomotive *Mallard* had put completely in the shade the 114 m.p.h. of Stanier's L.M.S.R. *Coronation* in the previous year. Then there were the L.N.E.R. streamline trains themselves, setting standards of comfort and *décor* never previously attained in Great Britain, or, for that matter, even equalled and much less beaten in later years. In these and many other ways we eventually felt that the L.N.E.R., in those halcyon years just before the 1939-45 war, was a company to which we were proud to belong.

This book attempts to translate those feelings into print. Whilst I myself have enjoyed recounting the technical and operating achievements—the "Way and Works", locomotives and rolling stock, train services, marine activities and so on—this book would have fallen far short of completeness had I not had the invaluable co-operation of Edward G. Marsden, who comes of North Eastern stock, and through much of the memorable 1930 decade was on the staff of the Chief General Manager at King's Cross, subsequently serving with the Railway Companies' Association and becoming Secretary to the Railway Executive. To him I am indebted for much information relative to the formation of the Company, its administration and financial problems, and the personalities involved. Warm acknowledgement is also due to Mr. O. V. S. Bulleid, Mr. B. Spencer and Mr. E. D. Trask, who with their wide knowledge and experience have helped at long last to solve the mystery as to how the historic locomotive exchange of 1925 between the London & North Eastern and Great Western Railways actually came about. Finally, I have to acknowledge the courtesy of the Public Relations and Publicity Officers of the Eastern and North Eastern Railways for the loan of a number of the photographs which have been included. I can only hope that readers will find in this volume an adequate survey of a truly great enterprise.

CECIL J. ALLEN

I

The Aftermath of War

IT WAS on 1st January, 1923, that the London & North Eastern Railway, second largest of the railway companies created by the amalgamation of existing companies under the provisions of the Railways Act, 1921, came into being. Born out of the ashes of conflict of one world war, its active and independent existence continued until September, 1939, when a second world conflagration engulfed the nation, and the dead hand of Government control once again extended itself over the railway network of Great Britain. Moreover this grip was not relaxed until the four group railways, after an existence of precisely a quarter of a century, lost their identity by being swallowed up in nationalisation.

Fully to appreciate the significance of the changes in the railway economy brought about by the 1921 Act, it is necessary briefly to review the historical events which led up to the passing of this Act. On the outbreak of the First World War, in August, 1914, the Government took control of the railways of the country and their ancillary services, vesting this control in a committee of General Managers known as the Railway Executive Committee. The procedure adopted for this step was slightly archaic. An Order in Council, made in pursuance of Section 16 of the Regulation of the Forces Act, 1871, declared that an emergency had arisen, and the President of the Board of Trade, acting under a warrant issued and renewed each week, thereupon took and retained possession of all the principal lines. In effect there was little, if any, interference by the Government with the work of this Committee, which under the distinguished chairmanship of Sir Herbert Walker, General Manager of the London & South Western Railway, proved itself a most competent and effective instrument of management.

Its work was reported upon in the following terms by the Select Committee on Transport appointed by the House of Commons in 1918:

"The success that has attended the operation of the railways throughout the war, which has been superior to that witnessed in any other of the belligerent countries, affords conclusive proof, both of the adequacy of the arrangements which have been made in advance, and of the capacity of those who have been concerned with their execution. There has been little dislocation notwithstanding that, in addition to a very large Government traffic, the volume of civilian traffic, both of passengers and goods, has been heavier than in pre-war days, that large numbers of the staffs have been inexperienced, and that considerable demands have been made upon the railways for rolling stock and materials of all kinds for use with the armies abroad".

This same Select Committee also expressed certain views as to the future organisation of transport in Great Britain. These far-reaching proposals were as follows:

"Your Committee considers:

1. That the organisation of the transport agencies of the country—and particularly of the railways—cannot be allowed to return to its pre-war position.

2. That the temporary arrangements for the control of railways and canals during the war would not be satisfactory as a permanent settlement.

3. That unification of the railway system is desirable under certain safeguards, whether the ownership be in public or private hands."

After considering this report, the Government of the day decided to create a Ministry of Transport, charged with the control and development of transport in Great Britain, to which the existing powers of Government Departments would be transferred, and on which extensive new powers would be conferred. Effect was given to this decision by the Ministry of Transport Act, 1919.

The Prime Minister's choice for the new Minister of Transport was Sir Eric Geddes, who after experience in the United States and India had joined the North Eastern Railway in 1904, and had risen rapidly to become Deputy General Manager of that company in 1911. Soon after the outbreak of war Lloyd George, who had become Minister of Munitions, picked on Geddes to become Deputy Director General for Munitions Supply. This was after the North Eastern Railway Board, in May, 1915, had offered the services of Geddes to the Government, explaining that the duties of management of the N.E.R. were divided between the General Manager and the Deputy General Manager, and that under the wartime control of the Railway Executive Committee, of which the General Manager (Sir Alexander Butterworth) was a member, for the time being the duties of the Deputy General Manager were largely in abeyance. In these circumstances the directors felt it right to place the latter's services at the disposal of the Government. In the letter conveying this offer there followed a paragraph of great significance:

"A few years ago the North Eastern Board made very special arrangements with Mr. Geddes, by which his services were retained to the North Eastern Railway with a view to his succeeding the present General Manager. But for this there is no doubt he would before now have been Manager of a large Railway Company".

The fact was that Eric Campbell Geddes was an ebullient personality possessed of great driving power, an incisive brain, and the capacity fully to utilise the brain-work of the brilliant men whom he always gathered round him. Of him Lloyd George wrote in his *War Memoirs*:

"He had the make of their powerful locomotives. That is the impression he gave me when one morning he rolled into my room. He struck me immediately as a man of exceptional force and capacity. I knew that he was a find, and I was grateful to Lord Knaresborough, the Chairman of the Company, for offering to release him during the period of the war. He turned out to be one of the most remarkable men which the State called to its aid in this anxious hour for Britain and her Empire." Geddes was then 39 years of age, and the relevance of his life story to the present history will be apparent a little later.

His rise in Government service was as rapid as it had been on the North Eastern Railway. By October, 1916, he had become Director-General, Military Railways, War Office, and then the first Inspector-General of Transportation in France, with the rank of Major-General. He was "mentioned in dispatches" by the Commander-in-Chief, Sir Douglas Haig, who, normally undemonstrative, wrote him an unusually cordial letter of appreciation of his services when he relinquished this appointment, in May, 1917, to become First Lord of the Admiralty. Next came a brief period when Geddes was put in charge of the demobilisation section of the War Cabinet, and then, towards the close of 1918, Lloyd George wrote him (with a Ministerial split infinitive!) in the following terms:

"After that work"—the demobilisation of the Fleet—"has been accomplished, I hope that the Government may be able to still have your services for the organisation of the immense questions of transportation and its development, which I am convinced will so vitally affect the welfare and prosperity of the nation". In short, Geddes was being invited to become Minister of Transport, with a seat in the Cabinet.

Now here a hurdle of substantial dimensions had to be overcome. It was as an emergency arrangement only that the North Eastern Railway Board had loaned Geddes to the Government, and they felt it entirely wrong that the question as to who should become their next General Manager should thus be left in the air, for as already mentioned their memorandum offering the services of Geddes to the Government had made it clear that by the special arrangements they had made he was in the direct succession for this post. It was regarded, very properly, that it would be impossible for Geddes to undertake the duties of Minister of Transport and still to remain in the service of the N.E.R., and that a clean cut of this connection must therefore be made. After a brief negotiation between Lord Knaresborough, Chairman of the Company, and Sir Eric, a compromise was amicably agreed whereby the latter would sever his North Eastern connection, abrogating his agreement with the Company, in consideration of the payment of £50,000. When news of this very substantial "golden handshake" leaked out, there was widespread comment, particularly from shareholders, culminating in questions in the House of Commons.

However, the directors undoubtedly had acted for the best. They insisted that the Prime Minister should be fully informed both of the reasons why the Board considered this to be the only satisfactory solution of the difficulty, and also of the nature and terms of the agreement made.

Sir Eric Geddes duly advised Lloyd George, who on 30th December, 1918, replied as follows:

"My dear Geddes,

I have received your letter of to-day.

The arrangement you have made with the Directors appears to me to be no bar to your serving the Government as Minister in charge of Transportation questions, as it is clear that all connection with the North Eastern Railway is severed before you take any part in the consideration of such matters.

I appreciate the action of the Board of the North-Eastern Railway in arranging to give you for the service of the State.

Yours sincerely,

D. Lloyd George."

The way was thus made clear for Sir Eric to enter his new duties as the first Minister of Transport in this country, which he did immediately the Bill become law.

Two points are to be noted here. Geddes was not chosen to be Minister primarily because he had been a railwayman, but rather because of the ability with which he had carried out the diverse assignments which had fallen to his lot during the war years. The pertinence to this history of his railway connection is that had he remained in N.E.R. service after the war it is more than likely that he would have become the first Chief General Manager of the London & North Eastern Railway, and we can but wonder how differently history might have been written had that happened. The second point is that the new Ministry was not intended to become merely a Ministry of Railways; its remit related to all forms of transport. But although it came into being at the time when road transport was becoming seriously competitive with the railways, for nearly ten years afterwards little or no attention was given by the Ministry to this emergent type of transport. Only then, after persistent agitation by the railways, as we shall see later, were some steps taken to regulate transport on the roads. Had Sir Eric remained as Minister it is probable that something substantial would have been done in this direction, and at a much earlier date.

In 1919, however, immediate preoccupation with the railways was required of the new Ministry. The Ministry of Transport Act continued the wartime Government control of the railways for a period of two years, during which the Ministry was charged with formulating proposals for their future organisation. At first there was every indication that Geddes intended to run the railways from Whitehall, and appointments were made to the Ministry staff which could only have been justified on this assumption. But in the country there was strenuous opposition to this policy, both by the railways and by trade and industry, and it was soon abandoned in favour of a plan to amalgamate the railways into "groups". When this became known, there was a hurried exodus from the Ministry of railwaymen who had taken up positions there, both during the war and later, and in the fullness of time some of these men were appointed to responsible posts on the amalgamated lines.

The task of preparing an acceptable scheme for the grouping involved the Ministry in protracted and intricate negotiations with the railways, conducted through the Railway Companies' Association, and with representative bodies of traders. An early proposal to form the railways of Scotland into an independent group might have appealed to nationalistic feelings were it not that the canny Scots realised that they would be considerably better off financially with a finger on the purse-strings of the wealthier English companies. Eventually agreement was reached, and the Railways Act, 1921, became inscribed in the Statute Book.

But the passage of the Bill through Parliament was far from easy. There was strong opposition to many of its clauses, including the amalgamation provisions. One of its most prominent opponents was Sir Frederick Banbury, Chairman of the Great Northern Railway and Member of Parliament for the City of London. So persistent and determined was his opposition that most people forecast that he would not be prepared subsequently to take any part in the direction of the London & North Eastern Railway. True to his convictions, he did not become a director of the L.N.E.R., but under the next Government, in 1924, he was solaced by elevation to the peerage as Lord Banbury of Southam.

As well as ordering the future shape of the country's railway system, the Railways Act, 1921, embodied important provisions for paying compensation to the companies in respect of arrears of maintenance of both rolling stock and way and works, and also of abnormal increases in working expenses due to standardisation of the staff's conditions of service during the period of Government control. It also provided for the establishment of Central and National Wages Boards; for the regulation of light railways; for the compilation of statistics; and, not least, for the establishment of the Railway Rates Tribunal and the complete revision of railway rates and charges. These last provisions were based on the proposals of the Rates Advisory Committee, and undoubtedly were influenced by the thinking of Sir William Acworth and his doctrinaire colleagues at the London School of Economics.

They would have been suitable enough, say, in the last decade of the previous century, but they were outmoded by the time they reached the Statute Book in the commercial conditions of 1921. Hindsight is easy; foresight—particularly in the economic sphere—is desperately rare. It is not surprising, therefore, that the scheme as envisaged was never fully implemented, while its formulation cost the amalgamated companies many years of hard work, during which progress in the field of competition largely stagnated, and the road hauliers were able firmly to establish themselves. Until now British Governments have always shown themselves unwilling to give the railways, national asset that they have always been, the same freedom to act commercially as that enjoyed, say, by the local undertaker; yet transportation is the vital service rendered by both.

To revert to the amalgamation proposals, the first schedule to the Act set out the "Constituent" and the "Subsidiary" railway companies that were to form each group. Before 1st January, 1923, the constituent companies might submit to the Minister of Transport an agreed scheme of amalgamation, and the amalgamated groups might submit schemes for the absorption of the subsidiary companies. Failing agreement, the proposals were to be settled by the Amalgamation Tribunal set up under the Act. Under the heading "North Eastern, Eastern and East Scottish Group" the schedule listed the following companies which were to be amalgamated and absorbed, and from the beginning of 1923 to form the London & North Eastern Railway:

Constituent Companies

Great Northern; Great Central; Great Eastern; North Eastern; Hull & Barnsley; North British; and Great North of Scotland; actually the Hull & Barnsley amalgamated with the N.E.R. in 1922, between the passing of the Act and the formation of the L.N.E.R.

Subsidiary Companies

Brackenhill Light; Colne Valley & Halstead; East & West Yorkshire Union; East Lincolnshire; Edinburgh & Bathgate; Forcett; Forth & Clyde Junction; Gifford & Garvald; Great North of England; Clarence & Hartlepool Junction; Horncastle; Humber Commercial Railway & Dock; Kilsyth & Bonnybridge; Lauder Light; London & Blackwall; Mansfield; Mid-Suffolk Light; Newburgh & New Fife; North Lindsey Light; Nottingham & Grantham Railway & Canal; Nottingham Joint Station Committee; Nottingham Suburban; Seaforth & Sefton Junction; Sheffield District; South Yorkshire Junction; Stamford & Essendine; and West Riding Railway Committee. The vast majority of these lines had been built under independent auspices, and still had retained their identity so far as finance was concerned, but had been worked for so long by the major railways that few other than those intimately concerned would have realised that they were not integral parts of the companies that operated them.

Finally, there were the railways owned jointly with constituent companies of the London Midland & Scottish group, of which the largest and most important were the Cheshire Lines Committee and the Midland & Great Northern Joint Railway. These, subject to special financial arrangements, now became the joint property of the London & North Eastern and London Midland & Scottish Railways.

In the succeeding chapters we have to look first at the constituent companies, which had a good many features in common, though the accident of geography had induced certain differences in outlook. The three English "Greats"—Great Northern, Great Central and Great Eastern—with the North British, were strongly competitive, as compared with the more aloof attitude of the North Eastern and Great North of Scotland, which enjoyed a virtual monopoly in the territories they served. All, other than the Great Northern, owed much to their links with sea-borne traffic, though even the G.N.R. enjoyed some share in the

Grimsby traffic and had its own small wharf at Boston. The G.E., G.C., N.E. and N.B. were port and dock owners on a substantial scale, and directly or indirectly were steamship owners of some standing. All the companies had excellent stocks of locomotives designed to suit their particular needs, and their coaching stock for main line services in general was of a high standard. Main line passenger services by 1922 had recovered from the strain of war, and on the whole were well planned and efficiently operated, and freight services, especially those for the carriage of coal, were satisfying the needs of trade and industry in their time.

Each company, of course, had its own special characteristics, and the silhouettes that follow may help the reader to understand the problems that were to be thrown up, not only in the process of agreeing the terms of amalgamation, but also subsequently. For, just as a nation is made up of the men and women living within its geographical bounds, so an industrial undertaking, and particularly a railway, is what it is by reason of the outlook and the energies of those who manage and staff it, and these qualities are formed and tempered by their environment, training and experience.

II

The Constituent Companies

1. THE GREAT NORTHERN RAILWAY

A COMPARATIVE newcomer to the galaxy of principal British railways, the G.N.R. did not receive the Royal Assent to the Act authorising its construction until 1846, and then only after bitter battles in the commercial, legal and Parliamentary fields. Very likely this quarrelsome beginning influenced the mentality of the infant, for this company was always a litigious one. It was laid out as a single operation, a trunk route all the way from London to Yorkshire, and was opened for traffic in August, 1850, except for King's Cross terminus, which was not ready to receive trains until October, 1852. At first its connection with the North Eastern Railway had to be made by using Lancashire & Yorkshire tracks from Shaftholme Junction, 4½ miles north of Doncaster, to Knottingley; not until 1871 did the North Eastern Railway complete the direct line from Shaftholme to York, essential link in the East Coast Route from London to Scotland.

A comment on the Great Northern by W. J. Gordon in his book *Our Home Railways* was that "It was built for speed and it has been used for speed". Notwithstanding its longer route, it even put up a spirited competition with the London & North Western and Midland Railways for the passenger traffic between London and Manchester, exercising running powers over the Manchester, Sheffield & Lincolnshire Railway from Retford to Manchester until after that company had transformed itself into the Great Central and built its own extension to London. With the Midland it competed strongly for the traffic between London and Leeds, Bradford and other West Riding towns, and, perhaps the most important of all, in conjunction with its North Eastern and North British partners it formed part of the East Coast Route, in equally strong rivalry with the West Coast Route of the London & North Western and Caledonian Companies on the other side of the country. Sometimes it was felt that this concentration by the Great Northern on its long-distance business was at the expense of towns of lesser importance on its main line, for which the service provided was mediocre, though possibly adequate at the time. Great Northern competition was not only in the passenger sphere; its fast freight trains between London and Manchester, the West Riding of Yorkshire and Scotland, in which it was a pioneer, gave admirable service to traders.

With two notable exceptions, King's Cross in London and Victoria in Nottingham (though the latter was built as a joint enterprise with the Great Central), the Great Northern had nothing much to boast about in its stations; indeed, on one occasion its Chairman, Sir Frederick Banbury, was heard to remark "There is no money in stations". Even King's Cross, behind its graceful frontage, had internal arrangements which by the end of G.N.R. history had been allowed to fall behind current standards, and it was not until L.N.E.R. days that any serious attempt was made to improve and modernise its amenities. By contrast, Great Northern hotels and train catering were of a high standard; as to the latter, it is worth recalling that the G.N.R., in 1879, was the first railway in the country to run a dining car in one of its trains. One distinctive feature of the Great Northern scene was its "somersault" signals, copied elsewhere in the country only by one or two of the minor railways in South Wales.

In Sir Frederick Banbury the Great Northern had a Chairman of strong personality who was not afraid to nail his colours to the mast on any issue on which he considered that he was in the right, as in his opposition in Parliament in 1921 to the Railways Bill, described in Chapter I. Charles Hastings Dent, the last Great Northern General Manager, was one of the rare mechanical engineers who have attained the highest administrative post on a British railway; he started his railway career as a pupil at Crewe of the redoubtable F. W. Webb, and had been General Manager of the Great Southern & Western Railway of Ireland from 1903 until coming to the G.N.R. as General Manager ten years later. Though conservative in outlook, the management of the company did not hesitate to experiment with several changes in railway organisation which had largely been inspired from across the Atlantic, though soon reverting to the older departmental form of organisation more generally favoured in this country.

2. THE GREAT CENTRAL RAILWAY

Until the close of the Nineteenth Century a provincial line, the former Manchester, Sheffield & Lincolnshire Railway had pursued a power-politics course in its relations with the trunk lines which connected it with the Metropolis. In this game the "railway flirt", as it became known, had tended to overplay its hand, and thereby had caused these railways to develop towards it an attitude of wariness and reserve. This was certainly justified when, under the powerful influence of Sir Edward Watkin, who was not only its Chairman but also that of the Metropolitan and South Eastern Railways and had an interest in the Channel Tunnel Company, the Great Central, as the M.S.L.R. now became, pushed southwards through the shires to London to a new terminus at Marylebone, opened in 1899. The vision of Watkins extended to a through rail route from Manchester to Paris. This effort exhausted the company financially, and the completion in 1912 of a great new dock on the Humber at Immingham, near Grimsby, at a cost of £2,600,000, though an earnest of the Great Central's faith in its future and thus a courageous venture, for the time being worsened the financial position still further.

The build-up of traffic on the London Extension was slower than had been hoped; it is by no means easy, even with the most lavish inducements, to get regular travellers to change their habits. To begin with, the G.C.R. seemed slightly doubtful as to the pattern its principal passenger services should follow. It even tried running through trains between Marylebone and both York and Leeds, but could not compete in time with the old-established competitors, and these experiments were soon abandoned. In the end, the main line trains from London were concentrated on Bradford and Manchester, giving *en route* an excellent service to and from Leicester, Nottingham and Sheffield, which certainly attracted a fair amount of patronage. The link with the Great Western Railway between Woodford and Banbury also was used to develop through services between North-Eastern England, Lancashire and Yorkshire and the South Coast, the West of England and South Wales.

Smart timings, punctual operation, comfortable rolling stock and ample restaurant car facilities, were all assets to the G.C.R. services. But the Great Central was always a restless neighbour; schemes of penetration and even further extension were often being hatched, and its traffic canvassing activities were extremely keen. Its chief handicap was the circuitous character of its routes to London from Manchester, to the west, and Grimsby and Immingham, to the east, which resulted in much freight traffic from these points being carried by the more direct routes of other companies.

In Lord Faringdon, better known to an earlier generation as Sir Alexander Henderson, the company had a Chairman who was widely recognised as an able financier and man of business. But the chief drive came from the bearded and dapper Sam Fay, General Manager from 1902 to the end of G.C.R. history in 1922. Like knights of old, he had the honour of knighthood conferred on him on the field of achievement, by the spontaneous act of King George V at the opening of Immingham Dock in July, 1912, the King borrowing a sword from his Naval Equerry to bestow the *accolade*. During the 1914-1918 war Sir Sam Fay served as Director of Movements at the War Office, though persistently refusing any military rank or uniform; later he regaled the public with an account of his experiences in a book with the slightly sardonic title of *The War Office at War*. Had he survived to the present day, he would have been most distressed at the proliferation of accountants in high places; he was once heard to remark that "accountants are backward-looking folk, studying what has happened; the boss man should have his eyes firmly fixed on what lies ahead". This declaration well describes the attitude of a man who had plenty of courage and vision, but was unable to overcome the odds against him sufficiently to set the Great Central Railway on its financial feet.

3. THE GREAT EASTERN RAILWAY

Like many English county families, the Great Eastern Railway was far from being wealthy, but it could claim quite a few aristocratic attributes. It served the Royal estate at Sandringham in Norfolk, which called for the frequent provision of Royal trains, and doubtless had some influence in the choice of Royal blue for the livery of its passenger locomotives. If the North Eastern Railway could boast, among its directors and officers, a future Foreign Minister and Minister of Transport, the Great Eastern could go even further, in that one of its Chairmen, the Marquess of Salisbury, became the Prime Minister of Great Britain and Ireland. Up to the close of the Great Eastern's independent history, also, it was a fine old aristocrat, Lord Claud Hamilton, then approaching his 80th year, who was still its Chairman.

The G.E.R. had strong links with the Episcopacy, serving as it did the cathedral cities of Ely, Peterborough, Norwich, Lincoln, and Bury St. Edmunds, joined in later years by Chelmsford; bishops and deans were almost as plentiful at Liverpool Street as at Paddington. So also were dons, in view of its service of the university town of Cambridge. Architecture played a part in its reputation, as, for example, the fine station frontages at Bury St. Edmunds and Stowmarket. On a more mundane, or, should we say, maritime level, the Great Eastern steamer services between Harwich and Continental ports had a high reputation all over Northern Europe; its hotels and its restaurant car catering also won general esteem.

But the G.E.R. had some heavy burdens to carry, and in particular that of bringing into London daily, and returning at night, the vast army of commuters living in the dormitory of the north-eastern suburbs. Yet even in this matter the Great Eastern won renown for the punctuality with which this suburban service was operated. Although finance was not available for much-needed electrification, in 1920 the Great Eastern won distinction by introducing the most intensive service ever operated entirely by steam power, at the peak periods with 24 trains per hour running over the same metals and providing 350 passenger seats every minute.

Although laid in the nominal flatness of the Eastern Counties, the Great Eastern main lines were by no means easily graded, as the formidable climb of the Colchester main line past Brentwood bears witness; also there were numerous speed restrictions compelled by curves. This was due to cheapness having been the chief consideration in laying the original lines; and for the same reason locomotive power was restricted by limitation of the loading gauge and by underline bridges which could not carry more than moderate weights. With such handicaps Stratford Works did some most praiseworthy work with its locomotive designs, but it is not surprising that the Great Eastern had to content itself with no more than leisurely progress by most of its express trains. For some years the company was unique in using oil-firing for many of its express locomotives, first introduced in order usefully to employ the residue from its oil-gas making plant at Stratford, and later developed on an extensive scale until the rising price of oil caused this method of firing to become more expensive than with coal.

For much of Great Eastern history its passenger rolling stock was of a somewhat Spartan description, especially in the London area, where the density of the suburban traffic made maximum accommodation in minimum space absolutely essential. For this reason the G.E.R. was the first railway in the country to build suburban coaches seating six passengers a-side. Main line stock also was not notable for luxury, though a substantial improvement set in from the middle 1900s onwards. But the Great Eastern could at least claim the credit, with the Midland Railway, of being the first to admit third class passengers to all trains, and the exclusive distinction of being the first to allow these humble patrons into the exclusive sanctity of a dining car.

The Great Eastern exercised sovereignty over a large area of the Eastern Counties, with one infiltration only into its territory—that of the Midland & Great Northern Joint Railway across from Peterborough to King's Lynn, Cromer and Yarmouth. From the earliest days it had used every possible endeavour to extend northwards, culminating in the incorporation in 1879 of the Great Northern & Great Eastern Joint Railway, which gave G.E.R. passenger trains access to York; its freight and particularly its coal trains also from now on enjoyed a direct route from Yorkshire and the Midlands to the Eastern Counties and London, though the coal traffic never increased to the extent that had been hoped. At the south of its territory the Great Eastern was barred from unfettered access to the Thames by the London, Tilbury & Southend Railway, and the position here was made worse when, in 1912, after negotiations conducted in complete secrecy, the L.T. & S.R. was acquired by the Midland Railway.

It was this unfortunate happening which forced the premature resignation of Walter Henry Hyde from the G.E.R. General Managership and precipitated the storm of criticism aroused by Lord Claud Hamilton when he declared that as he had not been able to find anyone in Great Britain suitable to occupy the vacant post, he had enlisted the services of an American, Henry Worth Thornton, until then General Superintendent of the Long Island Rail Road in the United States. Thornton had little opportunity of showing his powers, however, as a few months after his taking office there came the outbreak of the First World War, and in 1917 he was appointed as Deputy Director of Inland Waterways and Docks. Following this he became Deputy Inspector-General of Transportation on the Continent, and finally Inspector-General, with the rank of Major-General and the honour of knighthood. When he finally returned to the G.E.R., it was in the hampering conditions of continued Government control, and though he succeeded in effecting certain improvements in the Great Eastern services, all too soon his railway became swallowed up in the London & North Eastern group, and his connection with it came to an end.

4. THE NORTH EASTERN RAILWAY

Largest, wealthiest and most influential of all the constituent companies brought into the London & North Eastern group, the North Eastern Railway had the distinction of having incorporated, as part of its system, the first railway in the world to offer itself for the public transport with steam power of passengers and goods—the Stockton & Darlington, opened in 1825. As the years passed, the North Eastern Railway won for itself a leading place among the railways of Britain. Eventually it was of considerable size and handled vast traffics with efficiency; it was held in high esteem by the travelling public; it pursued an enlightened policy towards industrialists and traders; and it was financially powerful. It occupied the counties of Durham and Northumberland and the North and East Ridings of Yorkshire to the almost entire exclusion of any other major railway, and it had a substantial stake in the West Riding of Yorkshire also. By virtue of running powers over the North British it was able to run its own trains across the Scottish Border into Edinburgh, and its branch lines penetrated westwards into Cumberland and Westmorland.

Although the North Eastern enjoyed a near monopoly of the territory it served, it exercised this with benevolence. The success of this policy once led Sir George Gibb, when General Manager, to declare that there was no belief connected with railway policy and administration which he held with greater confidence than that each district should, in the public interest, be served by one undertaking under one management, thereby securing the highest combination of efficiency with economy of effort. How interesting it is that the French held the same view; there was no overlapping of their railways until the day when their entire railway system became nationalised.

It was Sir George Gibb, more than any other man, who was the principal means of putting the North Eastern into this commanding position, during a General Managership which extended from 1891 to 1906. Drawing the best from the practice then current in the United States, which he visited with some of his officers, and adapting this to English conditions, he thoroughly modernised the organisation and working of the line. One of his outstanding successes was the policy he pursued of drawing from outside into N.E.R. service young men of promise, and giving them the opportunities for training which would prove if they could become competent railway officers. From this beginning sprang the well-known N.E.R. (and later L.N.E.R.) traffic apprenticeship scheme, the benefits of which are still being felt to-day by British Railways.

While in the latter half of the Nineteenth Century there was a strong Quaker tradition attaching to the North Eastern Railway Board—derived from the continuing connection with Darlington and the Pease family—this had largely disappeared from 1900 onwards. In the first decade of the present century the Board represented an amalgam of industrialists, statesmen and country gentlemen, of liberal outlook, all distinguished in their respective fields, and most of them intimately associated with the various districts served by the railway. Among them was Sir Edward Grey, destined to become Foreign Secretary in the Asquith Government of 1905.

The N.E.R. served a territory rich in its natural resources of coal, iron ore and limestone, which gave rise to the wealth of heavy industry that prospered in close proximity to its rivers and ports. Among British railways it was the largest dock-owning company. Agriculture also provided much of the company's freight traffic. As to passenger traffic, it took the longest share in the working of the East Coast trains, over the 205 miles between York and Edinburgh; it could also lay claim to speed, for many years including in its timetables the fastest scheduled run in the British Empire, from Darlington to York, 44.1 miles, in 43 minutes, at 61.7 m.p.h. Its station at York was one of the most impressive in the country, and it had reason to be proud also of those at Newcastle Central, Hull Paragon, Darlington and Middlesbrough. It also led the way in tasteful displays on its station premises and in artistic railway advertising.

York, incidentally, provided hospitality for the trains of no fewer than five other railways—the Great Northern, Great Central, Great Eastern, Midland and Lancashire & Yorkshire (and, in earlier years, even the London & North Western), a remarkable working out of George Hudson's *dictum* of many years earlier, "Mak all t'railways cum t'York". All these lines worked into York with their own engines, while in the years both before and after the First World War restaurant car trains of Great Western and London & South Western (later Southern) stock were seen daily in York station. Hull Paragon similarly entertained the locomotives and trains of the Great Central, Lancashire & Yorkshire and London & North Western Railways.

Among examples of the forward-looking policy of the North Eastern directors was their initiative in recognising the Trades Unions and in setting up, in 1908, in advance of and on broader lines than those of the other railways, a Conciliation Board. Other developments of note were the establishment of a Commercial Agency charged with the responsibility for watching trade movements and inducing industrialists to establish new factories on the N.E.R. system; the compilation and intelligent use of statistics; and, in the operating realm, the use of high capacity wagons.

The electrification of the Newcastle suburban lines on North Tyneside, of which the first section was brought into use at the end of March, 1904, was the first provincial venture of its kind in Great Britain, beating by a single week the opening of the Lancashire & Yorkshire electrification from Liverpool to Southport, on the other side of the country. One minor but interesting innovation, not copied by any other railway, was the issue of first class 1,000-mile coupon tickets, each coupon covering a mile of travel, at a rate which worked out at no more than $1\frac{1}{4}$d. a mile. These activities by no means exhaust the list, but are typical of many progressive ideas worked out by the N.E.R. in the halcyon days before the First World War.

Chairman of the company in the last ten years before the end of its independent history was the first Lord Knaresborough, who came of railway stock, for his father, Sir Harry Stephen Meysey-Thompson, Bart., had succeeded the redoubtable George Hudson as Chairman of the former York & North Midland Railway, and had been Chairman of the N.E.R. from 1855 to 1874. A landed proprietor and former Liberal-Unionist Member of Parliament, Lord Knaresborough was a man of marked ability, but in his later years felt that the times were out of joint and that he had little in common with current trends.

As recorded in Chapter VI, the last North Eastern Railway General Manager was Ralph Lewis Wedgwood, but his appointment in 1921 was mainly due to his predecessor, Sir Alexander Kaye Butterworth, having voluntarily stepped down to enable Wedgwood to achieve managerial status before the grouping took place. Butterworth had qualified as a solicitor, and in the Legal Department of the Great Western Railway had become a recognised authority on railway rates and charges. From 1890 he had been Solicitor to the N.E.R. and his direct translation from that office to the post of General Manager in 1906, in succession to Sir George Gibb, was a surprise to many.

But the judgment of the Board proved to have been a sound one, and "A.Kaye.B.", as he so often signed himself, though small in stature, ranked among the giants for his outlook, capacity and attainments. He was wise in leaving to his competent officers the day-to-day working of the line, and was completely trusted by his staff. After his resignation, the services of Sir Alexander were retained by the North Eastern Railway Board so that he might be consulted on all questions connected with the amalgamation. Thus it was that on his death, in 1946, the obituary in *The Times* contained this passage: "It was largely through his work in negotiation and consultation that the merger which came to be known as the London & North Eastern Railway was brought to a successful conclusion".

5. THE HULL & BARNSLEY RAILWAY

At the time of the passing of the Railways Act, 1921, the Hull & Barnsley was still an independent railway, though in 1922, before the London & North Eastern Railway came into existence, it had amalgamated with the N.E.R. after more than forty years of conflict between the larger company and this intruder into its territory. In his little monograph on the North Eastern Railway, C. M. Jenkin Jones relates how "Hull had never taken the N.E.R. to its heart, as had other ports and trading centres further north, and any scheme to break the N.E.R. monopoly could count on the support of the City Corporation and many of the trading bodies of Hull". This was a more than tolerant picture of the situation, however.

Years of dissatisfaction, real or imaginary, with the N.E.R. and the shortcomings of the Hull Dock Company had resulted in a number of projects for independent rail access to the city. Thus it was that in August, 1880, the Royal Assent was given, despite strenuous opposition from the N.E.R. and the Dock Company, to a Bill authorising the Hull, Barnsley & West Riding Junction Railway & Dock Company. This was for a new railway, 53 miles long, from a junction with the Midland Railway at Cudworth into Hull, and a new dock with an original water area of nearly 50 acres, to be one of the largest and best-equipped in the country.

Construction, which so far as the railway was concerned involved cutting through the Wolds, with three tunnels between Little Weighton and South Cave of which the longest, Drewton, measured 2,116 yards, was very expensive, as also was that of the Alexandra Dock; indeed, by the opening of both five years later the original estimated cost of about £4,000,000 had swollen to nearly £10,000,000. Not surprisingly, also, construction had been retarded because of financial difficulties. Various branches of the railway were brought into use later, bringing its total length up to 93 route miles.

At first the traffic carried was disappointing. A rate war with the N.E.R. and the Dock Company had serious results for all concerned, though the North Eastern had more room for manoeuvre, by traffic arrangements with other railways such as the grant of running powers, variations in routing and rate concessions. More than once it seemed likely that the Midland Railway would absorb the Hull & Barnsley, but the former was defeated by the determination of the Hull Corporation to maintain the complete independence of its *protégé*. There was equal opposition to closer working arrangements, and even to amalgamation, with the North Eastern. Finally, however, after nearly twenty years of acute controversy, agreement was reached between the two companies, and was given statutory force in the Hull Joint Dock Act of 1899. This authorised the construction of a new deep water dock to be the joint property of both railways, and also the acquisition of the existing Dock Company by the North Eastern Railway. From now on relations between the two companies improved, much to the advantage of the Hull & Barnsley Railway, the shortened name adopted by that company in 1905.

The main task of the Hull & Barnsley was the movement of coal from South Yorkshire pits to Hull Docks for shipment; it had but little miscellaneous freight traffic. Its passenger traffic also was limited, though up to the 1914-1918 war it ran a few express trains with its own locomotives in each direction between Hull and Sheffield, using Midland metals from Cudworth onwards, in competition with the Great Central Hull-Sheffield service. It is a commentary on whether or not the building of the railway part of the Hull & Barnsley enterprise was justified that its main line was one of the first to be closed under the economies enforced by nationalisation.

As previously mentioned, to such an extent had the relations between

KING'S CROSS TERMINUS, PAST AND PRESENT.   *Above*, before the centre carriage lines were displaced in 1926 by the new platforms Nos. 7 and 8. In platform 10 the "Harrogate Pullman" is headed by ex-Great Central 4–6–0 No. 1164 *Earl Beatty*.

[*F. R. Hebron*

Below, Nos. 7, 8 and 10 platforms as now. In 1961, well into the diesel age, British Railways still rely on Gresley A4 Pacific No. 60028 *Walter K. Whigham* and the former Great Northern and North Eastern Royal saloons (second and third from engine) to carry Her Majesty the Queen to York for the wedding of the Duke of York.   [*British Railways*

LIVERPOOL STREET TERMINUS. *Above right:* The West Side, as in Great Eastern Railway days, with the large central clock and a G.E.R. "Claud Hamilton" 4-4-0 in foreground. *Right:* In L.N.E.R. days, with the queue for a main line train. *Above:* The frontage, with the clock tower, which was later partially destroyed by enemy bombing. Morning commuters are streaming up the slope.

[British Railways

Above: The frontage of Fenchurch Street terminus of the former Great Eastern Railway. Centre: Cambridge Station exterior. The canopy was added in later years to the original frontage. Below: The unique 1,254 ft. long main platform at Cambridge, used by both down and up trains.

[British Railways

Left: Nottingham Victoria Station, built jointly by the Great Central and Great Northern Railways and opened in 1900. Below: Sheffield Victoria Station of the former Great Central Railway, with the Royal Victoria Station Hotel to the left.

[British Railways

Right: A typical Great Northern main line station—Grantham. [British Railways

the North Eastern and Hull & Barnsley Railways been transformed by the 1899 agreement that amalgamation was agreed on, with the approval of the Railways Amalgamation Tribunal, from April, 1922, before the grouping compelled by the Railways Act, 1921, had taken place. The General Manager of the Hull & Barnsley Railway from 1905 until this amalgamation was Edward Watkin, previously Mineral Manager of the Great Central Railway, who thus perpetuated in railway administrative circles the name of his renowned uncle, Sir Edward Watkin. His was no easy task, but he carried it on with such ability that in the final year of his service he had the then unique distinction, while retaining his managerial office, of being elected a member of the Board also.

6. THE NORTH BRITISH RAILWAY

If not the most prosperous, the North British was certainly the largest of the railways in Scotland. The only Scottish railway to have its headquarters in the capital, Edinburgh, it was wise enough to locate its Goods Manager in the commercial centre of Glasgow. Edinburgh, however, from which its main lines radiated in all directions, was its principal focal point. Here was Waverley, one of the finest Scottish stations; but by comparison its Queen Street station in Glasgow and Tay Bridge station in Dundee were poor affairs. Its longest tentacle was the West Highland line, which reached Fort William in 1894 and Mallaig in 1901, and was taken over by the N.B.R. in 1908. Other long branches which penetrated into the territory of other railways were the Waverley route from Edinburgh to Carlisle, with its extension to Silloth on the Cumberland coast; and the Border Counties line, crossing the Border to run south to Hexham in Northumberland, from which Newcastle was reached by running powers over the North Eastern Railway. Access to Aberdeen was obtained only by running powers over the tracks of its arch-enemy, the Caledonian Railway. Although a traffic agreement had been in force between these two companies for many years, few, if any, North British men would have a good word to say for their rival; and no doubt the antipathy was mutual.

Scenically the North British Railway possessed some of the most glorious stretches of line in the country. It was proud to run its trains over two of the most notable bridges in Great Britain, spanning the Firths of Forth and Tay, though of the former it was a part owner only. It could boast admirable hotels in Edinburgh and Glasgow, and was joint owner with the Caledonian and Highland Railways of the Station Hotel at Perth. Its train services no doubt were adequate, though the extremely steep gradients of its main lines precluded anything in the realm of high speed. Apart from its share in the East Coast Joint Stock, and with the Midland in the Midland & North British stock (of Midland design), most of its coaches were of a Spartan description.

In the through trains to and from the Midland line which the North British Railway operated over the 98 miles between Edinburgh and Carlisle it was a slightly reluctant partner, and it demanded from the

Midland annual payments if such were needed to make up the receipts from working these trains to a certain agreed minimum per mile. In respect of the summer "Highland Express" leaving St. Pancras at 7.15 p.m., for example, the Midland paid the North British a subsidy of £6,097 between 1903 and 1907, and on the Edinburgh portion of the 1.30 p.m. from St. Pancras, for the four years to June, 1908, £5,090. Thus, despite the longer haul of the Midland trains as compared with the 57½ miles of the East Coast trains between Berwick and Edinburgh, not unnaturally the N.B.R. set a good deal more store by the latter traffic, which was on a far more ample scale, even though the North Eastern Railway actually worked these trains into and out of Edinburgh.

As to the water, the North British was the largest dock-owning company north of the Border, and obtained a considerable share in the traffic to and from the docks of other owners at Leith, Dundee, Aberdeen and on the Clyde, specialising in the shipment of coal. It ran its own passenger steamers to the Clyde resorts from its pier at Craigendoran, and was joint owner with the Caledonian Railway of the steamers on Loch Lomond. It also operated a ferry service between Granton (Leith) and Burntisland, relic of pre-Forth Bridge days, and also across the Forth between South and North Queensferry.

Alone among Scottish railways, the North British had, as a fundamental part of its operating organisation, a comprehensive traffic control system, based largely on Midland methods. Of this the mainspring was C. H. Stemp, the Operating Superintendent, who came to Scotland from the Great Eastern Railway, brought up in that company's tradition of punctual and efficient working. "The Major", as he was generally known, was a martinet, but soon the N.B.R. showed the beneficial effects of his G.E.R. training. He continued for some years to serve the London & North Eastern Railway after the grouping. His immediate Chief from 1922 was James Calder, the General Manager, who had worked himself up from the humble position of station clerk by sheer hard work and application.

The outstanding North British personality was its Chairman, William Whitelaw. Son of a wealthy Scottish ironmaster, after a short spell as a Member of Parliament he joined the Board of the Highland Railway in 1898, and three years later, at the early age of 32, he became its Chairman. The Highland at that time was in financial difficulties, but the economies effected by Whitelaw so improved the position that it was no surprise when he was invited in 1912 to become Chairman of the larger North British Railway, while still continuing with the Highland as Deputy Chairman. During 1915 and 1916 he had the unique distinction of acting as Chairman of both companies simultaneously.

A battle of note in which Whitelaw was one of the two chief protagonists was the action of the North British against the newly formed Ministry of Transport, after the First World War, concerning the delay in the payment of its war and post-war claims against the Government for compensation. This contest dragged on for nearly two years, and was a *cause célèbre* watched anxiously by the other railways. None could doubt that the fight was really between Whitelaw and Sir Eric Geddes. Eventually, by dint of hard effort and close attention to detail the N.B.R. vindicated its claim, but the issue could have been settled much sooner and with less cost to all concerned had there been more good will on both sides.

With little doubt it was the reputation that William Whitelaw thus established that influenced his election as the first Chairman of the London & North Eastern Railway, as described in Chapter V. Incidentally, in L.N.E.R. days he used humorously to remark that three locomotives had been named after him—the Gresley Pacific *William Whitelaw*; the North British "Scott" class 4-4-0 *Wandering Willie*; and the veteran North British 0-6-0 *'Ole Bill*.

7. THE GREAT NORTH OF SCOTLAND RAILWAY

Smallest of all the constituent companies was the Great North of Scotland, owning no more than 334 route miles of line. With brisk train services, praiseworthy cleanliness of coaches and stations, and a progressive spirit permeating its activities, it was a game little company which had served its own territory around Aberdeen faithfully and well. But in its youth and middle age it had been in trouble through being too game, and the legal squabbles in which it had seemed to delight had been expensive affairs. It was Aberdeen's own railway; but about a hundred miles away there was another Royal Burgh called Inverness, where they also bred a fighting race, and although the G.N.S.R. set out bravely to reach Inverness, its own metals never reached as far, for Inverness had its own railway too!

It may be significant that the Great North of Scotland was launched in 1844 at a meeting held "within the writing chambers of Messrs. Adam & Anderson, Advocates, in Aberdeen". So it was that during the first half of its existence its representatives were constantly in and out of Advocates' chambers, and although by 1922 its litigious days were long over, it was perhaps most fitting that its last Chairman was named in the records as "Mr. Alexander Duffus, Advocate, Aberdeen". He succeeded to the Chair in 1921 and became the Great North's nominee on the London & North Eastern Board.

Aberdeen General passenger station was owned jointly by the Caledonian and Great North of Scotland Railways. The original station was nothing to boast about, but the commodious present station, completed in 1914, ranks among the finest in Scotland. The Great North of Scotland owned three first-class hotels, two of them, oddly enough, in the one city of Aberdeen and the third at Cruden Bay, on the coast just over 20 miles to the north. The latter was built in the 1890s, and was provided with a golf course and branch line of its own, but this venture never achieved the success that had been hoped. The pride and joy of the Great North of Scotland, however, was its ownership of the Deeside line, the terminus of which at Ballater, 43 miles from

Aberdeen, served the Royal residence of Balmoral Castle. From Queen Victoria's day, therefore, the G.N.S.R. had the privilege of working Royal trains along the branch whenever the Sovereign took a holiday at Balmoral, as well as the special "Messenger Trains" which carried dispatches between Ballater and Aberdeen in connection with the London trains.

The Great North of Scotland was a pioneer among British railways in providing road transport to connect with its trains. As early as 1904 a service of motorbuses was put in operation between Ballater and Braemar. Parliamentary powers were obtained to develop these road services for both passengers and freight, regular and seasonal, and by 1922 the company owned 38 passenger road coaches and 11 mechanic-ally-propelled lorries. It is rather ironical that the company's pro-gressive spirit should have been responsible for introducing into the area what in later years would become the railways' most formidable and indeed destructive competitor.

8. JOINT RAILWAYS

In the grouping various railways which had been the joint property of two or more of the constituent companies presented no difficulties, but there were others owned jointly with companies which from 1923 onwards became a part of the London Midland & Scottish system, and which from now onwards, therefore, were the joint property of the L.N.E.R. and L.M.S.R. Of these the most important was the Cheshire Lines Committee, with 143 route miles of line. In this the L.N.E.R. became the predominant partner, as the previous joint owners had been the Great Central, Great Northern and Midland Railways—two L.N.E.R. constituents to one of the L.M.S.R. The original owners, at the incor-poration in 1865, had been the Great Northern and Manchester, Sheffield & Lincolnshire Railways; not until 1866 did the Midland come in, and from that time onwards the ownership of the system was shared equally by the three companies.

The Great Northern share was of interest, seeing that Great Northern trains could only reach the nearest point on the C.L.C. system by travel-ling over 56 miles of the Great Central line from Retford to Godley Junction, or 54 miles of the Midland from Codnor Park Junction in the Erewash Valley to Chorlton Junction, outside Manchester. But with the aid of running powers the Great Northern for many years ran highly competitive through express trains between King's Cross and Manchester *via* Retford, and right up to the grouping operated through freight trains with its own locomotives to its large Deansgate goods station in Manchester. A minor point of interest is that the popular refreshment and dining rooms in both Manchester Central and Liverpool Central stations were staffed by the G.N.R.

This mention of Manchester and Liverpool bears witness to the fact that the title of the Cheshire Lines Committee was misleading; certainly a branch of the C.L.C. extended as far as Chester, but by far the major part of the system was located in Lancashire. Its principal main line ran for 34 miles between Manchester Central and Liverpool Central, with a loop serving Warrington, and was notable for providing one of the first even-interval passenger services in Great Britain; its "Punctual Expresses", leaving each terminal at 30 minutes past the hour and taking 45 minutes for the run with a Warrington stop, were probably the best patronised of any of the three routes connecting the two cities. Other routes of importance were that serving Southport, and the line diverging from the Liverpool-Manchester line at Glazebrook and cutting through Stockport to reach the Great Central Manchester-Sheffield main line at Godley Junction. The latter was used by the through Liverpool-Sheffield-Hull trains, and also, as far as Cheadle Heath, by the Midland trains for St. Pancras. Manchester Central, of course, was the terminus of the Midland express service from London.

The Cheshire Lines Committee possessed its own passenger rolling stock, but its motive power, other than on the through Midland trains running into Liverpool, was provided by the Great Central Railway. It had the monopoly of the important freight services from and to the Trafford Park Estate at Manchester, and other freight operations on a large scale were conducted in Manchester and at the extensive Brunswick sidings, on the River Mersey just outside Liverpool. Each of the three owning companies was represented on the Board by three directors; after the grouping this composition was altered to five L.N.E.R. and two L.M.S.R. directors, with an eighth brought in from outside. The rolling stock came under the supervision of the L.N.E.R. Chief Mechanical Engineer and the "Way and Works" under that of the L.M.S.R. Chief Civil Engineer.

Another joint system of importance was the Midland & Great Northern Railways Joint Committee, an amalgamation of various smaller companies which had succeeded in penetrating the territory of the Great Eastern Railway, and finally combined in 1895 under a single management located at King's Lynn. The Great Northern arm of the line ran eastwards from Peterborough, while an end-on connection with a Midland branch from Saxby, near Melton Mowbray, ran through Spalding to join the line from Peterborough at Sutton Bridge. From here the main line continued through King's Lynn to Melton Constable, where it branched into three, one line to Sheringham and Cromer, a second to Yarmouth, and a third to Norwich. In later years agreement with the Great Eastern resulted in the building of joint coastal lines in Norfolk and Suffolk between Cromer, Mundesley and North Walsham, and Yarmouth, Gorleston and Lowestoft.

The Midland & Great Northern was a completely self-contained railway, with its own locomotives, coaches and wagons, maintained at Melton Constable. Its directorate comprised three Midland and three Great Northern representatives—a proportion which continued unchanged after the grouping—and John J. Petrie was its Traffic Manager at King's Lynn; but its most notable personality was William Marriott,

who at Melton Constable combined the joint responsibilities of Civil
Engineer and Locomotive Superintendent.   At the grouping these two
offices were separated, though the headquarters of both remained at
Melton Constable.   After nationalisation the Midland & Great Northern
was one of the first casualties, and only a fraction of its 194 miles of line
still remains in use to-day.

A third L.N.E.R. & L.M.S.R. joint line of importance was that built
jointly by the Great Northern and London & North Western Railways
between Bottesford, on the Grantham and Nottingham line, and Welham
Junction, near Market Harborough, with branches 45 miles in all.
This gave the L.N.W.R., by running powers over the G.N.R., direct
access for passenger and freight traffic into Nottingham, and the G.N.R.
by a branch of its own from Marefield, similar access to its own passenger
and goods stations in Leicester.   Passenger traffic never grew to any
sizeable dimensions, and ceased soon after nationalisation, but along
the main trunk line, even though various of the branches have closed
down, there still remains a fairly substantial freight traffic.   There were
many other short stretches of joint line, and also joint stations, which
remained the joint property of the London & North Eastern and London,
Midland & Scottish Railways after the groups had come into being.

Most important of the lines jointly owned by L.N.E.R. constituent
companies which on the grouping came into exclusive London & North
Eastern ownership was the Great Northern & Great Eastern Railways
Joint Committee, with 123 miles of line extending from Grassmoor
Junction, March, in Cambridgeshire, through Spalding, Lincoln and
Gainsborough to Black Carr Junction with the Great Northern main
line, just south of Doncaster.   Its construction was really the outcome
of the strenuous efforts of the former Eastern Counties Railway to break
out of its limited sphere as an agricultural railway and find a paying
outlet for its products to the north, with a return traffic of coal to the
south.

These hopes were finally realised, after a whole series of fierce battles
with competing interests, by the passage of a Bill in 1879 which led to
the opening of the G.N. & G.E. Joint Line three years later.   By running
powers over the Great Northern and North Eastern Railways this gave
the Great Eastern Railway access to York for its passenger trains, but
passenger service over the route has always been on a small scale.   As
to freight, however, this still remains one of the most important traffic
arteries in the country.

To conclude this chapter, Tables 1 to 6 inclusive set out the principal
statistics of the six main constituent companies of the London & North
Eastern Railway at December 31st, 1922—the last day of their independent history.   These include the issued capital (Table 1), the dividends paid over a period of years (Table 2), the gross receipts and expenditure (Table 3), the total of passengers and freight conveyed (Tables
4 and 5), and the mileage, rolling stock and staff (Table 6).   The one
feature of these tables that stands out more than any other is the dominant

position in every respect of the North Eastern Railway, so prosperous that at the end it was paying 7½ per cent. on its Ordinary stock (or "Consols"), whereas the other companies in the group could manage nothing more than 4 per cent. in the case of the Great Northern, 2¾ per cent., the Great Eastern, 1½ to 1 per cent., the North British and Great North of Scotland with their Deferred Ordinary stock, and nothing at all the Great Central. It is small wonder that, as related in the succeeding chapters, the North Eastern claimed so commanding a role in the new company.

Table 1

Capital issued by the L.N.E.R. Constituent Companies as at December 31st, 1922

Constituent Company	*Debenture Stock & Loans*	*Preference Stock*	*Ordinary Stock*	*Total*
	£	£	£	£
Great Central	23,872,708	20,567,488	10,658,020	55,098,216
Great Eastern	18,884,629	20,826,335	15,362,886	55,073,850
Great Northern	15,802,467	23,195,260	22,804,768	61,802,495
North Eastern*	28,042,882	27,707,612	34,152,966	89,903,460
Great North of Scotland	1,611,171	3,415,408	1,795,350	6,821,929
North British	17,304,753	27,575,852	21,579,287	66,459,892
Totals	105,518,610	123,287,955	106,353,277	335,159,842

**Including Hull & Barnsley Railway.*

Table 2

Representative Financial Results of L.N.E.R. Constituent Companies, 1900-1922

Dividends paid on Ordinary or similar stocks

Railway	*Stock*	1900	1910	1911	1921	1922
		%	%	%	%	%
Great Central	5% Preference (1894)§	Nil	Nil	½	2½	4½
"	Preferred Ordinary	Nil*	Nil	Nil	Nil	Nil
"	Deferred Ordinary	Nil	Nil	Nil	Nil	Nil
Great Eastern	Ordinary	3	3⅛	3⅜	2¾	2¾
Great Northern	Ordinary	3	4⅛	4⅜	4¼	†4
Hull & Barnsley	Ordinary	1½	3⅝	3	4⅛	‡
North Eastern	Ord. (N.E. Consols)	6⅜	6	6¼	7½	7½
Great N. of Scot.	Preferred Ordinary	2½	3	3	3	3
"	Deferred Ordinary	Nil	¼	¾	½	1½
North British	Preferred Ordinary	3	3	3	Nil	1
"	Deferred Ordinary	¾	½	1	Nil	1

**Last previous dividend, ¼% in 1898. †Preferred Converted Ordinary. ‡Amalgamated with N.E.R. §Latest Preference stock issued; shown because G.C.R. capital structure included preponderating amount of Debenture and Preference stock.*

Table 3

Gross Receipts and Expenditure of L.N.E.R. Constituent Companies in Year 1922

Constituent Company	Gross Receipts	Expenditure	Net Receipts*
	£	£	£
Great Central	11,874,770	9,715,618	2,363,304
Great Eastern	12,606,550	10,970,895	2,073,493†
Great Northern	12,928,174	10,398,127	2,848,194
North Eastern‡	22,178,008	18,144,052	4,723,709†
Great North of Scotland	1,092,261	865,031	282,153†
North British	10,344,039	8,011,516	2,441,170

*Including miscellaneous receipts. †Including proportion of amount receivable under Section 11, Railways Act, 1921. ‡Including Hull & Barnsley Railway.

Table 4

Number of Passengers conveyed and Season Tickets issued by L.N.E.R. Constituent Companies during year 1922

Railway	Ordinary Tickets				Annual Season Tickets
	1st Class	2nd Class	3rd Class	Workmen's	
Great Central	361,587	—	16,181,360	7,120,324	23,932
Great Eastern	1,473,400	1,512,094	57,326,831	26,369,206	91,015
Great Northern	605,154	211,752	23,406,834	6,972,069	58,970
North Eastern*	846,698	—	46,443,402	11,043,250	45,565
Great North of Scotld.	103,224	—	3,512,913	269,680	3,815
North British	961,393	—	24,158,227	6,931,536	39,560

*Including Hull & Barnsley Railway.

Table 5

Freight Tonnage and Live Stock conveyed by L.N.E.R. Constituent Companies Year 1922

Railway	Merchandise	Coal & Coke	Other Minerals	Live Stock
	tons	tons	tons	head
Great Central	5,143,328	22,566,032	5,141,410	578,305
Great Eastern	5,083,584	5,055,166	2,095,922	1,279,937
Great Northern	5,034,001	13,550,075	3,673,897	810,977
North Eastern*	9,927,147	42,621,427	7,948,102	2,542,221
Great North of Scotland	523,023	417,264	74,060	416,547
North British	5,011,426	18,739,108	4,064,845	2,654,951

*Including Hull & Barnsley Railway.

Table 6

Mileage, Rolling Stock and Staff of L.N.E.R. Constituent Companies at December 31st, 1922

Railway	Total Mileage		Loco-motives †	Vehicles			Total Staff
	Route	Single Track‡		Psngr.	Freight	Service	
	miles	miles	No.	No.	No.	No.	No.
Great Central	855¼	2,698¼	1,356	2,727	35,330	2,963	31,456
Great Eastern	1,191	2,637½	1,336	5,548	27,213	2,898	38,006
Great Northern	1,051¼	3,124¾	1,353	3,474	38,706	2,870	35,874
North Eastern*	1,864½	5,407	2,141	4,065	123,823	3,964	63,063
Gt. North of Scotland	334½	526	122	766	3,603	124	3,082
North British	1,377¾	2,764¾	1,075	3,576	55,806	3,164	29,518

*Including Hull & Barnsley Railway.   †Steam.   ‡Including sidings

C

III

The East Coast Joint Service

THE ORIGINS of the East Coast Route go back to the earliest days of railways. George Hudson, the "Railway King", was behind the idea, no doubt influenced by his policy of putting York as prominently as possible on the railway map. Be that as it may, at first the only rail route from London to Edinburgh was for most of the distance up the east side of the country. In the 1840s passengers for the north travelled by train over the London & Birmingham Railway from Euston to Rugby, the Midland Counties from there through Leicester to Derby, the North Midland on to Normanton, the York & North Midland into York, and by May, 1844, the first through train was run from London to Gateshead, across the Tyne opposite Newcastle, using Great North of England metals from York to Darlington, and those of the Newcastle & Darlington Railway for most of the remaining distance.

By 1850 the all-important High Level Bridge across the Tyne and the Royal Border Bridge across the Tweed, with the connecting Newcastle & Berwick Railway, and the North British Railway from Berwick to Edinburgh, had been completed, and from now on an all-rail route connected the English and Scottish capitals. For by 1850 the Great Northern main line also had been completed from London to a point north of Doncaster, and the use of Lancashire & Yorkshire tracks from Shaftholme Junction to Knottingley permitted a link-up with the York & North Midland and provided access to York for the Great Northern trains. One or two short cuts, such as that from Shaftholme to York through Selby, had still to be built, but by 1852, with the opening of King's Cross terminus in London, the East Coast Route had come into being.

This resulted in the abandonment of Euston as the London terminal, to the chagrin of the "Euston Square Confederacy", the railway mandarins who had so bitterly opposed the Great Northern project. Finally, in 1854, the incorporation had taken place of the North Eastern Railway; ten years previously the North British Railway also had been incorporated; and the nucleus thus had come into being of an East Coast alliance which, although it had its uneasy moments, was destined to be permanent. It is of interest to recall that with the amalgamation in 1865 of the North British and the Edinburgh to Glasgow Railways Glasgow in effect became the northern end of the East Coast main line, and thus from its earliest days the true Scottish terminal of the East Coast Route.

In the succeeding years this alliance proved to be a remarkable partnership of three great railways. Each gave the highest priority to its share of responsibility for all the arrangements involved, and for the actual working of the trains. The latter were composed of special East Coast Joint Stock, each coach lettered "E.C.J.S." and bearing the distinctive coat-of-arms of the alliance; moreover these coaches in later years were, with the possible exception of those of the Midland Railway, the finest examples in the country at that time of the coach-builders' craftsmanship.

Friction there may have been from time to time between the three companies; sometimes it was said by the Great Northern and North British supporters that the contribution of the North Eastern was merely to pull the trains, whereas the burden of developing the traffic fell exclusively on the other two partners, but this claim made little allowance for the substantial patronage of the route extended by Tees-side and Tyneside. A rather ugly squabble did blow up in 1894 by the North British management objecting to the working of the East Coast trains by the North Eastern Railway with its own locomotives into Edinburgh; this even led to litigation, and, from the beginning of 1897, to the N.B.R. insisting on all these trains being stopped at Berwick and worked between there and Edinburgh by North British locomotives. But as the dispute was largely due to the North British objection to paying the North Eastern the modest sum of £2 10s. for every through working by the latter's locomotives, the N.B.R. soon found that the altered arrangements were a great deal more expensive, and after no more than a year, under a ruling of the Railway & Canal Commission, the previous method of working was reverted to. Such troubles, however, were of no more than minor importance.

Indeed, in the light of to-day's inordinate emphasis on specialisation of management, it is interesting to reflect that the considerable work of supervising the administration and operation of the joint service, additional as it was to the domestic affairs of each company, was handled without difficulty by the management of each railway. There was a regular conference of those concerned, and a small office at York known as the East Coast Trains Department, but its work was mainly that of *liaison*; the actual management of the extensive facilities and all that they involved was taken in their stride by the departmental officers of the three companies. It might have been thought impossible to-day to perform the service so given without the creation of a separate company or some elaborate organisation; yet the plan worked with the greatest efficiency. To some extent it set a pattern of working still closely followed in London & North Eastern days, and there can be no doubt that the close association of the various departments with each other on East Coast matters created a feeling of common purpose which was of great value when the L.N.E.R. came into being.

The East Coast Route has long stretches suitable for fast running, and has always been noted for speed. The East Coast "Flying Scotsman" handsomely beat its West Coast rival in the 1888 "Race" from London to Edinburgh, and impartial judges do not consider that the tables were completely turned in the 1895 "Race to Aberdeen". It cannot be forgotten that on the last night the West Coast cut their racing train down to a featherweight of no more than three coaches, of 70 tons weight, running a second train to serve the surplus passengers and those who would have joined or left at certain intermediate stops omitted by the racing train.

Moreover, judging by the recently published communications which passed between the General Managers of the competing companies, those of the East Coast were reluctant competitors, not a little apprehensive of the risks involved in the reckless disregard of many speed restrictions by the drivers of the racing trains. Anyway, there were many sighs of relief by railway officers when by mutual consent the contest came to an end. From then on minimum times for the day trains between London and both Edinburgh and Glasgow were agreed to by both sides, and imposed a dead hand on acceleration for more than a quarter of a century. But when at last speeding up began, in 1932, culminating with the streamline trains of 1937, the London & North Eastern Railway 6-hour "Coronation" from King's Cross to Edinburgh still beat by 30 minutes the 6½-hour London Midland & Scottish "Coronation Scot" from Euston to Glasgow.

The fact that Edinburgh Waverley was not primarily a terminal, but in effect an intermediate station on the East Coast Route, was of great significance, and still is so to-day. It meant that the same trains of one trunk route from England could serve both the Scottish capital and all the other principal centres of population and industry—Glasgow, Perth, Dundee and Aberdeen. This has always permitted a flexibility in train working arrangements; up to the years between the wars, for example, the "Flying Scotsman" carried through coaches from London to all the four cities mentioned, and until the introduction of third class sleeping cars added greatly to the weight of the night trains, some of these also incorporated numerous through portions.

Overall times at night are always of less importance than those of the day trains, so that the East Coast Companies, and later the L.N.E.R., could obtain plenty of patronage for through sleeping cars between London and Glasgow, even though over a route 38½ miles longer than that from Euston. It is not without note that until March, 1965, the East Coast "Talisman" provided a 7-hour service between King's Cross and Glasgow, which was faster than any train by the rival route during the years that part of the latter was in course of electrification.

One interesting feature of the East Coast service was that in the early 1900s it was possible to leave Edinburgh at 7.50 a.m., with the luxury, unusual in those days, of a breakfast car to Newcastle, and to be in London by 4.10 p.m., whereas the Glaswegian had no West Coast London-bound train earlier than the 10.0 a.m. from Glasgow Central, due in Euston at 6.20 p.m. This East Coast advantage still persisted during recent years; after the withdrawal of the West Coast 8.30 a.m. "Caledonian" from Glasgow, passengers could leave Glasgow Queen Street at 7.0 a.m., change at Edinburgh into the 8.0 a.m. "Talisman", and be into King's Cross by 2.0 p.m., nearly $3\frac{1}{2}$ hours ahead of the Euston arrival of the 10.0 a.m. "Royal Scot" from Glasgow Central. But with the electrified timetable of the London Midland Region, from April 1966 this advantage has disappeared; a new 7.40 a.m. from Glasgow Central now reaches Euston by 2.15 p.m., and the 10.15 a.m. "Royal Scot" runs up to London in $6\frac{1}{2}$ hours. The East Coast, however, even though a change at Edinburgh is involved, still offers by far the fastest service between London and Perth, and is now the only recognised route between London and both Dundee and Aberdeen.

When the London & North Eastern Railway came into being it was in some respects not merely the expansion but the embodiment of the East Coast Route. This is not to say that nothing else mattered within the wider range of the company's activities, but—and especially with a Scottish Chairman—nothing else mattered quite so much.

IV

The New Company—Its Formation

THE 1921 ACT provided that the "railways shall be formed into groups . . .
and the principal railway companies in each group shall be amalgamated, and other companies absorbed in the manner provided by this
Act". The grouping therefore was not on a strictly geographical basis;
it was achieved by the amalgamation of *companies* with due regard to
their geographical affinities. In their competitive early days some of
these companies had penetrated extensively into one another's territories,
with the result that in the grouping there was considerable overlapping
in the "fringe" areas. One has only to look at the former railway map
of, say, the West Riding of Yorkshire or Nottinghamshire to realise the
competitive potential of this interweaving of lines after grouping had
taken place. In the general climate of opinion forty years ago this was
not regarded as a bad thing, in all probability, and any proposal for
the truncation of railway routes, in order to avoid overlapping, no
doubt would have aroused bitter opposition, as well as involving an
accounting exercise which might have taken years to bring to a conclusion.

Regret has sometimes been expressed that a Midland group was not
established which might have absorbed the "problem child", the Great
Central. At first sight such a plan might seem to have had its attrac-
tions. The London & North Western and Lancashire & Yorkshire
combination, effected in 1922, was financially sound and would not
have been weakened; reduction in size of the eventual London Midland
& Scottish Railway would have been an advantage; and much overlapping of the L.N.E.R. and L.M.S.R. in the Midlands, Lancashire
and the West Riding of Yorkshire would have been avoided. On the
other hand, the effect on the Eastern group would have been serious.
The major dock installations at Grimsby and Immingham would have
been put into fierce competition with those of Hull; direct access of the
L.N.E.R. to Sheffield, Manchester and Liverpool would have been
cut off; and the Great Northern Railway's joint interest in the Cheshire
Lines Committee's system would have been reduced to nothing more
than an investment.

There was a further consideration. The Great Northern, Great
Central and Great Eastern Companies—the "Three Greats" as they
were sometimes known—for many years had worked closely together.
So closely, in fact, that in 1909 they had promoted a Bill for their con-

solidation as a single undertaking, to be managed by a Great Northern, Central & Eastern Railways Committee, somewhat on the same lines as the South Eastern & Chatham Railway Companies' Managing Committee, which had come into existence ten years earlier. But in 1909 our legislators were fearful of permitting anything in the nature of a monopoly, and when it became clear that the Bill would not become law without onerous conditions being imposed, the three companies withdrew it after a very costly and abortive fight. Yet only twelve years later the same capricious Mother of Parliaments compelled the complete amalgamation of the same three railways within the wider framework of the Eastern group!

After having come so closely together, the "Three Greats" might be thought to have no difficulty when it came to fulfilling the amalgamation requirements of the 1921 Act. But it must be remembered that the problem was now quite different. In the 1909 scheme each company was to have preserved its identity, and as a body corporate would have received from the Managing Committee its share of the net receipts accruing to the joint undertaking; the agreed proportions were to be 37.39 per cent. to the Great Eastern Company, 35.73 per cent. to the Great Northern and 26.88 per cent. to the Great Central. The 1921 Act, on the other hand, was for the complete amalgamation of the companies and the merging of their assets in a new capital structure. The terms on which this was to be done would vitally affect the wellbeing of their shareholders, and there were, moreover, three other partners all equally anxious to secure the best deal possible for their proprietors. And one of these, the North Eastern, was quite formidable—indeed, the most formidable—in its overall size and financial strength.

The dominant position of the North Eastern Railway caused it to be the fulcrum of the negotiations leading to amalgamation; this also gave rise to jealousies and to the strong feelings inevitable in such a situation. The amicable settlement reached by the North Eastern and Hull & Barnsley Railways in their 1922 fusion unhappily provided no precedent for what was to follow. A tremendous task lay ahead. Not only had the terms of the amalgamation to be agreed, involving the equation of the various companies' stocks and shares in the new capital structure; but the new Board of Directors also had to be agreed, the new Chairman elected, the new General Manager appointed for the whole undertaking, and an organisation laid down suitable for the needs of the new and very large company.

All this had to be done concurrently with the settlement of the claims of the individual companies against the post-war Railway Compensation Account, and anxiety to get an adequate share of this £60,000,000 weighed heavily with each company. All the complex negotiations involved had to be carried out at the top level, with the full authority of the six Boards concerned, on the initiatives of their Chairmen; never before had so much work fallen to the lot of railway directors! And the time was short. Not until August 19th, 1921, did the Railways Act, 1921, receive the Royal Assent, and it was laid down that if the constituent companies had not presented an agreed scheme of amalgamation before January 1st, 1923, a scheme would be prepared and imposed by the Amalgamation Tribunal set up under the Act, which was certainly the last thing that any of the companies wanted! So, with no more than 16½ months in which to prepare, there was no time to be lost.

As we have seen in Chapter II, the Chairmen of the Great Northern, Great Central and Great Eastern Railways were all strong and active personalities. In Scotland, William Whitelaw of the North British was not only a man of great force of character, but also, more than any of the others, was steeped in the practical side of railway administration. It may have been for that reason, or because of his strong desire to bring his company into more affluent circumstances than it had enjoyed in the past, that his approach to the problems to be faced, though no less firm, was at least less contentious than that of two of his principal London colleagues.

The North Eastern Railway Chairman, Lord Knaresborough, was of a different type altogether. Greatly respected though he was by all who came into contact with him, he had no personal ambitions in the "brave new world" that had been ushered in by the 1921 Act, which he realised would eventually sever his family's unbroken connection with railways from their earliest days. Seventy-six years of age, and impatient of London influence, his anxiety was as to how the prosperous position of North Eastern shareholders might be preserved despite their having to admit poorer relations "into the house". These considerations induced in him a somewhat diffident and aloof attitude, and the cut and thrust of the negotiations that lay ahead were not to his taste at all.

In August, 1921, Sir Hugh Bell, a director of the N.E.R. and the well-known Tees-side ironmaster, wrote to Sir Alexander Butterworth, the General Manager, in a somewhat pessimistic vein: "It is most disheartening to think that the handling of the North Eastern interests is left to so undecided a person as our Chairman and that we can do nothing to counteract the intrigues which are no doubt going on to the great prejudice of our interests." Sir Hugh was nothing if not outspoken; but it was an outspokenness born of sincerity and sharpened by impatience, for he certainly had a great respect for the Chairman.

Sir Hugh Bell was not alone in his anxieties, however. Early in September, 1921, he received a letter from Sir George Gibb, the former General Manager, who was always watchful of the welfare of his beloved North Eastern Railway. This communication reviewed the whole situation in some detail, and weighed the effect that the conduct of the negotiations might have on North Eastern interests; it is evident that he was by no means happy at the course that events were taking. "Small things at the outset may affect future developments", he wrote. "For example, it was very unfortunate that the first meeting of Chairmen should be at the Great Northern offices. It should have been in the North-East."

Right: The handsome North Eastern Railway head-quarters building at York, in which took place many of the discussions prior to the formation of the L.N.E.R. *Below:* Interior of York Station, showing main through platforms 8 and 9 and the graceful curved roof.

[*British Railways*

THE RAILWAY CENTENARY
1925. *Above:* Early locomotives on exhibition at Faverdale Works, Darlington. On the right the Hetton Colliery locomotive, with the Stockton & Darlington *Derwent* behind; on the left the Canterbury & Whitstable *Invicta.*

Left: The Hetton Colliery locomotive, once again in steam, leads the Centenary procession from Stockton to Darlington.

Below: The train of tableaux in the Centenary procession passing the grandstand.

[*British Railways*

Above: Patrick Stirling's 8 ft. single-driver No. I of the former Great Northern Railway in the Centenary procession.

Below: The last North Eastern Railway design, Raven's Pacific No. 2400 *City of Newcastle*, heads the "Flying Scotsman" train past the grandstand.

Below: The Raven express passenger electric locomotive, built for the N.E.R. main line electrification from York to Newcastle which never materialised.

[All British Railways

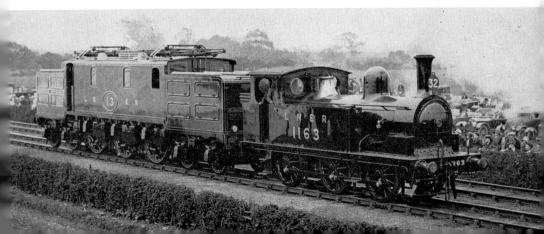

Above: An interesting group at the reopening after the 1939–1945 war of the York Railway Museum. On the right Sir Ronald Matthews, Chairman of the L.N.E.R. from 1938 until 1947; at the back Miles Beevor, acting Chief General Manager for the last six months of L.N.E.R. history; on the left C. M. Jenkin Jones, Divisional General Manager, North Eastern Area, L.N.E.R., from 1936 to 1947.

[*York Press Agency*

Below: Some of the exhibits in York Railway Museum. In the centre Britain's first Atlantic locomotive, Ivatt's No. 990 of the former Great Northern Railway; on the left No. 1275, a former North Eastern Railway 0–6–0.

[*British Railways*

He stressed the importance of bringing the management into the matter, rather than leaving it entirely to the directors. "It would be easy, however, under existing conditions", he continued, "for some of the Chairmen temporarily to grasp the control of group affairs, just as they got the nominal control of all proceedings at the Railway Association (and got into sad messes often in consequence)". He urged that Sir Alexander Butterworth should take the lead in these affairs, adding: "It is certain that Butterworth's leading position will be accepted by the Managers and also by the directors of other companies. . . . But Butterworth needs support . . . I do not believe that Lord K. has any real desire to retain the Chair during the interim period. He would probably be glad to get rid of the work and responsibility."

Various expedients were considered. One idea was to put all matters connected with the amalgamation into the hands of a responsible committee of directors, to be known as the Interim Joint Board, under Viscount Grey. To this, however, Lord Grey was reluctant to agree. "I don't want it", he wrote, "and if I am put in the Chair it must be because only in that way can agreement be secured or because Lord Knaresborough does not want to do it." This proposal died a natural death, but the North Eastern Railway set up a Special Committee to keep in touch with the course of affairs, under the Chairmanship of Lord Knaresborough, comprising Lord Joicey, Viscount Grey, Sir Hugh Bell, Sir Arthur Pease, Sir Alexander Butterworth, Walter K. Whigham and others; also Sir George Gibb, who attended from time to time as adviser.

Without much regard to the powers of the Railway Amalgamation Tribunal to impose a scheme of amalgamation if agreement were not reached between the companies by the end of 1922, Sir George Gibb urged that, rather than enter into a hurried amalgamation without complete unanimity in regard to finance and organisation, there should be an interim period during which each company would continue to work independently, on pre-war lines, as far as practicable with voluntary co-operation. But this, of course, was impossible.

The North British Board, taking advantage of a contact between Sir Harry Hope, one of their directors, and Murrough J. Wilson of the N.E.R. Board (both Members of Parliament), caused a hint to be dropped diplomatically that these two companies should get together for discussion at the earliest opportunity. To this suggestion Sir Alexander Butterworth returned an equally diplomatic answer: "Many thanks for your note, which is very satisfactory as far as it goes. I am trying to keep in touch with the North British, as far as possible, mainly through their Solicitor, Mr. James Watson, who is one of the ablest of the railway lawyers, but it is not very easy, as there is no getting away from the fact that on the question of allocation of stocks our interests and those of the North British are not identical. At the same time the relations between the two companies are, I believe, thoroughly friendly."

The North Eastern Railway Board finally found a solution to its difficulties by handing over the major part of its heavy responsibility to Sir Alexander Butterworth, who from time to time reported to the N.E.R. "Special Committee". For reasons explained in Chapter VI, Butterworth had relinquished his General Managership of the North Eastern in the autumn of 1921, and his resignation had been accepted by the Board with the qualification "that he be requested to remain in the service of the Company pending the formation of the Amalgamated Company for the purpose of advising the Board upon all questions relating to the Amalgamation". This wise step surprised no one, and such was his reputation that Butterworth was soon recognised as one of the principal figures in all the comings and goings among the Eastern group companies that led finally to agreement.

Comings and goings there certainly were. A contemporary observer recorded that "There was a great haggle among the constituent companies about the financial terms of consolidation. Throughout the lengthy negotiations, Mr. W. K. Whigham and Sir Alexander Butterworth upheld the claims of the North Eastern stockholders and secured for them a fair basis for the exchange of their holdings into the stocks of the new Company." But it would be impossible to follow the negotiations through their many vicissitudes. The "great haggle" was very tough going, and wounds were inflicted that were slow to heal.

Writing to Lord Knaresborough on a point that had arisen, Butterworth remarked: "May I suggest that you should write direct to Lord Faringdon, or that Dunnell should write to the G.C. Solicitor? I am afraid I am not exactly *persona grata* at Marylebone these days. I am afraid Lord Faringdon has never really forgiven me for some of my outspoken remarks in the early days of the Grouping controversy and he knows I was not prepared to go as far in his favour as Whigham did in the matter of the financial terms".

Eventually agreement was reached just before the deadline in time, but only at the cost of inflating the capital structure of the new company (set out in Table 7), as compared with the total paid-up capital of its

Table 7
Capital Structure of London & North Eastern Railway Company as at January 1st 1923
Debenture, Guaranteed, Preference and Ordinary Stock

		£
3 per cent. Debenture ⎫ ranking *pari passu*		66,352,793
4 per cent. Debenture ⎭		33,617,629
4 per cent. First Guaranteed		29,838,251
4 per cent. Second Guaranteed		27,329,739
4 per cent. First Preference		48,145,988
4 per cent. Second Preference		65,683,531
5 per cent. Preferred Ordinary		41,873,116
Deferred Ordinary		35,514,228
	Total	348,355,275
Total Loan Capital: £99,970,422.	Total Share Capital £248,384,853	

constituents, by more than £13,000,000, and this was to prove a serious burden to the London & North Eastern Railway in the days that lay ahead. It is of interest that the "Statistical Scrap Book" compiled by Sir Alexander Butterworth during the course of the financial negotiations is still in existence. In its 185 pages of foolscap size there are figures relating to all aspects of railway affairs, financial and traffic, some written in longhand, and others with statements or appreciations gummed on to the book's pages, while other pages contain extracts from annual accounts or from other officially published sources, not all relating exclusively to the constituent companies of the Eastern group. It is a mine of information going back in many aspects to the previous century.

Concurrently with the financial negotiations, discussions were taking place between the companies on other matters of major importance, such as the composition of the new Board, the appointment of the Chairman and General Manager, and the name by which the new company would be known. As to the Board, at this stage it was not a matter of names, but how many directors each constituent company was to nominate to serve on it, and as may well be imagined this proved to be a thorny subject. In August, 1921, Butterworth wrote to Lord Grey: "It was quite clear from the last meeting of Chairmen and General Managers that we were entering upon a stage of manoeuvring for position and influence, and it was ominous that our claim to something approaching one-third of the voting power in the Group was going to be seriously challenged by our London partners".

Notwithstanding the size and influence of the N.E.R., this claim no doubt was regarded by the Boards of the other constituents as being disproportionate; thus it was that Sir Alexander's fears proved to be well grounded. Arguments continued until July 19th, 1922, but at a meeting held that day in the North Eastern Railway's Westminster office it was thought, to the relief of the majority, that agreement had been reached. This relief was shattered, however, when a few weeks later Lord Knaresborough received a letter dated October 6th, 1922, and written from King's Cross, from Sir Frederick Banbury, Chairman of the Great Northern Railway, in the following terms:

"We had a Board Meeting here to consider the draft preliminary scheme.

"My Board feel that in view of the position of the Great Northern Railway they are entitled to five Directors in the New Company; this could be arranged by increasing the number of Directors to twenty-seven.

"The position then would be that the Company with the largest share in the New Company would have nine Directors, the next largest five, the three next four, and the smallest one.

"You will remember that the Great Northern declined to agree to the proposed allocations of Directors suggested at the meeting of our Financial Committee on July 19th at Cowley Street.

"Should you agree to our suggestion my Board would be prepared to select their Directors to serve on the new Company on the 19th of this month.

"I am sending a similar letter to the other Chairmen".

From the figures given earlier in this chapter concerning the agreed proportions of the division of net profits, had Parliament permitted the amalgamation of the Great Northern, Great Central and Great Eastern Companies in 1909, it is by no means certain that the Great Northern was the "next largest" constituent in the new group; that position might well have been claimed by the Great Eastern. Anyway, Lord Banbury's suggestion met with no favourable reception at York.

Lord Knaresborough acknowledged the letter, adding, tersely, that the impression of the N.E.R. representatives was that "the number of directors was settled by agreement on the 19th July, but I note your statement that the G.N.R. dissented". He also wrote to Butterworth: "I enclose a letter received this morning from Banbury . . . you will see that it contains a suggestion *and* a threat, viz., that if we do not agree he will not select his directors. He is very anxious to postpone the amalgamation until July 1923 . . . You will know better than I do how far he can obstruct. . . . He is evidently out for mischief!"

Two days later Lord Knaresborough wrote again to Sir Alexander: "I *suppose* we cannot go to our shareholders till this preliminary scheme is agreed to by *all* the Companies in our Group? Unless, I suppose, we agree to absorb or amalgamate, leaving out the G.N.R. Banbury is evidently for some reason or other catching at every straw to postpone amalgamation. But is this straw of fighting for five directors for the G.N.R. a substantial branch to hold on to? I mean if he hangs on to it can he stop us from presenting a scheme or preliminary scheme to the Tribunal? . . . Can Banbury absolutely hang up all advance? I suppose his Board are in his pocket till the new directors are chosen. It seems to me that you had better be careful in view of all this about the date of your resignation. . . . I wonder what Faringdon's attitude is about the five directors. Banbury did not indicate whether the G.N.R. would accept five for them also".

To these letters Butterworth replied: "The Great Northern can of course drive us to the alternatives of going their pace or leaving them out of the scheme, and I suppose if they made it impossible for us to start the scheme on January 1st next, we should accept the second alternative, much as we should regret it. As to their demand for a fifth director, it is very late in the day to put this forward, and not quite fair to the N.E.R. since the composition of the Board was treated by us as a vital matter when the financial terms were under discussion. But technically I think Sir F. B. is right in saying that the G.N. never expressly assented to the numbers of Directors. My own feeling is that if this concession will really and finally bring the G.N. cordially into line, we might assent to it without doing ourselves or anyone else much harm. But I am not at all sure what line the other Companies will take. In the past the G.N. have had very few friends except myself."

As one of the constituent companies' Chairmen, William Whitelaw had received a copy of Sir Frederick Banbury's letter, and he displayed some native Scottish caution in handling it. Writing to Butterworth, he said: "I presume you will have seen the letter written by Sir Frederick Banbury to the Chairmen. . . . In replying, I am not committing myself to any opinion; before doing so I shall want to know the views of the N.E. representatives. Some months ago I worked out various figures based on length of road, single track mileage, capital and gross and net revenue, and apportioned 24 directors among the five large companies accordingly. I enclose a copy of this statement, the last column of which gives the full result of the calculations. On these figures the G.N. is really more entitled to five than the N.E. is to eight. Personally I do not attach importance to this matter but perhaps others may take a different view".

The statement referred to by Whitelaw appears on p.46 (Table 8); it is of exceptional interest as an illustration of the meticulous care and practical application with which he approached most problems and his readiness to work things out for himself with, if needs be, a home-made formula. It was typed by himself on a machine whose fount of type, certainly not of the most modern, was to become very familiar in L.N.E.R. days. To Whitelaw's communication Butterworth's reply was to communicate to him the terms of Knaresborough's acknowledgement of Banbury's letter, adding: "I do not think I can add anything until we have had our meeting at York, but my own feeling is that if it would ease matters with the Great Northern it would be as well to let them have their extra director. I think, however, that if this is done it should be without prejudice to a reduction of the Board in the future, for I think twenty-six is already larger than the Board ought to be".

To cut a long story short, however, eventually the Great Northern demand for an extra place on the amalgamated company's Board was defeated by the other constituents, and that company—or should we say its Chairman?—became resigned to the inevitable. The business of nominating the directors who were to take up the assigned places went on behind the closed doors of the various Board Rooms, and no record remains of what transpired. There were few difficulties in the case of the North Eastern Railway. It had been tacitly agreed that one place would be given to a member of the Board of the recently absorbed Hull & Barnsley Railway, but when the list was made public it was seen that this place was additional to the eight seats claimed by the N.E.R. Following is the complete list:

Appointed by the North Eastern Railway (Eight)
> Rt. Hon. Lord Joicey.
> Sir Hugh Bell, Bart., C.B.
> Rt. Hon. Viscount Grey of Fallodon, K.G.
> John Henry Brunel Noble.
> Sir Arthur Francis Pease, Bart.

Table 8

Statement prepared by William Whitelaw to show, on a proportional basis, the number of Constituent Company Directors entitled to sit on the L.N.E.R. Board

(Figures based on 1913 Accounts)

Railway	Length of Road First Track	Proportion of Directors	Single Track including Sidings	Proportion of Directors	Capital Expended Account No. 4	Proportion of Directors	Gross Revenue Account No. 8 (above the line)	Proportion of Directors	Net Revenue Account No. 8	Proportion of Directors	Average Proportion of Directors
	miles		miles		£		£		£		
G.C.R.	824	3.2	2,570	3.8	56,569,000	4.5	6,549,000	4.1	2,218,000	3.8	3.88
G.E.R.	1,191	4.6	2,616	3.9	53,783,000	4.3	6,713,000	4.2	2,173,000	3.8	4.16
G.N.R.	1,032	4.0	3,064	4.6	53,746,000	4.3	6,949,000	4.5	2,463,000	4.3	4.42
N.E.R.	1,752	6.8	4,886	7.4	84,862,000	6.7	12,235,000	7.7	4,454,000	7.7	7.26
N.B.R.	1,375	5.0	2,704	4.0	51,110,000	4.0	5,576,000	3.5	2,427,000	4.2	4.14
Total	6,174	—	15,840	—	300,068,000	—	38,022,000	—	13,735,000	—	23.86
1/24th	257	—	660	—	12,503,000	—	1,583,000	—	572,000	—	—

Oswald Sanderson.
Walter Kennedy Whigham.
Murrough John Wilson, M.P.

Appointed by the N.E.R. from the Hull & Barnsley Railway (One)
Col. Charles William Trotter, C.B.

Appointed by the Great Central Railway (Four)
Rt. Hon. Lord Faringdon, C.H.
Walter Burgh Gair
Edwin A. Beazley
Hon. Eric Butler-Henderson

Appointed by the Great Eastern Railway (Four)
Rt. Hon. Lord Ailwyn, P.C., K.C.V.O., K.B.E.
Hubert T. Bailey
Col. William Johnson Galloway
Sir Eric Hambro, K.B.E.

Appointed by the Great Northern Railway (Four)
Frederick Liddell Steel
Hon. Rupert Evelyn Beckett
Oliver Robert Hawke Bury
Bernard Alexander Firth

Appointed by the North British Railway (Four)
William Whitelaw, J.P.
A. Reith Gray
Lt.-Col. Hon. Arthur Cecil Murray, C.M.G., D.S.O., M.P.
Andrew Kirkwood McCosh

Appointed by the Great North of Scotland Railway (One)
Alexander Duffus

The new Board thus consisted of twenty-six members. It included some famous names, and was representative of various walks of life, notably "The Establishment"; the Law; the City, Finance and Banking; Trade and Industry, and heavy industry in particular; Mining; and Shipping. One point of note was that three of the former Chairmen saw fit to retire, including, not surprisingly in view of his difficult attitude throughout the negotiations, Lord Banbury; the remaining Chairmen appointed to serve on the new Board were Lord Faringdon and the two Scots, William Whitelaw and Alexander Duffus. The question now exercising many minds, and dealt with in Chapter V, was who would occupy the responsible position of Chairman of the new company.

V

The New Company—Its Chairman

IT IS not in the least derogatory to the memory of that great character, William Whitelaw, to say that he was elected, *faute de mieux*, as the first Chairman of the London & North Eastern Railway. He himself shared in the general surprise created by his election: "They had much better have chosen Sir Alexander Butterworth" was his comment on hearing the news. It has always been assumed that he was influenced, in accepting the appointment, by the prospect of an occupation which would act as an anodyne to his grief at losing two sons in the 1914-1918 war.

Be that as it may, he had been Chairman of two railway companies for a total of 23 years, and had looked on the Railways Act, 1921, as signalling the end of his tenure of that office. Though it could not have been foreseen in 1922, the L.N.E.R. was to have financial difficulties, and the selection of a Chairman who already had presided over the fortunes of two railways which were far from "comfortably off" might have been held to show prophetic wisdom. Yet Whitelaw remained in office longer than the Chairmen of all the other three railway groups, over a further span of 15 years guiding, with dignity and unerring touch, the destinies of the new company.

But surprise there certainly was when it was known who was to occupy the chair. Forebodings were expressed that he might treat this new concern, made up of seven major railways and sixteen subsidiary undertakings, merely as an enlarged North British Railway. Lord Claud Hamilton of the Great Eastern—and strangely, perhaps, for one bearing his surname, though actually he was an Ulsterman—was troubled on nationalistic grounds; "The Chairman of a Scottish railway for one of the 'Big Four' ", he said, "is asking for trouble". Sir Eric Geddes is alleged to have been even more forthright, declaring of Whitelaw: "He represents the bygone feudal system of railway management, when railway directors regarded the General Manager much as they would their bailiff or gamekeeper." But such doubts were soon dispelled.

On the other hand, viewed from within the circle of the major constituent companies, there were good reasons for the choice of William Whitelaw. Age and other considerations eliminated the Chairmen of three former companies—Lord Claud Hamilton of the Great Eastern, approaching his 80th year; Lord Knaresborough of the North Eastern, 76; and Sir Frederick Banbury of the Great Northern, 78—even though we had not yet reached the era when men were regarded as "too old at sixty". This left Lord Faringdon of the Great Central and Whitelaw. As far as possible the latter had avoided clashes with other companies; not so with Lord Faringdon, as the restless history of the Great Central had proved. This may have swayed opinion in Whitelaw's favour; and in addition, as will be seen in a moment, Faringdon had some distinctly heterodox views about the Chairmanship. But the issue was a long time in getting settled.

Initially there had been a strong movement in favour of making Sir Alexander Butterworth the Chairman of the new company. He himself was aware of this, for in August, 1921, he wrote as follows in a letter to Viscount Grey of Fallodon: "Since I saw you I have learnt from a reliable source that my name has been canvassed in connection with the future Chairmanship to a greater degree than I had any idea of, and I have reason to think that it would be favourably received by every company except the Great Northern. I am told that Sir Frederick Banbury's attitude is that he recognises the prior claim of Lord Knaresborough, but that failing Lord Knaresborough he considers that he has something approaching an indefeasible claim to the position, and that on no account will he accept your humble servant".

Viscount Grey's reply to this was of great interest:

"Fallodon,
August 21, 1921.

"My dear Butterworth,
"I am obliged for your letter. This business of choosing a Chairman of the Group has become, as such things always do, the subject of intrigue and manoeuvring.

"The post of Chairman is going to be of full time work that will absorb all the time and energy of the man who holds it. It must be settled on merits and not on prescriptive right, as Banbury apparently suggests.

"These inside manoeuvrings may result in an outside Chairman being chosen on his merits, with you as G.M. of the Group, or they may result in you being chosen as Chairman—also on merits. I distrust my own qualifications for the post. Being on a railway Board is just what I like, and I should be glad to be on the Board of the Group even though it will mean more work and attendance than the N.E.R. alone. But the Chairman will have to live mostly in London and give up leisure and other interests in life for some years. I have had enough of office to know what it means and I don't like it.

"Yours sincerely,
Grey of F."

Butterworth's acknowledgment opened on a slightly plaintive note, but he then proceeded, quite casually, to drop a bombshell. Whether or not this was done with the idea of overcoming Grey's reluctance to put himself forward for the office can be no more than a matter for conjecture to-day:

D

"Cowley Street, S.W.1.
24 August 1921.

"Dear Lord Grey,

". . . I quite appreciate your feeling about the Chairmanship, but you will also appreciate that had it been possible to have been the General Manager of the Group under yourself as the Chairman that would have been just the position I should have liked, and if you found you had had enough of it after two or three years, and the new Board had been willing that I should succeed you, my content and happiness (officially speaking) would have been secure for all time, but I can quite see that these are 'castles in the air' that will never be realised.

"One thing I am determined upon and that is that I will not lend myself to manoeuvre or intrigue. If anything comes to me I hope it will be on merits, or supposed merits, and I shall gratefully accept it. If not, I shall retire, and will try to do so as gracefully as possible.

"At the moment, I think things point to a Chairman from outside, and the only two names I have heard suggested are Granet and Geddes. There are signs which seem to point strongly to the latter desiring it, if not actually angling for it. Granet, I believe, would like it, but I doubt whether he would 'stand for it' in opposition to Geddes. On the other hand, I cannot conceive that Geddes will be chosen. I find, however, that some people think there are more impossible things in the world, and one objection, viz., that a certain number of the staff would at once leave, would be to some extent, if not entirely, got over by his ability to bring his own staff with him from the Ministry. . . . At present, however, I think there is nothing to be done except get such holiday as is possible, and think of other things.

"Yours sincerely,

"A. Kaye B."

Sir Guy Granet at the time was Chairman of the Midland Railway, and from the formation of the London Midland & Scottish Railway in 1923 became its Joint Deputy Chairman; but he occupied the post of Chairman of that company from 1924 until succeeded by Sir Josiah Stamp, his nominee, in 1927. Sir Eric Geddes, as we have seen already in Chapter I, had been Deputy General Manager of the North Eastern Railway up to the outbreak of war in 1914, and was under special agreement with the N.E.R. Board to succeed eventually to the post of General Manager. He had then been loaned to the Government, and by 1919 had become the first Minister of Transport, but only after his connection with the North Eastern had been definitely severed.

It would be pleasant to imagine that Butterworth accepted his own advice and went quietly away on holiday to "think of other things". If he did so he might have spared a thought for the effect that the blast from the explosion that he had set off would have on the North Eastern Board, who only three years before had paid Geddes £50,000 on the consideration that "all connection between Sir Eric Geddes and the Company shall come to an end". Several of the N.E.R. directors expressed themselves forcibly when the Geddes idea began to circulate. Sir Arthur Pease observed: "Gibb first mentioned to me the Geddes rumour and afterwards Butterworth in a private note. It seems to me the proposal is impossible on several grounds". Sir Hugh Bell wrote, "I cannot help feeling that it would put the North Eastern Board in a very awkward position indeed if, after all that has happened, Geddes came back to us in any such position as that suggested. If I were satisfied that the solution were a good one, I should not mind the adverse views which would, I have no doubt, be expressed, though I confess it would be very distasteful to me to serve on a Board with him". To this letter to Lord Joicey he added, "Kitson and Noble who happen to be here to-day concur in thinking Geddes' appointment quite out of the question." Lord Joicey was Deputy Chairman of the North Eastern Railway at that time, and John Noble and Roland Dudley Kitson were directors.

In a longer letter to Viscount Grey, written about the same time, Sir Hugh Bell wrote: "There seems to be no doubt Geddes is trying to be made either Chairman or Managing Director. I do not know how you would view such an outcome, but it seems to me it would place the North Eastern directors in a very awkward position and would lay us open to extremely unpleasant criticism. I think it would be extremely unpopular. I very much question whether it would work satisfactorily, and unless I am very much mistaken, I think it would very considerably complicate the arrangements as to management which we thought would be best. It would, I fear, involve the loss of Butterworth's services entirely".

The last sentence is of particular interest, and not less significant is the reference to the position of "Managing Director". Although this was a post hitherto unknown on any British railway, it is now known that many years before Sir George Gibb had suggested to the North Eastern Railway Board the creation of such a post, but his enthusiasm for it was not reciprocated, and he dropped the idea. Nevertheless Geddes would have known of this plan, as also would Sir Hugh Bell, so that this reference tends to confirm the personal interest of Sir Eric Geddes in the course of affairs at this particular stage. As a body, therefore, the North Eastern Railway directors were resolutely opposed to the return of Geddes to any directorial or executive position in the new company. But not all the directors of the other constituent companies shared the same view. There is every indication that Lord Faringdon, Chairman of the Great Central, if not himself the originator of the idea, was a strong supporter of the proposal to nominate Geddes as the Chairman of the new company.

Commenting in a letter to Sir Alexander Butterworth on the appointment from January 1st, 1922, of R. L. Wedgwood as General Manager of the North Eastern Railway, William Whitelaw wrote, in somewhat guarded terms: "The proposed appointment of Mr. Wedgwood will have the support of the North British Company. This does not mean that I am anything but disappointed at your not occupying the position for several years at any rate. I only hope that I shall not find that this bargain with Lord Faringdon covers something else; anyhow I have always had in view that the N.E. Board were entitled to select the General Manager, as well as to nominate a Chairman if they could find someone for the latter position who was really qualified". To this Butterworth, who, it may be added, was by now 67 years of age, replied: "Thanks for your kind letter. No, there is no 'bargain' with Lord Faringdon . . . and if his idea still is to get Sir Eric as Chairman, we are entirely opposed to him."

At that time, November, 1921, it is clear that the idea of persuading Viscount Grey of Fallodon to accept the Chairmanship had not been abandoned, and it was undoubtedly a great disappointment to a number of influential directors of various of the constituent companies that he would not allow his name to be put forward. It is of interest that the North British Railway Board was unanimous in agreeing that the Chairman of the London & North Eastern Railway should be Lord Grey, the Chief Officer Sir Alexander Butterworth, notwithstanding his age, and the Headquarters at York. But, as we have just seen, Lord Grey was not prepared to "play". What, then, of the chances of Butterworth to become Chairman rather than General Manager?

There is some evidence to show that, contrary to Butterworth's impression that the Great Northern Board was the stumbling block to his nomination to the Chair of the new company, actually Lord Faringdon of the Great Central, resenting some of Butterworth's outspoken remarks on financial terms, was the rock on which foundered any chance that the latter might have had of becoming either Chairman or Chief General Manager. On the other hand, there is no evidence to suggest that the thought of bringing in Sir Guy Granet from outside as Chairman aroused any strong feelings of antagonism.

This is not really surprising. In Midland days Sir Guy had shown himself an able and astute General Manager of that company and later a most capable Chairman. He had always been on excellent terms with Sir George Gibb and Sir Alexander Butterworth, and with his city interests he was in every respect a personality of distinction who inspired general respect. It is significant that as early as September, 1921, the possibility of Sir Guy coming to the Eastern group had been in the mind of Sir George Gibb, for in that month, to a letter expressing the hope that Lord Grey might be persuaded to take the Chairmanship, he added: "or perhaps Granet, if Lord Grey is, as I suspect, rather half-hearted in his willingness to act". It is possible that at that time Granet would not have been reluctant to accept such an invitation, as no doubt he did not altogether relish the role at first cast for him as Joint Deputy Chairman only of the London, Midland & Scottish Railway, rather than having the supreme command from the start. But as things turned out, a year later he became Chairman of that company, and from then on no offer from the London & North Eastern would have been likely to tempt him.

After the end of 1921 the intrigues and manoeuvrings for the supreme L.N.E.R. posts seem to have terminated.   There appears then to have been a tacit agreement all round to let the question of the Chairmanship take its course, and the names of Geddes and Granet were heard no more in this connection.   The great haggle between the constituent companies over financial terms was absorbing everyone's energies, and it was not until the end of 1922 that the election to the Chairmanship of the new company took place.   And this was, as we have seen, and to his own surprise, William Whitelaw.   In view of the contention of Lord Grey's letter of August 21, 1921, already quoted, as to the demands that the Chairmanship would make upon the holder, it is worthy of note that Whitelaw held only one other directorship, that of the Bank of Scotland.   Apart from this, his only outside interest was in the affairs of the Church of Scotland, which caused him to be both a regular attender and also a not infrequent speaker at the General Assembly in Edinburgh.

VI

The New Company—Its Chief General Manager

NOT SURPRISINGLY, it was from an early date that the question of the Group General Managership began to exercise the minds of the leading spirits in the constituent companies. As things were in August, 1921, the situation was a complicated one. Of the occupants of this position on the five principal constituents, Sir Sam Fay of the Great Central was 65 years of age; Charles Hastings Dent of the Great Northern was slightly younger, but probably had little desire for the tremendous responsibilities that this major task would bring; much the same could be said of James Calder of the North British, then only 52, who was happy to remain in Scotland.

Sir Alexander Butterworth of the North Eastern, though 67, seemed oblivious of his age; in his case certainly "age did not weary nor the years condemn". Even so, it would have been a tough assignment at his time of life to tackle the formation and the initial management of so vast a concern as the new London & North Eastern Railway. Moreover, as we have seen already in Chapter V, by some he was being thought of in those days as the probable Chairman. There remained Sir Henry Thornton of the Great Eastern, then no more than 50 years of age, an American, of tremendous vigour, with a great record of achievement, both on the G.E.R. and in his wartime service. By now he had largely overcome the dislike which his appointment in 1914 had aroused in many quarters; surely he was the obvious choice!

But Thornton's biographer, D'Arcy Marsh, probably put his finger on the weak link, when he wrote: "Something in the story of his life, something in the character of the man himself, had made him into first-class newspaper 'copy'. He had become more than a railway executive; he had become, to the British public, something of a buoyant adventurer." And in those days such qualities were hardly likely to commend such a man to every Board Room of the railway "Establishment." When rumours of his impending withdrawal from the railway scene began to circulate, Sir Hugh Bell wrote: "It looks as if Sir Henry Thornton did not mean to remain as a full-time railwayman. If so one of our difficulties is removed."

Thornton's actual resignation from the General Managership of the G.E.R. did not come, however, until September, 1922. D'Arcy Marsh has related how J. H. Thomas, the secretary of the National Union of Railwaymen who later entered the Labour Government of 1924, was instrumental in putting him in touch with the Canadian National Railways. "How'd you like to go to Canada, Henry?" he is reported to have said to Thornton, and the more Thornton thought about the idea the better he liked it. The result was that his mind was pretty well made up "without waiting to see what delegation of managerial authority would follow on the consummation of the English merger", as D'Arcy Marsh polysyllabically puts it. So Thornton left these shores to become President of the Canadian National Railways—"before him," writes his biographer, "a task of overwhelming proportions, the glittering rewards of a fortune taken at the flood", but then, unhappily, "the shallows and the miseries of a swift ebb-tide".

Thornton's going made it almost certain that R. L. Wedgwood would become General Manager of the group. Indeed, there was no one else, unless Lord Faringdon or any others had insisted on bringing in someone from outside the service. But it would have been much more difficult to find a fully qualified outside candidate for this post than for the Chairmanship. Various ideas were canvassed. One which originated with some members of the North Eastern Railway Board was that Sir Alexander Butterworth should resign the General Managership of that company in favour of Wedgwood, but that the former should be created "Chief Officer" of the N.E.R., and as such become the North Eastern nominee for the post of Group General Manager. The object was to put forward a name of such weight that no possible objection could be raised; then, after a few years, Sir Alexander could retire and leave the way open for Wedgwood to succeed him. But the proposal did not appeal to Butterworth. "I thought the programme an inconsistent one", he wrote, "and that as regards myself the first move would militate against the success of the second. I admit that it is a matter of opinion, and in any event it is the opinion of the directors and not mine that must prevail".

As early as August, 1921, Sir Alexander had a talk with Wedgwood on the matter, and smoothed the way for the latter to discuss things with Viscount Grey, who subsequently communicated to Butterworth the outcome of the meeting: "My talk with Wedgwood brought out nothing new. The position is that he wants to become General Manager of the N.E. Rly. on equal terms with the General Managers of other lines, so that he will have an equal chance with them of making good his succession to General Managership of the Group. If he were in that position of General Manager of the N.E. Rly. he would decline an outside offer. . . . That is the impression I got. It must be talked over at our September meeting".

The North Eastern Directors, however, seemed unable to make up their minds. Writing to one of them on 2nd November, 1921, Butterworth urged the necessity of decision:

"I think that what the N.E. Board ought to direct their minds primarily to is the surest means of securing that the chief official position (not merely at the first start but for years) shall go to someone in whom the

North Eastern Board has complete confidence, recognising that it is more than likely that candidates will be put forward for that position whose qualities would not or might not entirely commend themselves to the North Eastern directors".

A few days later, obviously anxious alike at the lack of decision and the effluxion of time, Sir Alexander addressed a private memorandum to his Board on the subject. It was a lengthy and closely reasoned document breathing throughout the little man's loyalty to his company and his affection for his Deputy, Wedgwood. After calling for careful thinking in a complicated situation, and insisting that the interests of the North Eastern Railway must take precedence over any personal considerations, he wrote:

"I will merely point out that the answers might be different if Amalgamation were coming about on 1st January, 1922, from what they would be if it were going to be postponed till 1st January, 1925. But obviously, if W's best chance of becoming ultimate Group General Manager depends on *initial* appointment, the aim of the Directors should at once be directed towards making as good as possible his prospects of being accepted as first General Manager to the Group, e.g. by at once giving him a General Manager's status and experience. If, on the other hand, his best chance lies in the other direction (i.e. by succeeding B.) then the important thing is to do everything to improve and nothing to diminish B.'s chances of being chosen or accepted as the first Group General Manager. . . . Of course, the matter would be greatly simplified if you could arrange with a majority of the Group to support your programme, i.e., your nominee, and the most practical step would seem to be to try and bring this about".

The "B" in the passage just quoted was, of course, Butterworth's unassuming way of referring to himself, and the final paragraph of his memorandum revealed, no doubt unwittingly, the stature of the man who for nearly sixteen years had guided the destinies of his company:

"In conclusion, a word about myself. As I have said more than once, I have no wish to relinquish either my work or my salary as long as I am fit to discharge the one and earn the other, and I should like to work for the Group after Amalgamation, if I am still fit for work of that sort. But I should not like, and would not knowingly agree, to remain in my present or any other position a moment longer than the Directors thought it was to the interest of the Company that I should do so. I have had a good innings, and the last thing I should like would be in any way to outstay my welcome. Besides, I am not unmindful of the kindness I have always received from the Directors both individually and collectively. Therefore they need have no hesitation in telling me that in their view the time has come when it would be in the interest of the Company that I should relinquish the reins in favour of a younger man. I shall comply without any sense of grievance and I shall be ready to retire wholly or to undertake other work for the Company, as the Directors may think to be most in the interests of the Company".

Admirable indeed—but even at the age of 67, not an entirely unqualified *Nunc Dimittis*.

This document was at last successful in bringing the North Eastern Railway Board to the point of decision. At their next meeting, on 11th November, 1921, the following Minute was drawn:

"In view of the approaching amalgamation of the Companies forming the North Eastern, Eastern and Scottish group, the question of the General Managership of the Company pending such amalgamation and the bearing which any change might have upon the selection of the first General Manager of the Amalgamated Company were considered by the Board, and Sir Alexander Butterworth having expressed his desire that the Directors should not allow any considerations of his personal interests to stand in the way of the adoption of whatever course the Board considered would be in the best interests of the Company and having stated that the Directors might regard themselves as having a tender of his resignation in their hands, it was RESOLVED:

1. That Sir Alexander Butterworth's resignation of the position of General Manager be accepted as from 31st December next, but that he be requested to remain in the service of the Company at his present salary pending the formation of the Amalgamated Company for the purpose of advising the Board upon all questions relating to the Amalgamation.

2. That Mr. R. L. Wedgwood be appointed General Manager of the Company from 1st January next. . . .

3. That it be placed on record that it is the intention of the Board to make Sir Alexander Butterworth when his connection with the Company ceases an adequate financial grant in recognition of the most valuable services he has rendered to the Company during his association with it first as Solicitor and then as General Manager".

As Sir Alexander had suggested, the North Eastern Directors then took the further step, through their Chairman, Lord Knaresborough, of informing the Chairmen of the other companies in the Group of their decision, and intimating that they were putting forward R. L. Wedgwood as their candidate for the General Managership of the new company. William Whitelaw's support for this nomination has been noted already; that of Lord Faringdon, Chairman of the Great Central, was rather more reserved. "I think you have done well in appointing Wedgwood as your General Manager", he wrote to Lord Knaresborough. "He will have my support when the bigger question of a General Manager for the grouped lines comes up for consideration. No one man, however, will be able to take working control of so large a system as the Eastern Group. I quite anticipate that it will be found necessary to have a *consortium* of managers, at any rate to begin with"—an intelligent anticipation of the divisional system of organisation, with Area General Managers, which the London & North Eastern Railway eventually adopted.

So it was that R. L. Wedgwood took over the General Managership of the North Eastern Railway for the last year of its separate existence, towards the end of which the directors-to-be of the new Company unanimously appointed him Chief General Manager from 1st January, 1923. It is of interest to add that in later years there existed between him and Lord Faringdon, who became Deputy Chairman of the L.N.E.R., a mutual relationship of high regard and esteem.

It is not inappropriate here to give a brief sketch of the life of the man who was at the helm for just over 17 out of the total quarter of a century's history of the London & North Eastern Railway. Ralph Lewis Wedgwood was born on 2nd March, 1874, the third son of Clement Francis Wedgwood and great-great-grandson of Josiah Wedgwood, founder of the far-famed pottery firm bearing his name. He was thus inheritor of the great radical and intellectual traditions associated with Wedgwood and Darwin; his great-uncle by marriage was, indeed, Charles Darwin himself. Ralph was educated at Clifton and Trinity College, Cambridge, where at the age of 22 he took a first in the Moral Philosophy Tripos. Forthwith he was invited by Sir George Gibb to join the staff of the North Eastern Railway, and accepted without hesitation. That this young intellectual, scion of a distinguished family, should have opted for what might well have seemed to him anything so mundane as railway service is explicable because from his early days, like so many "spotters" of later years, he had developed a deep interest in, and affection for, railways and trains. His brother Frank had been bitten in the same way, and it is not without interest that the latter became a director, first of the North Staffordshire and later of the London, Midland & Scottish Railway.

Ralph Wedgwood started his railway career on Tees-side, there gaining familiarity with traffic and dock working, and becoming District Superintendent at Middlesbrough in 1902. Then, in 1904, at the early age of 30, he was appointed Secretary to the North Eastern Railway. His interest, however, was in the Traffic Department and a year later, at his own request, he returned to that department as Divisional Goods Manager at Newcastle. In 1911 he became Assistant Goods Manager at York, and succeeded Eric Geddes as Chief Goods Manager on the latter being appointed Deputy General Manager in the same year. When Philip Burtt, the N.E.R. Passenger Manager, retired in 1914, Wedgwood added the duties of this office to his own, and in all these appointments thus gained an exceptionally wide experience of the traffic side of railway business.

Then came the First World War, in which Wedgwood volunteered for service, being transferred, after a spell in the Transport Establishment in France, to the Ministry of Munitions. From 1916 to 1919 he was Director of Docks, under the Director-General of Transportation in France, with the rank of Brigadier-General. Much of his life during this period was spent in a sleeping car, and he often used to look back with nostalgia on this existence in such typically railway surroundings. His war service was rewarded by the bestowal of the C.B. and the C.M.G.

He then returned to the North Eastern Railway in 1919 as Deputy General Manager, and, as we have seen, succeeded Sir Alexander Butterworth as General Manager from the beginning of 1922, finally becoming Chief General Manager of the London & North Eastern Railway from the formation of the Company in 1923.

In 1924 he received the honour of knighthood, and in 1942, on his retirement from the Railway Executive Committee, a baronetcy was conferred on him. Among many other activities of a busy life, Wedgwood was President of the Confederation of Employers' Organisations for the year 1929-1930, a member of the Weir Committee on Main Line Electrification in 1930-1931, and a member of the Central Electricity Board from 1931 to 1946; he was also Chairman of the Committee of Enquiry into Indian Railways in 1936 and 1937.

As Chief General Manager of the L.N.E.R., Sir Ralph was the embodiment of the classical quality *gravitas*, and, certainly to the younger elements, a somewhat awe-inspiring figure. To some extent this austerity of demeanour and outlook was accentuated by the form of organisation adopted by the company, with the Chief General Manager at the summit of a pyramid, supported by the Area General Managers, who coped with much of the hurly-burly of daily work. But the awe owed much more to the intellectual power which Wedgwood brought to bear on every item reaching his desk, and the lucidity with which his views and judgments were expressed. His letters on major subjects, and his policy directives, were couched in language which had all the force and authority of Papal encyclicals. The recipients therefore were under some compulsion to put forth their best into any action that was necessary, or any reply that they were required to make.

But with all this, it must not be thought that Wedgwood ever ceased to be a railwayman to the core. The railway lore acquired in his earliest days, and the practical first-hand experience of railway working that he had gained on Tees-side in the tough first years of his railway life, never left him. Thus he was always able to appreciate every detail of the proposals and plans put before him by his officers, and to master, not only their intrinsic merits, but also their significance in the general scheme of things. The officers sponsoring major schemes, as in discussion he sat opposite them in isolation at his desk, realised that he was just as familiar with what was being proposed as they were.

His great gifts showed at their best when he was in the witness-box. It was no small satisfaction to the railway lawyers when, in any major case, they were to have him as witness. He was always a complete master of his brief, for as a preliminary he would go to the greatest lengths in order to marshal all the relevant facts, foreseeing any possible line of attack that opposing counsel might take. Moreover, his alert mind was proof against any surprise question shaking him in cross-examination, and not infrequently he caused counsel on the other side to retire frustrated.

One outstanding tribute to Wedgwood's competence in this field was paid by a former Chief Officer of the London Midland & Scottish Railway, A. J. Pearson, in his book, *The Railways and the Nation*, in which he wrote: "Sir Ralph Wedgwood's name was a household word on British railways between the wars. One of the beacons of his career was the evidence he gave to the Railway Rates Tribunal in the great revision of railway charges of 1920-1927 when he was in the witness-box day after day under cross-examination. It was a wonderful performance, and his patience and endurance were remarkable". A tribute to his powers also was made by Lord Brabazon when the latter was Minister of Transport during the early part of the Second World War. After sitting-in at a session of the Railway Executive Committee, the Minister remarked that it all seemed very complicated to him, but added that nowhere, even among the top echelons of the Civil Service, had he heard such quick and incisive arguments as those of Sir Ralph.

If, at these Olympian heights, Wedgwood was sometimes felt to be a little aloof from the rhythm of the railway, it was because smoking concerts and similar "get-togethers" were not altogether in his line of country, and it was not his way to assume any unnatural semblance of heartiness. On the other hand the Chairman, William Whitelaw, had a natural gift for presiding acceptably on such occasions, and Wedgwood was therefore wise enough to leave the representation of the higher command as far as possible to Whitelaw at such social events. Nevertheless, behind a somewhat formidable exterior the former concealed a very human personality. His pithy and pertinent comments of any item of news, or his witty sallies provoked by quite ordinary incidents in daily life, were a joy to hear. And when once, in the quiet hours of the day at Liverpool Street Station, he was seen to try walking up a descending escalator, remarking "I've always wondered how difficult it was", one felt that the eternal boy was not far below the surface.

This being so, it is not surprising that the policy of introducing Britain's first high speed streamline train, the "Silver Jubilee", was one for which he was personally responsible. In this he was fortunate in having the collaboration, as Chief Mechanical Engineer, of Sir Nigel Gresley, who produced the fine locomotives and rolling stock needed to make this express and its successors, the "Coronation" and "West Riding Limited", the outstanding success that they were. His admiration for Sir Nigel was great, and the two men, so unlike in many ways, were close friends. On being told of Gresley's untimely death in 1941, Sir Ralph was deeply moved. His comment, so typical of the speaker, might well have been used as Sir Nigel's epitaph: "A great Englishman whose ancestors fought at Agincourt".

Such, in a few words, is a portrait of the man selected to be the Chief Officer of the London & North Eastern Railway for the 16 years from the company's inauguration in 1923. Some have held the view that he was too much of an intellectual and too remote in consequence; others may have felt that by comparison, say, with Sir Josiah Stamp of the London, Midland & Scottish his leadership was too much in the background; nevertheless the general opinion has been that no better appointment could have been made.

Under his guidance a number of large corporations, each with its own traditions and loyalties, were moulded in a comparatively few years into a loyalty to the London & North Eastern Railway without experiencing any of the troubles that beset the L.M.S.R. in its early years, which finally made it necessary for the latter company to bring in a personality from outside to accomplish this by no means easy task. Wedgwood saw the L.N.E.R. through the difficult peace years, with the financial anxieties and labour troubles described in later chapters, and when in 1939 the nation had once again to resort to arms because of German aggression it was Sir Ralph, by then retired from railway service, who was selected by the Government to be Chairman of the Railway Executive Committee, charged with managing all the railways of the country. Through his railway life it was a long, rather lonely, and very hard furrow that Sir Ralph Wedgwood was destined to plough, but plough it he did, and looking back we can see that the furrow was straight.

VII

The New Company—Its Name

AMONG ALL the other complicated preparations that had to be made for the amalgamation, one that occasioned a great deal of argument was the all-important choice of a name. And when at length "London & North Eastern Railway" was decided on, it was a title which by no means pleased everyone. Some thought it unnecessarily cumbersome. Others regarded it as an attempt to perpetuate the name of the London & North Western Railway, now just about to disappear, but with "Eastern" substituted for "Western". Why was it necessary to incorporate "London" in the title, when none of the constituent companies acknowledged its link with the capital in this way? The objection of some of the Southerners was all the greater, as this name might indicate that the new group was to be a glorified North Eastern Railway, from now on firmly linked to the Metropolis by a line of its own. And then there was the practical objection that the use of five initials—or four if the *serif* were omitted—would add to the cost of lettering rolling stock, station signs, and so on.

It was certainly very late in 1922 before the final decision was taken; in October discussion was still active. In a letter dated 9th of that month, William Whitelaw told Sir Alexander Butterworth: "I have written to Lord Faringdon and Sir Frederick Banbury about the name of the Company. I do not like 'North and Eastern'; I think a much better name would be 'The Great North Railway Company'. Was not the original foundation of the North Eastern named 'The Great North of England'? Our main line runs alongside what in these motor days is so well known as the Great North Road; one of the Scottish companies is in part called the 'Great North', and the initials 'G.N.' are already on some 1,300 engines, 3,500 coaching vehicles and 40,000 wagons, which will belong to the new company. The name is short, geographically accurate, and historic".

To this Butterworth replied the following day: "Personally I rather like your idea of the 'Great North Railway Company'. It would please the Great Northern and hurt nobody else that I can see, and we have on our North Eastern the Great North of England Clarence and Hartlepool Railway which is one of our oldest bits of line and is being absorbed into the Group, for up to the present it has been worked by the North Eastern under a 999 years lease, and then there are also the Great North of Scotland Railway and the Great North Road. At the same time I am not quite sure that our directors will like all reference to the word 'East' or 'Eastern' being left out of the title. What do you say to the 'East Coast Railway Company'? Perhaps that rather seems to ignore the Great Central, but after all they come out upon the East Coast at Grimsby and Immingham". It is not without a wry smile that 42 years later we find the railway directors of 1922 being influenced in any favourable way by the existence of the Great North Road.

Three days later Butterworth followed his letter to Whitelaw by another in which he wrote: "I mentioned to Lord Knaresborough your suggestion that the name of the new Company might be 'The Great North Railway Company', and he writes 'Great North would rather take the wind out of the sails of the Western Group, and there is no Company on the East of us to lose by leaving out the East or Eastern.' I know that Lord Knaresborough prefers 'North' or 'East', or 'North and East' to 'Northern' and/or 'Eastern', and I must confess my preference goes entirely in favour of as concise a title as possible, and certainly the initials should be as few as possible.

"On the whole I think I should vote either for 'North East Railway Company' or 'Great North Railway Company', and between these two I think I should, like yourself, give preference to the former. It would have the advantage of leaving the lettering of our huge stock of wagons just as it is". Lord Knaresborough certainly had strong views on the shortened form of the adjective; "You do not talk of the Northern Star or the Northern Pole or the Northern Wind or the Eastern Wind or the Eastern Riding", he wrote. This was perhaps rather a curious stand to be taken by the Chairman of the North *Eastern* Railway, though in fairness it must be added that this title had been settled long before he took office.

As a former General Manager of the North Eastern Railway, Sir Alexander's preference for "North East Railway Company" can be understood, but in retrospect it seems a pity that the fine title of "Great North Railway" was not adopted. It would have satisfied the geographical considerations more completely than "London & North Eastern Railway" did, when one thinks of the company's interests in Lancashire, Carlisle, Glasgow and the West Highland Line. As Whitelaw had claimed, the former was a grand traditional name, associated from the earliest days with a great trunk route from the south to the north of Great Britain, and might have pointed very neatly to the railway as successor to the great highway whose name was so widely known.

But it was not to be. Eventually the title of "London & North Eastern Railway" was adopted—not even with the abbreviated "East" about which such strong views had been expressed. So five words had to be printed on all stationery, and the initials "L. & N.E.R." applied to locomotives, coaches, notice boards, and much else, all of which involved unnecessary labour, printer's ink and paint. Only on the wagon stock was there any abbreviation, freight vehicles being merely lettered "N.E." from the start, which permitted the lettering of the North Eastern Railway's 120,000 wagons to remain unaltered.

Within a short time the initial letters of the company were shortened to "L.N.E.R.", and aesthetically and practically this was an advantage. Later, under the stress of war conditions, when every possible economy was essential. Sir Charles Newton, who had succeeded Sir Ralph Wedgwood as Chief General Manager, sanctioned the abbreviation to "N.E." on locomotives and coaches also. How much happier it might have been, right from the start, to have used the letters "G.N." !

VIII

The New Company—Its Organisation

ONCE THE Boards of the constituent companies had come to grips with the fundamental financial problems of the amalgamation, and were making progress towards their solution, attention began to be focussed on the way in which the new company was to be organised. Drawing attention to a chart which had been published showing what had been done in the reorganisation following the fusion in 1921 of the London & North Western and Lancashire & Yorkshire Railways, Sir Alexander Butterworth remarked: "I think it is obvious that some of its features were largely suggested by personal considerations, and it remains to be seen how much of it will remain when all the companies in the Group are amalgamated. One noticeable feature is that whereas the chart provides for an all-line Engineer, Mechanical Engineer and Goods Manager, the work of the Superintendent is divided up into two geographical divisions, so again while there is an all-line Estate Agent and Accountant, there seems to be no all-line Storekeeper or Hotels Manager".

Sir Hugh Bell, of the North Eastern Railway Board, took a particular interest in the subject, largely because, as he said, in a letter to Butterworth, "I am just at this moment engaged in organising what will, I hope, be a very important enterprise. My very competent colleagues at an extremely early stage in our co-operation prepared a diagrammatic scheme on which we should build up our management. I was the more ready to fall in with this plan as many months ago I had expounded it in general outline to Wedgwood much as I stated it to you and Gibb the other day. Since then I have put it on paper."

But Sir Alexander was a little sceptical. "On the one hand", he wrote in reply, "I do not think it is possible to treat the organisation of a British Railway Company quite in the same way as any private industrial undertaking, however large and important, and less than ever now that the size of the Railway Companies is multiplied threefold. On the other hand, whoever be the party or parties that initiate a scheme of organisation, or whatever be their position, sooner or later, and probably at a very early stage, the matter must become one for discussion and criticism, and whatever part the Directors may play in the matter (and obviously the final settlement of the organisation is a matter for them and them alone) I am convinced that at a comparatively early stage they will require the advice of their experts.

"The question whether there shall be a General Manager of the new

E

company in the full sense of the term as understood hitherto on British Railways is entirely a question for the Directors—just as the procedure of the Directors themselves—and one upon which I expect they would not look for very much advice or assistance from their Officers. On the other hand, the question whether in local areas there shall be a corresponding official (either under denomination of Chief Officer or District General Manager or what not), which I believe will ultimately be found to be the crucial and controversial point in your scheme, is to my mind a question which any body of Directors will find very difficult to settle satisfactorily without expert advice". Re-echoes of this problem have been heard from time to time since, and not least since nationalisation has taken place!

It is probable that Butterworth was aware that the directors-to-be of the new company had the matter of reorganisation in hand, and that as it could be of no more than academic interest to himself at that stage he was anxious not to commit himself to any specific plan, though at the same time trying to guide the exuberance of Sir Hugh Bell into realistic channels. In point of fact, as early as April, 1922, Sir Alexander had been in possession of a detailed memorandum, twelve foolscap pages in length, which had been prepared at his request by Wedgwood, setting out a possible scheme of Group organisation. This he thought it advisable to have available in case of enquiry; judging by various pencil annotations he had studied it carefully, though there is no evidence that any use was made of the document.

A further and shorter memorandum was prepared by Wedgwood six months later, weighing up the relative merits of locating the Group Headquarters in London or York, and, it is interesting to note, concluding that London would be the more convenient, but he thought that a central position such as York might make for greater efficiency. Though there is nothing to prove that any use was made of this later document either, it is clear that in the form of organisation finally adopted the directors realised that it would be undesirable to over-concentrate the managerial staff in London.

The final decisions were made by the directors who had been nominated to serve on the Board of the new company, and who met, under the Chairmanship of William Whitelaw, in the elegant Westminster offices of the North Eastern Railway in Cowley Street. The threads of some of the preliminary thinking described in previous chapters can be traced in the scheme that was evolved. The "Chief Officer" concept found expression in the creation of the post of Chief General Manager; Lord Faringdon's idea of a "consortium of General Managers" came to life in the appointment of a Divisional General Manager for each Area; and the insistence of the N.E.R. directors on some degree of local autonomy was largely realised in the constitution of Area Boards. One of these was to be located at York, in order to look after the affairs of what had been the North Eastern Railway, and was henceforward to be the North Eastern Area of the L.N.E.R.

Broadly, the new organisation was based on the creation of three large geographical divisions, or areas. The Scottish Area comprised the former North British and Great North of Scotland Railways; the North Eastern Area the North Eastern and Hull & Barnsley Railways, actually amalgamated in the year before the Grouping; and the Southern Area the Great Northern, Great Central and Great Eastern Railways. As a sop to Scottish susceptibilities, Scottish affairs were entrusted to the care of a General Manager (Scotland); those in charge of the North Eastern and Southern Areas were known as Divisional General Managers; it was also decided, as might have been expected, that the Headquarters of the Chief General Manager would be in London. Divisional General Managers were to be allowed to authorise expenditure in their Areas within prescribed limits; projects involving heavier expenditure, or matters of policy, were to be submitted for approval to the Chief General Manager, and, wherever of sufficient importance, to the Board. Under each Divisional General Manager departmental officers were to be appointed to take charge of the various departments which were traditional in the organisation of British railways. The only all-line appointments, other than that of the Chief General Manager, were to be the Chief Mechanical Engineer, Chief Stores Superintendent, Chief Accountant, Chief Legal Adviser, Advertising Manager, and Secretary to the Board.

Mention has been made of the Area Boards. There was one for each Area, and they were to comprise the directors of the company who in each case were associated with, or specially interested in, the work of the Area concerned. These Area Boards would have little actual authority; their function was to keep the Board as a whole in touch with local developments, as well as to cultivate good relations with the staff and with the public in each Area.

Meantime the task of absorbing the minor companies had been proceeding smoothly, and in September, 1922, Sir Alexander Butterworth was able to assure Lord Knaresborough that "the only subsidiary company, the purchase of which presents any difficulty, is the South Yorkshire Junction Railway, and that is mixed up with an agreement with the Denaby Colliery Company with regard to which Wedgwood is in negotiation". With the disappearance of these subsidiaries many old, and in some cases extremely interesting, legal agreements and working arrangements were terminated.

It is of interest to set on record the first major appointments made by the future Board of the London & North Eastern Railway; with the location of their offices they were as follows:

All-Line

Chief General Manager	Kings Cross	R. L. Wedgwood, C.B., C.M.G.
Asst. General Manager	Kings Cross	R. Bell
Asst. Gen. Manager (Staff)	Kings Cross	Kenelm Kerr
Joint Secretaries	Marylebone	James McLaren
		G. F. Thurston

Chief Legal Adviser	Marylebone	Sir Francis Dunnell, Bart., K.C.B.
Chief Accountant	Kings Cross	C. L. Edwards, C.B.E.
Chief Mechanical Engineer	Doncaster	H. N. Gresley, C.B.E.
Technical Adviser	Westminster	Sir Vincent Raven, K.B.E.
Chief Stores Superintendent	Doncaster	W. T. Weeks
Advertising Manager	Kings Cross	W. M. Teasdale

Southern Area

| Divisional Gen. Manager | Liverpool St. | S. A. Parnwell |

North Eastern Area

| Divisional Gen. Manager | York | Alexander Wilson, O.B.E. |

Scottish Area

| General Manager (Scot.) | Edinburgh | James Calder. |

While a few changes in the actual personnel took place within the first year or so of the new company, and there were certain gaps to be filled and minor adjustments to be made subsequently, there was nothing amorphous about the shape of the organisation which the new Board had worked out with such efficiency. Indeed, it is a remarkable tribute to their work that the plan which they devised in 1922 survived all the vicissitudes of the years, and was practically unchanged when nationalisation took place in 1948. Even to-day, under nationalisation, the North Eastern and Southern Areas of the L.N.E.R. still in effect continue as the North Eastern and Eastern Regions of British Railways.

Needless to say, the original organisation had its critics. There were those in the other Groups who prided themselves on the quickness of the decisions which could be taken by one Chief at the head of a vast department covering an entire railway system as compared with the L.N.E.R. triplets of officers, from the Divisional General Managers downwards, who shared many of the responsibilities. But appearances can be deceptive, and decisions could be reached quickly enough on the L.N.E.R. when rapid decisions were needed. Moreover, when three experienced officers put their heads together the decisions eventually taken were usually pretty sound, which was not always the case with some of the other monolithic organisations; neither were the latter always so quick in action as has been claimed. The London & North Eastern pattern can certainly be said to have fostered a high morale, and to have made possible the closest contact between the higher officers and the trading community in various parts of the country.

If the L.N.E.R. organisation had one weakness it was, perhaps, that like the wheelbarrow it needed someone to push it. It did not work automatically, and without constant supervision from the Chief General Manager's office there might have been a tendency for the several Areas to fall apart and become slightly self-sufficient. That they did not is in itself a tribute to the co-operation between Headquarters and the Areas which enabled the company to give first class service and to survive the many economic vicissitudes in its history related later.

IX

The Way Ahead—1923-1925

ONLY THOSE who lived through the years immediately following the 1914-1918 war can have any conception of the atmosphere that then prevailed. The guns were silent; the holocaust was over; the "war to end all wars" had been fought and won. The Prime Minister had spoken of hanging the Kaiser, and his chosen associate, Sir Eric Geddes, in one of his political utterances had promised that the Germans should be "squeezed until the pips squeaked". This general feeling of optimism, born largely of relief, endured for a short time, and when the Coalition Government was swept away, and with it both Lloyd George and Geddes, neither ever to return to the political area, the succeeding Government, still buoyed up by the prevailing spirit, adopted the theme of "tranquillity" as its guiding principle.

It was into this atmosphere that the four new railway companies emerged, full of high hope for the future. Nationalisation had been avoided; the work of national reconstruction lay ahead; and the railways had now to enjoy their share in this worthwhile task. Actually, however, in the British railway world, as in the national and international spheres, there was little solid ground for such optimism after the surface had been scratched.

For seven years the Government had hired the railways of the country at a rental equivalent to the net revenue earned by the individual companies in 1913, although during the intervening period the value of money had halved. Without its normal maintenance, railway equipment had been worn down under the pressure of war transportation, and vast arrears of upkeep had to be undertaken at costs far in excess of those current before the war. True, the railways had been given a lump sum of £60,000,000 as compensation, but it is significant that within a few years the nation was spending annually an equivalent sum, favouring the railways' chief competitor, on the highways of the country.

During the period of Government control the wages of railway employees had been increased, and in 1917, without consulting the railway managers, the Government had committed them to the introduction of an eight-hour day as soon as the war was over. William Whitelaw calculated that in 1923, by comparison with 1913, there had been an increase of no less than 148 per cent. in the railway wages bill. The cost of coal was now from 80 to 90 per cent. above that before the war, and such had been the inflation of steel prices that, following on the purchase in 1921 by the Great Eastern Railway of steel rails from a Belgian firm, in 1923 the London & North Eastern Railway placed orders on the Continent for wheels and axles, for the lowest British quotation at that time was 70 per cent. higher than that of the Continental suppliers. By contrast, however, whereas freight rates when the war ended were about 100 per cent. and passenger fares 75 per cent. above the 1913 level, both had since been reduced to between 50 and 60 per cent. above the pre-war figures in order to combat the falling off in trade and the steady growth of road competition.

Such was the hard world into which the London & North Eastern Railway was launched. The fact was that the railways were handed back by the Government to private enterprise in conditions, both as to labour and charges, which were suited to a monopoly, and this at a time when that monopoly was ceasing to exist. Only in years to come would it be fully revealed how incompatible with the day and age were these rates and charges, and the standard revenue provisions of the Railways Act, 1921, but already these considerations were influencing the L.N.E.R. Board in its dividend policy. To enable the Company to pay, in respect of the 1923 results, what the Board felt entitled to regard as the minimum dividend secured on the deferred stock under the Act, £550,000 was taken from the Compensation Fund and disbursed to the stockholders.

Defending this action, at the L.N.E.R. annual meeting held early in 1924, Whitelaw said, "In our view this is the proper policy to pursue when we have reduced our rates and fares below the point at which we can in the meantime earn that rate of dividend". These rugged facts of life were not immediately apparent to or appreciated by the staff of the new Company, though their interest was keen and was titillated by various manifestations of the change that had taken place, as, for example, in the new colours and lettering of rolling stock and various similar developments.

The year 1924 closed with claims pending from the Unions for improved wages and conditions, which if granted in full would cost the Company an additional £13,000,000 annually. "I cannot help thinking", said Whitelaw, "that those responsible for the programme of the Unions have not fully realised the effect of their demands upon the industry on which they, as well as ourselves, are dependent." More ominous, perhaps, was the falling off in coal exports, which resulted in a decline of 5,250,000 tons or $11\frac{1}{2}$ per cent. in the coal hauled by the L.N.E.R. to the East Coast ports for shipment. Indeed, whereas the total tonnage of coal handled by the L.N.E.R. in 1923 was 102,000,000 tons, by 1924 the figure had contracted to 93,000,000 tons and by 1925 to 87,000,000 tons, and as coal was one of the staple traffics of the Company, the seriousness of this shrinkage will be appreciated. The situation in the mining industry generally was creating anxiety, which was to grow more intense until it culminated in the General Strike of 1926.

The fact was that the immediate post-war boom was over, and the nation was facing that long and miserable period of bad trade, with its unhappily high level of unemployment, that was to last for many years and to create an ugly scar on the national life. Over the North of England and industrial Scotland trade was stagnant and many collieries, shipyards and iron and steel works were being wholly or partially closed down. The old days of prosperity were gone, and L.N.E.R. revenues were being supported, to a far greater extent than anyone would have thought possible a few years ago, by its Southern Area. Nevertheless, in a national effort to create work, largely at the instigation of Bonar Law, then Prime Minister, the L.N.E.R. Directors continued their policy of renovating their property and overtaking arrears of maintenance. New work was put in hand also; amongst other projects, one undertaken jointly with the London Midland & Scottish Railway, after a slight brush with that Company, was the depositing of a Bill for the construction of new joint lines to serve developments in the Nottinghamshire coalfield.

Another Bill, however, was rejected in March, 1926, by the House of Commons. It was to establish a new Superannuation Fund, and the rejection was largely the result of the combined opposition of the Railway Clerks' Association and the annuitants of the existing Funds. Also the public spirit shown by the L.N.E.R. Directors in providing work in the national interest struck no echoing chord in Government quarters when it came to the competition of road transport which by that time was seriously, and in the opinion of many unfairly, affecting railway traffics. This problem was engaging the close attention of the Railway Companies' Association, and was to continue to do so for many years to come.

Singularly enough, it was only the former Great Eastern Railway, which at the time of the Grouping might have seemed to be no more than a poor relation, that was providing any real satisfaction to the proprietors of the Company. Largely owing to the introduction of sugar beet as a staple crop in the Eastern Counties, and to the establishment of beet sugar factories, freight traffic over the G.E. Lines by 1925 had expanded by 20 per cent. over the pre-war figure. This increase had resulted in some operating difficulties, but although these had been successfully overcome, the Directors had come to the conclusion that some infusion of new capital into this part of their undertaking would be justified. So a new traffic control office was established at Cambridge, and—a much bolder venture—it was decided to lay out at March, in Cambridgeshire, a new marshalling yard of great size and with all the latest mechanised electric equipment, at a cost of over a quarter of a million pounds, as described in Chapter XIV. This was a farseeing decision which ever since has been most beneficial to railway operation in East Anglia.

Another practical step towards improved performance and efficiency taken in these early years was the institution of a Central Wagon Control for the entire system, working through the district operating officers. The headquarters was established at York, and most suitably so, seeing that the organisation was the brain child of the vigorous C. M. Jenkin Jones, then Superintendent of the North Eastern Area; he now assumed the title of Freight Rolling Stock Controller of the Group, while still retaining his position as Superintendent. The Control was superimposed on the existing organisation for freight organisation, and was not integrated with the train working, like that devised some years earlier by Sir Cecil Paget for the Midland Railway, the first of its kind in the country. However, any such weakness in the L.N.E.R. scheme was more apparent than real, for the former functioned efficiently, and served the Company well until the end of its independent days.

Early in its life the London & North Eastern Railway obtained a grant of a coat-of-arms, and adopted as its motto the word "Forward" which had formed part of the Great Central Railway's crest. It always seemed a pity that more use was not made of this fine L.N.E.R. heraldic device. The constituent companies up to the time of amalgamation had emblazoned their crests on their locomotives and coaches, but the L.N.E.R. abstained from this display, and its locomotives and coaches were the losers in consequence.

In the years 1924 and 1925 the London & North Eastern Railway took part in two exhibitions of considerable importance; in that of 1924 it was a participant but for that of 1925 it was entirely responsible. The former was the British Empire Exhibition at Wembley, where the Company exhibited one of its latest Gresley Pacific locomotives, No. 4472 *Flying Scotsman*. The brochure issued to celebrate this display declared: "The many visitors to the British Empire Exhibition at Wembley in 1924, and in particular those who make their way to the Palace of Engineering, will hardly fail to be attracted to the stand of the London & North Eastern Railway Company. Here are exhibited, and available for close and detailed inspection, two most interesting locomotives—the original which on the 27th September, 1825, drew the first passenger train in the world, and alongside it a veritable Goliath of modern railway engineering science, one of the 'Pacific' type of locomotives, the largest and most powerful passenger engines in Great Britain".

Flying Scotsman, in impeccable condition, certainly made a most impressive display, but the last sentence just quoted was not to go unchallenged. For alongside the L.N.E.R. stand was that of the Great Western Railway, on which was exhibited one of their latest 4-6-0 locomotives, *Caerphilly Castle*. Although both in appearance and in reality the G.W.R. engine was obviously smaller and lighter than its imposing L.N.E.R. companion, yet with its higher working pressure—225 lb. per sq. in. as compared with 180 lb.—the formula normally used gave it the advantage in tractive effort. As related in Chapter XVII, an actual exchange of locomotives between the two companies took place in the following year, for comparative trials, in which the G.W.R. "Castles" did prove their superiority over the L.N.E.R. Pacifics, and the result was certain modifications in the design of the latter which greatly improved their performance.

Above: The Royal Border Bridge, Berwick, completed in 1850, with 28 arches of 61 ft. 6 in. span, 2,160 ft. in length. It is being crossed by the southbound "Coronation"
[*M. W. Earley*

Right: Welwyn Viaduct, Hertfordshire, also completed in 1850, with 40 arches, 1,560 ft. long and 89 ft. in maximum height. [*G. H. Lake*

Below: The flyover between Manor Park and Ilford, built in preparation for the Great Eastern electrification from Liverpool Street to Shenfield and beyond, to carry the electric lines over the main lines.

[*British Railways*

Above: One of the massive steel viaducts on the L.N.E.R. line from Darlington to Tebay: Belah, 1,040 ft. long and 196 ft. in maximum height. A photograph taken after nationalisation; the viaduct has since been demolished.

[*J. W. Armstrong*

Left: Northbound express amid the latticework of the world-famed Forth Bridge, 8,296 ft. long, with two main spans of 1,710 ft. each, giving 157 ft. clearance above the Forth at high water.

[*E. R. Wethersett*

Below: For many years the longest viaduct in the world—the Tay Bridge, 10,711 ft. long, with 85 spans, 13 of them 227 ft. across. The stumps of the ill-fated first Tay Bridge are seen to the right of the present bridge.

[*British Railways*

Above: Robert Stephenson's double-deck High Level Bridge cross the Tyne, with six 125 ft. spans, 1,337 ft. long and 112 ft. in maximum height. In the foreground is the swing-bridge which formerly carried the Great North Road.

[*British Railways*

Right: Across the Wear between Sunderland and Monkwearmouth, the 300 ft. span bridge opened in 1879, with the much later steel arch road bridge behind.

[*Thos. H. Mason*

Below: The Queen Alexandra double-deck bridge carrying rail and road across the Wear near Sunderland, opened in 1909; main span 330 ft.

[*British Railways*

Above: Bramhope Tunnel, 3,761 yds. long, the most lengthy bore of the former North Eastern Railway, opened in 1894. This is the north portal.

[*British Railways*

Left: The ornamental south portal of Audley End Tunnel, Great Eastern line.

[*Timothy H. Cobb*

Below: The Western portal of Woodhead Tunnel, 3 miles 66 chains long. The original Great Central tunnels, of which the first was completed in 1845, are on the left, and have now been abandoned; the double-line tunnel bored in preparation for electrification, on the right, was opened in 1954.

[*British Railways*

The second exhibition, that of 1925, was one which attracted world-wide interest. It celebrated the Centenary of Railways, the first railway in the world opened for public traffic having been the Stockton & Darlington, in September, 1825. In order to coincide with the 1925 meeting in Great Britain of the International Railway Congress, the celebration was moved forward to July. There was, first of all, an exhibition of items of historical interest at the Faverdale Wagon Works, Darlington, but overshadowing everything else was the procession of ancient and modern locomotives and rolling stock over the actual route of the former Stockton & Darlington Company. Fortunately fine weather favoured the occasion, and the entire route was lined by thousands of spectators, the grandstand having, among its distinguished occupants, the Duke and Duchess of York, later King George VI and Queen Elizabeth.

In the procession there were 53 items in all. The oldest participants were a locomotive built for Hetton Colliery in 1822, and George Stephenson's *Locomotion No.* 1, designed by that famous pioneer and driven by himself in person on the Stockton & Darlington opening day. For the Centenary a replica train had been built, comprising open "chaldron" wagons and the covered coach *Experiment*, all occupied by men and women in the costumes of 1825. Whereas the Hetton Colliery locomotive, which during its life had gone through several rebuildings, ran under its own steam, it was not deemed safe to steam the boiler of *Locomotion No.* 1, which was moved by a petrol motor cunningly concealed in the tender, while masses of oily waste were burned in the firebox to produce smoke from the chimney and provide the necessary illusion of steam transport.

London & North Eastern steam power of all kinds, needless to say, was seen in great variety, up to and including both Gresley and Raven Pacifics, one of the two big Gresley 2-8-2 freight locomotives and the mammoth articulated six-cylinder Garratt 2-8-8-2 locomotive, just fresh from the builders, destined for duty banking heavy coal trains up the Worsborough 1 in 40 incline, between Barnsley and Penistone. All the other railway groups were represented by complete locomotives and trains, including a Great Western "Castle" with the G.W.R. Royal train, a London Midland & Scottish Hughes 4-cylinder 4-6-0 and a Southern "King Arthur" 4-6-0. There was even a glimpse of the future in the 4-6-4 electric locomotive—hauled, needless to say, by a steam rival—built by the North Eastern Railway in preparation for the projected electrification of the main line from York to Newcastle over which, nevertheless, this locomotive never had the opportunity to run.

"A first impression of the Railway Centenary", wrote an observer of the procession, "was that as a spectacle it was unique. Slow, stately, magnificent, irresistible—never before can there have been its equal in the whole realm of pageantry on land, unless it be the Jubilee procession of 1875. The gradual unfolding of the history of steam locomotion in this living picture was bound to impress those who were privileged to witness it; to those who have made a lifelong study of the locomotive and have been seized with its peculiar fascination, the 'show' proved unbelievably thrilling. I was seated among a number of old-time railway employees, some of whom had actually been connected with the Stockton & Darlington line, and their comments on past *versus* present were alone worth going a long way to hear. To see the locomotives which have formed the subject of his enthusiasm greeted with cheers and clapping by the vast crowds that had assembled at various points to witness the procession, also, could hardly fail to warm the heart of the real railway enthusiast."

The whole affair was superbly organised and the success of the celebration owed much to the backing and support of William Whitelaw. It was, moreover, an outstanding tribute to his greatness that at the official banquet he was content to reply to the toast of the L.N.E.R., leaving the post of honour as chairman of the occasion to be occupied by Viscount Grey of Fallodon. The Centenary certainly gave the L.N.E.R. staff a "shot in the arm" and helped to boost morale.

One interesting outcome of the Centenary celebrations was the decision to establish a permanent museum of railway relics. The first location suggested was Darlington, but eventually York was decided on as being more generally accessible, and in 1928 the York Railway Museum came into being, on the site of the first York station. The exhibits ranged from documents, bills, prints, and a great variety of examples of equipment, to full size locomotives.

Eventually to the locomotives of North Eastern Railway origin—the 2-2-4 tank engine *Aerolite*, Stephenson long-boiler 0-6-0, Fletcher and Tennant 2-4-0s and Worsdell 4-4-0—there were attracted locomotives of other railways. These comprised a Great Northern Stirling 8 ft. 4-2-2 with small and large-boilered Ivatt Atlantics; the London Brighton and South Coast 0-4-2 *Gladstone*; and the Great Western 4-4-0 *City of Truro*, credited with being the first engine in this country to attain a speed of just over 100 m.p.h. In more modern times British Railways have established another museum, at Clapham, which houses various London & North Eastern types, including the record Gresley A4 Pacific *Mallard*, whose 126 m.p.h. in 1938 established a world record for steam power. A list of locomotives of the L.N.E.R. and its constituent companies now preserved or scheduled for preservation appears in Table 12, page 148.

Reverting to the Centenary, its effect, of course, was purely psychological, and did nothing to dispel the growing anxieties caused by diminishing coal traffic and increasing road competition. As it was, a more hopeful trend set in towards the end of 1925, though none could foresee the tragedy that was to overtake the railways in the following year.

X

1926 and the General Strike

THE SLIGHTLY more encouraging outlook towards the close of 1925, mentioned in the last chapter, continued into the early part of 1926. In the first four months receipts from railway and ancillary businesses increased by £440,000, while expenditure decreased by £486,000; given a continuation of these trends, it was confidently felt that the net receipts for the year would show an increase in the region of £2,000,000. But this was not to be. The threatened troubles in the mining industry came to a head in May, 1926, with the calling of a strike, which flared into the General Strike called so ill-advisedly by the Trades Union Congress, and in which the railwaymen decided to join in support of the miners. This was a disaster for the railway industry, and no less, of course, for the men themselves.

The railwaymen's decision to stop work, so unconstitutionally, was a severe shock for the management, which had a high regard for its work-people, and was astonished that they could take their responsibilities so lightly. For ten unhappy days the normal railway services came to a standstill. On the L.N.E.R. an emergency organisation came into being, almost overnight; volunteers were enlisted in considerable numbers; and after the lapse of a day or two skeleton services were improvised over most main lines and many branches, as well as in the London suburban area. By the time the strike collapsed these improvised services were becoming fairly regular, and the obvious determination of the general public to assist in every way possible no doubt was of considerable help in breaking the strike. The nation was appalled by the vicious action of certain strikers at Ashington, in Northumberland, who derailed an express train from Edinburgh to London by removing a rail from the track; many other acts of sabotage, though not quite as serious as this one, were perpetrated.

But with the collapse of the railway strike the troubles of the railway managements were by no means over. The wretched mining strike dragged on until the autumn, and the supplies of home-produced coal with which to run the trains gradually dried up. Reserve stocks were used up, and the Directors, who were determined to carry on limited services to the best of the Company's ability, had to purchase coal from the Continent and from America. A number of these overseas contractors failed to fulfil their obligations, and showed themselves quite unscrupulous by delivering their coal to other purchasers, at prices higher than those that they had agreed with the L.N.E.R. At one time in October railway coal supplies were so reduced that many trains had to be cancelled; moreover, the imported fuel was of such poor quality that keeping steam with it in locomotive boilers was a herculean task for firemen. Commenting on the situation, William Whitelaw remarked, "The task imposed by Pharoah upon the Israelites of making bricks without straw was a mere joke compared with the work drivers and firemen had to perform in raising and maintaining steam on some of the material which in the name of coal was supplied to them."

For the Company 1926 was a disastrous year financially. As a result of the General Strike, the second period of the year showed a drop in receipts of £10,526,000, although the management had succeeded in reducing expenditure by £4,239,000—a figure which, but for the increased cost of coal, might well have approximated to £6,000,000. The L.N.E.R. staff lost some £4,000,000 in wages as the result of their folly in striking. On the year's results the best that the Directors could do for the shareholders was to pay a dividend of ½ per cent. on the Preferred Ordinary stock. The Chairman showed himself conscious of the hardship inflicted on a large number of stockholders, as the result of the virtual disappearance of any dividend, by declaring: "One of the most melancholy results of the upheaval has been that it is upon the really poor people who had neither strike pay nor dole that the burden of the catastrophe has fallen most heavily".

So it was that the end of 1926 marked the end of a stage in London & North Eastern history—"the end of the beginning", to use a phrase coined later by one of the most distinguished of Englishmen. What had been the course of the financial fortunes of the Company from the date of its inauguration? In the first year, 1923, the total net income had been £14,047,221; in 1924 the figure had dropped to £11,717,667 and by 1925 to £10,129,069; while 1926 had seen a catastrophic fall to no more than £4,636,878. From 1923 to 1925 the Preferred Ordinary dividend had been maintained at 5 per cent., while in 1926, as we have just seen, only ½ per cent. could be paid. As to the Deferred Ordinary stockholders, whereas in 1923 and 1924 they had received 2½ per cent. on their holdings, in 1925 1 per cent. was the maximum possible, while in 1926 their dividend disappeared altogether.

Truly it could be said, or sung, after four brief years, that:
"The radiant morn hath passed away,
    And spent too soon her golden store".
But throughout this period the Board and the management of the Company had exhibited outstanding qualities of resilience and of determination, in face of whatever difficulties there might be, to go forward, to give the public a first class service, and to maintain their property at the highest possible standard of efficiency.

XI

The Years of Depression—1927-1933

THE WOUND inflicted on the national economy by the General Strike and the protracted coal stoppage in 1926 was deep. It was, moreover, extremely slow to heal, and only after some years of industrial depression, accompanied by acute unemployment, was there any sign of better times. So seriously was the London & North Eastern Railway affected that an unprecedented arrangement was agreed to in 1928; it was that, to aid the Company's finances, the Directors, Chief Officers and the whole of the staff would accept a temporary reduction of $2\frac{1}{2}$ per cent. in fees, salaries and wages. By agreement with the Unions this reduction in remuneration continued until May, 1930, and both sides undertook not to seek any revision of pay or conditions of service before 12th November of the same year. Industrial history offers few examples of such co-operation; acceptance of any comparable personal sacrifice in the common cause would be unthinkable in the mood that prevails to-day.

Notwithstanding the shortness of money, the L.N.E.R. management showed no lack of enterprise in these difficult years. Some of the work put in hand included new sidings for handling the developing iron and steel traffic from the plants in North Lincolnshire, a new passenger station at Frodingham, and an additional pier at Salt End on the Humber to accommodate increasing oil imports.

In 1928 the four railway groups secured Parliamentary powers to run road transport services, and in the following year to provide similar services by air. Whereas the latter were not immediately exercised, the railways, including the L.N.E.R., purchased shares in various road undertakings, mostly passenger, though the L.N.E.R. did also take an interest in one or two road freight operators, such as Currie's of Newcastle. Following on these investments, certain unremunerative London & North Eastern passenger services were withdrawn, and in this way an estimated saving of £35,000 was achieved in 1930, and just over double that figure by 1931. By the end of 1930 the L.N.E.R. had invested a total of about £2,000,000 in road transport undertakings, on which it was receiving a return of $6\frac{1}{2}$ per cent. But one of the most important developments in this field took place in 1933, when the four railway groups, acting together, purchased the old-established road transport firms of Carter Paterson and the Hay's Wharf Transport Company, of which the principal subsidiary was Pickfords. In this way a large stake in road haulage was assured. The L.N.E.R. share in the purchase was £545,000.

As for passenger traffic on the railways, however, by the late 1920s the progressive loss was proving a major problem for the Company. Such had been the boost given to the private car and to public road passenger services by the General Strike of 1926 that between 1925 and 1927 the number of L.N.E.R. passenger journeys had dropped by no less than 47,000,000. In an attempt to compete on more nearly level terms with the bus, the London & North Eastern in 1927 revived the idea pioneered nearly a quarter of a century earlier by the Great Western Railway of the self-contained steam rail motorcar. But this was now available in a much more modern form, with high pressure boilers of an automatically-fired design, such as the Sentinel-Cammell railcars, of which a considerable number were introduced in the North Eastern Area from 1927 onwards, together with some other types powered by internal combustion engines. These were cheap to operate, but heavy on maintenance; their principal handicap was their inability to accommodate peak traffic, as at week-ends, and as a result their life was comparatively short. A new attraction to long-distance passengers, as related in Chapter XXII, was the introduction in 1928 of the first sleeping cars for third class passengers, on the same lines as the Continental *couchette* coaches of to-day.

In his Budget for 1928, the Chancellor of the Exchequer repealed the outmoded Passenger Duty, but on condition that the railways should spend on development a sum equivalent to the capitalised value of the duty, an amount assessed in the case of the L.N.E.R. at £1,500,000. The London & North Eastern Railway management accordingly proposed to the Ministry of Transport a series of major works, including a widening of the Great Eastern Colchester main line from Romford Junction to near Harold Wood, with new stations at Romford and Gidea Park; the creation of a new marshalling yard at Mottram, on the Great Central main line between Sheffield and Manchester; and new refuge sidings at various points on the Great Northern main line and what formerly had been the Great Northern & Great Eastern Joint Line. All these proposals were approved by the Minister and work on them began without delay.

In 1929 some improvement began to show itself in coal traffic; as compared with 1928 the volume of export coal through the North-East coal ports, including the Humber, increased by 27 per cent. In the Southern Area, due largely to the increase from 230,000 acres in 1927 to 347,000 acres in 1930 of the land in the Eastern Counties devoted to raising sugar beet, freight traffic in general was showing substantial growth; between 1928 and 1929 alone there had been a rise of 29 per cent. To assist in moving this increased freight, a most timely acquisition between 1924 and 1929 from the War Department Disposals Board had been that of 125 2-8-0 locomotives of the Great Central type designed by John G. Robinson; these had been built for war service, but many of them up to the time of this transfer had never turned a wheel. Most of them were drafted to the Great Eastern motive power depots at

Stratford and March and to the Great Northern at Doncaster. But this freight improvement turned out to be no more than temporary.

A more encouraging and persistent increase, however, was in the Continental traffic, particularly that passing through Harwich, which had been the special pride of the former Great Eastern Railway; it still so continued in London & North Eastern days, under the *aegis* of A. L. Gibson, the Continental Traffic Manager, himself an old Great Eastern man. The activity at Parkeston Quay had been further added to by the decision of the Zeeland Shipping Company, effective from the beginning of 1927, to transfer its daily sailings to Holland from Folkestone to Parkeston. Whereas in 1923 the net profit from the L.N.E.R. Continental traffic had been £80,000, in the three successive years the figure mounted to £104,000, £133,000 and £203,000 respectively, and between 1927 and 1928 alone there was an increase of 166,536 in the number of passengers carried by the Hook route. The additions to the L.N.E.R. fleet put on order to cope with this growing traffic are described in Chapter XXV.

But with all this enterprise, 1930 was a difficult year from the financial standpoint, and 1931, with the national financial crisis and the abandonment of the gold standard, was even worse. Apart from the general depression in trade, especially in the heavy industries, the prime cause was the increasing "bite" of road competition into railway traffic, both passenger and freight. In the second half of 1930 the L.N.E.R. management carried out some drastic measures of economy, which resulted in a saving of over £1,600,000 between July and December, and by the continuation of these economies through 1931 a total reduction of £4,250,000 was effected—a remarkable managerial achievement in so short a time.

Over the years the loss of dividends by the shareholders of the Company had given rise, naturally enough, to great dissatisfaction, and although, as we have seen, the Directors were extremely sympathetic, those who were suffering would have been less than human had they regarded sympathy as any adequate substitute for cash. Expression was given to these feelings by the formation, in November, 1927, of an L.N.E.R. Stockholders' Association. From the first this body was, and continued to be, highly critical of the L.N.E.R. Board, and it made repeated efforts, though always defeated, to get its own nominees elected to the Directorate.

The first such effort was to propose a reduction in the number of members of the Board to the statutory minimum of 16; but although this was defeated, it was not apparently without some effect, for the Board agreed to reduce its number from 26 to 24 at the 1932 Annual Meeting, and further to 22 at that of 1933, with a reduction also of the Directors' fees.

It was very likely with the activities of the Stockholders' Association in his mind that at the Annual Meeting of 1932 the Chairman, William Whitelaw, made an important statement concerning the financial policy of the Company. It was as follows:

"We have this year changed our policy of drawing on reserves to pay dividends. In past years reserves were drawn upon in order to pay a nominal dividend on the Preferred Ordinary stock, and so to keep our prior stocks in the Chancery Trustee list. This policy incidentally, of course, involved the payment in full of the dividend on the Second Preference stock. The situation to-day is quite different; we could not in any circumstances have paid a dividend even of a nominal amount on the Preferred Ordinary stock and therefore the question of maintaining the Trustee status did not arise, and the only point for decision was whether or not a transfer should be made from reserves in order to pay a more substantial dividend on the Second Preference stock. This is quite a different question from that which arose in past years when the maintenance of the Trustee status was within our grasp. We have no doubt that our duty to the stockholders generally requires us in the changed circumstances to leave our general reserve fund untouched".

This alteration in policy was clearly right in the prevailing circumstances. Lest the Company should be accused of prodigality in bolstering dividends by drawing on reserves during these lean years, it should be noted that no less than £8,000,000 had been spent on new capital works during the seven years from 1923 onwards. It is a further tribute to the hope of future improvement in traffic that in spite of all the difficulties which were besetting the Company, another £8,000,000, with Government assistance, was laid out in the succeeding eight years up to 1938.

Here, then, is the financial picture from 1927 to 1933. In 1927 the net L.N.E.R. revenue was £12,184,478; in 1928 there was a fall to £11,277,759 but 1929 saw a temporary recovery to £13,061,250. From then on the decline in net revenue was continuous—to £11,168,050 in 1930, £9,424,610 in 1931 and £7,166,858 in 1932, but with a faint recovery to £7,723,120 in 1933. Preferred Ordinary shareholders received a dividend of 3 per cent. in 1929, but ⅜ per cent. in 1927, no more than ¼ per cent. in 1928 and 1930 and nothing at all from 1931 to 1933; while Deferred Ordinary shareholders received nothing throughout this seven year period. Small amounts were paid from 1931 to 1933 on certain other stocks, such as the 4 per cent. First and Second Preference and 5 per cent. Redeemable Preference stock, but not more than 1 to 2 per cent. on the stocks first mentioned and 1¼ to 2½ per cent. on the Redeemable Preference.

It had been estimated that in 1930 as compared with 1924, after due allowance had been made for the bad trade position, the railways had lost in net revenue not less than £16,000,000 from road competition. Indeed, as by 1924 freight carriage by road already had reached considerable proportions, the figure just quoted may well have been a considerable understatement of the total loss. On the other side of the ledger the railways, in the same six years, had succeeded in reducing their expenditure by no less than £18,800,000—no mean achievement.

To these economies the L.N.E.R. had made its own substantial contribution. Between March, 1923, and March, 1932, the number of officers and clerical staff had been cut from 24,597 to 19,674; the number of other staff from 177,635 to 154,283; and the total cost of salaries and wages from £36,105,266 to £29,061,493. Since 1928 the stock of steam locomotives had been pared by 332 units, and a deliberate policy had been adopted of repairing, taking out of traffic and "tallowing down" certain types of locomotive, until by 1933 some 430 engines in all were in this condition, though ready for immediate service if and when needed. The number of wagons awaiting repair also was allowed at this time to increase by more than 6,000 above the normal standard, in order for the time being to limit the cost of wagon repairs.

That these policies were justified is seen in the fact that in 1932 freight traffic was still diminishing; the total of coal and merchandise carried by the L.N.E.R. in that year was 8,500,000 tons or 8 per cent. less than in 1931, though this loss was counterbalanced in some degree by a reduction of 7.63 per cent. in freight engine mileage. In the ten years following the 1923 Grouping, L.N.E.R. freight tonnage had been reduced by 45,000,000 tons and passenger journeys by 58,000,000. But for this vast loss of traffic to the roads the railways might well, in most years since the amalgamation, have earned more than the net revenue fixed by Parliament, and four-fifths of the surplus could have gone towards a reduction of rates and fares. As it was, it had been necessary to increase freight rates by about 7 per cent. in 1927, in an attempt to make ends meet, and this had further encouraged the diversion of freight traffic to the roads.

In 1931, however, the Railway Companies' Association made strong representations to the Minister of Transport that in common fairness there ought to be some adjustment of the economic balance between rail and road freight haulage. The upshot was the establishment in 1932 of a Conference, under the Chairmanship of Sir Arthur Salter, to review the whole position and to make recommendations. Its members consisted of the four railway General Managers, on the one side, and, on the other, four representative figures from the world of road transport. Thanks largely to the genius of its Chairman, the Conference was able to reach unanimous conclusions, and these were that the licensing system for road passenger services should be extended to goods haulage, that licence duties should be increased, that measures of regulation should be introduced to ensure the payment of fair wages, that there should be compulsory maintenance of road vehicles in a state of fitness, and that road hauliers should be required to keep records of their activities. Great pressure was needed by the Railway Companies' Association on the Government to induce it to move in this matter, culminating in a direct appeal to the Prime Minister, but at last these recommendations were embodied in a Road and Rail Traffic Bill which reached the Statute Book in the summer of 1933.

The system of licensing enacted by this legislation has persisted with but little variation to the present day. So practical did the scheme prove that not until 1964 did a present-day Government set up a Com-

F

mittee under the Chairmanship of Lord Geddes to review it. Whilst the Act enabled the railways to have some influence on the admission of newcomers to the road haulage industry, and on the expansion of existing undertakings, its weakness, of course, was that many large and influential road haulage firms by now were very firmly established; moreover, the unrestricted licensing of vehicles regarded as ancillary to the main business of any firm still left the railways suffering severely from their existing handicap, and completely unable to overtake their competitors and restore their former position.

However, there had at least been some improvement in the position as the result of this legislation, and with some restored optimism the railways entered upon what was to be the last chapter of their independent history feeling that from now on they would at least be able to contain their competitors. A useful step at this time in the direction of more economical working was an agreement entered into from 1st July, 1932, with the London Midland & Scottish Railway, and from 1st January, 1933, with the Great Western Railway, to pool the revenue from certain types of competitive traffic. The aim of these pooling arrangements was to concentrate traffic over the most economic routes, to co-ordinate terminal working, to eliminate competitive canvassing, and to give the public more extended availability of tickets over competitive routes.

The steps taken by the Government under the Finance Act of 1932 to boost the national economy certainly assisted trade and industry throughout the country, and the railways benefited to some extent by increased traffic. As an index of the beginnings of trade recovery, steel production, which in 1932 was averaging 438,500 tons a month, increased in 1933 to 583,500 tons a month, with a consequent boost to coal mining, and increased rail traffic between the mines and the steel plants. On the other hand, the tariffs imposed by this Act substantially reduced import traffic, and the latter year closed with a loss to the L.N.E.R. on its steamship account of £95,314, consisting mainly in £81,588 lost by the Harwich and Grimsby services.

During the passage of the Road and Rail Traffic Bill through the Commons the Chief General Manager, Sir Ralph Wedgwood, was taken seriously ill, and his absence at this critical time, with the loss of his foresight and counsel, was felt acutely by his colleagues. With little doubt his illness was the result of the strain to which his responsibilities, and his response to them, had subjected him. But the skill of his medical advisers and the devotion of Lady Wedgwood pulled him through, and he made an excellent recovery.

XII

The Years of Fulfilment—1934-1939

DURING THE five years immediately preceding the outbreak of the Second World War the London & North Eastern Railway reached the zenith of its achievements, and had no superior in Great Britain in the modernity and efficiency of the services that by now it was operating for both passengers and freight. As related in detail in Chapter XXIV, in the realm of speed it was the first railway in the country to introduce streamline trains and runs of more than 200 miles in length timed at over 70 m.p.h. from start to stop, and eventually, in 1938, Gresley's A4 Pacific *Mallard* achieved a speed record—126 m.p.h.—which has never been beaten by any other steam locomotive in the world. The streamlined "Silver Jubilee", "Coronation", and "West Riding Limited" provided entirely new standards of luxury, and captured the public imagination. Moreover, the general standard of L.N.E.R. passenger service also had been brought up to a high level by the acceleration of many less spectacular main line trains all over the system.

On the freight side regularly scheduled express freight trains, composed wholly or partly of wagons fitted with continuous brakes, could now be found in considerable numbers in the working timetables, in most cases with late afternoon or evening departures, but early morning arrivals guaranteed at most of the principal centres served by the company. This enterprising policy even extended to the regular operation of express coal trains between the principal provincial concentration centres and London. In an attractively produced brochure published in 1938 the L.N.E.R. claimed to be running the finest freight services in the world, with timings tailored to meet trading needs at each destination, and recommended the use of these trains, not merely for perishable traffic, but also for all urgent merchandise.

Movement of freight was being facilitated and expedited by various important new works. These included the widening of the North Eastern Area main line between Skelton Bridge, York, and Northallerton, brought into use in 1933; the new Fish Dock at Grimsby, opened in 1934; the marshalling yard at Mottram on the Great Central Sheffield-Manchester main line; and the magnificent new Inward marshalling yard at Hull.

In 1934 an agreement of major importance to London commuters was entered into jointly by the four main line railways and the London Passenger Transport Board. It was both for the pooling of suburban traffic and also for an ordered scheme of development to link up certain tubes with surface suburban lines which would be taken over by the L.P.T.B. So far as concerned the L.N.E.R., as related in Chapter XXI the Central London line was to be extended from Liverpool Street to an exchange station with the Great Eastern suburban services at Stratford, and the L.P.T.B. was eventually to take over the branch from Leyton to Loughton, Epping and Ongar, with the Newbury Park to Woodford line; while at long length electrification was to be undertaken of the Great Eastern lines from both Liverpool Street and Fenchurch Street to Shenfield. Not only was Government assistance to be provided for the carrying out of these projects, but also for the next 15 or 16 years Government loans were to be made available, at no more than $2\frac{1}{2}$ per cent interest, for the carrying out of other essential work. The L.N.E.R. management decided without delay to apply this infusion of money to works designed to improve the traffic flow, and the plans so made also are set out in detail in Chapter XIV.

During these years the company was very much alive to the need for protecting its essential railway business, and realised that such protection required penetration, if needs be, into the fields of its competitors. It will be remembered that as far back as 1928 the four main line railways had obtained Parliamentary powers to operate air services, and at last, in 1934, an attempt was made, in conjunction with the other three groups and Imperial Airways, to exercise these powers, a subsidiary company called Railway Air Services being formed for this purpose. Some limited air services actually were put into operation by railways in certain areas where they were forced by geographical considerations to make considerable circuits by rail which could be bridged in a fraction of the time by air—as, for example, across the Bristol Channel—but in the event the L.N.E.R. found no similar obstacles in the Eastern Counties, and never got "off the ground" in this venture. However, such assistance as was possible was given by the L.N.E.R. to the other railways, and a close watch was kept on the possibility of developing air services of this kind.

Meantime investments in the bus companies, which also had been authorised in 1928, were proving quite profitable. Not only were these giving a yield of 8 to 10 per cent., but savings also were being obtained by the closing of unremunerative branch lines and the reduction of local passenger services. Further, the railways collectively were making substantial loans to the road freight transport firms in which they had invested, to enable them to improve their equipment and their depot accommodation, in the hope of adding to the 5 per cent. return that they were obtaining from these undertakings. At the same time the L.N.E.R. adopted a forward policy of extending and mechanising its own cartage equipment, in order that its road vehicles might range widely over country districts and so compete more effectively with the ever-increasing activities of the independent road hauliers. On the shipping side also the whole of the Humber fleets owned by the L.N.E.

and L.M.S. Companies, using the ports of Hull and Goole, in 1935 were put under the control of a specially formed subsidiary company known as Associated Humber Lines.

Up to the middle 1930s the trading outlook was certainly improving, and the Directors and officers were feeling justified in the progressive policy they were pursuing. In 1934 the tonnage of freight carried by the L.N.E.R. rose by 9 per cent. over the corresponding figure in 1933, and there had been an increase of 3.28 per cent. in the number of passenger journeys. Agricultural traffic tended to lag in 1935 and 1936, but there was a marked improvement in the output of coal and steel, and also in shipbuilding; the culmination was an increase of 7.25 per cent. in passenger journeys in these two years, and of £672,000 and £868,000 in the net revenue from the carriage of general freight and coal respectively.

The Continental services via Harwich also had picked up from the crisis years, and for 1935 as compared with 1934 there had been an increase of 13 per cent. in the number of passengers and 5 per cent. in the tonnage of freight. Further, coming events were casting their shadow before by an addition of no less than 60 per cent. to the number of motor-cars accompanied by passengers that were being carried across the North Sea. With the interruption of the 1939-1945 war, however, many years were to elapse before the immense modern development of this type of traffic was to take place.

The recovery of railway traffic just described proved to be no more than temporary. For whereas in the previous four years the net revenue of the Company had increased steadily from £8,348,146 in 1934 to £10,107,442 in 1937, the year 1938 showed a disastrous fall to £6,653,167. Although no divided payment had been possible on the Preferred and Deferred Ordinary stocks in the four years mentioned, the First and Redeemable Preference stockholders had received payment in full in 1936 and 1937, and Second Preference holders ½ per cent. in 1936 and 1¾ per cent. in 1937. But the 1938 results could not justify any dividends whatever on the Preference and Ordinary stocks.

It fell for the first time to Sir Ronald Matthews, the newly appointed Chairman, to face some highly critical stockholders at the 1939 annual meeting of the Company. He explained that one of the worst difficulties with which the L.N.E.R. had to contend had been a setback in the steel industry, which accounted for more than two-fifths of the tonnage of freight, other than coal and coke, originating on the system; the fall in freight receipts, compared with 1937, due in part also to the continued loss of traffic to the road hauliers, had been 16¼ per cent. While warning that another year like the last would "seriously threaten our whole commercial existence", Sir Ronald held out the prospect of better things in 1939, especially from the results of the "square deal" campaign about to be mentioned. The *Railway Gazette*, in reporting this meeting, commented that the new Chairman "created a very good impression by his conduct of the proceedings on an exceptionally difficult occasion", and that the calming effect of his remarks resulted in the meeting dispersing "in good humour".

It is hardly surprising that the railway administrations were becoming seriously alarmed at the effects of the harmful competition of the road hauliers, to which they had no adequate means of reply because of the various statutory limitations on the railway charges. In November, 1938, therefore, they made representations to the Minister of Transport seeking early legislation to remove this statutory control of their charges for the conveyance of merchandise, and of all conditions which prevented them from competing on an equal footing with other forms of transport. It was felt that the Salter Road-Rail Conference of 1932 had not gone far enough in the direction of equalising the conditions in which road and rail respectively had to operate, and that greater freedom for commercial enterprise by the railways was essential.

The representations of the railways were accompanied by some high-powered publicity, which will go down to history as the "Square Deal Campaign". This telling title was due to the inspiration of Sir Ralph Wedgwood, who, when the question was being discussed as to what the campaign should be called, produced this as his suggestion, to the general acclaim of his colleagues. It did not please all those outside railway circles, however, and especially, it need hardly be added, the road hauliers.

The Minister of Transport referred the railway companies' case to the Transport Advisory Council, whose Chairman, Sir Arthur Griffith-Boscawen, was indefatigable in his endeavours to secure agreement between the conflicting interests represented on the Council. This eventually he succeeded in doing; the Council was given its remit on December 12th, 1938, and produced an agreed report on April 4th, 1939. The nature of this report, and the hopes to which it gave birth, were admirably expressed by the Railway Companies' Association in the following terms:

"The Report of the Transport Advisory Council contains recommendations to the Minister of Transport, and through him to the Government, for the orderly planning of the great transport industries of the country on a new and national basis best suited to meet the modern requirements of the trading community. These recommendations can only be implemented by legislation and this step is one of very great urgency. When Parliament has sanctioned the commencement of this new era in transport, practical advantage will immediately accrue to the country; in the first place, the railways will be enabled to evolve with the other transport interests a logical system of charges to meet the needs of every branch of trade and industry; and in the second place, the improved financial position of the railways will afford them an opportunity to initiate a comprehensive programme of improvement of their services both to industry and to the travelling public.

"The economic advantages which are likely to result from such sound and well-reasoned proposals as are found in the Council's Report must be far-reaching. On the one hand, the railways in a healthy state will be able to continue their annual expenditure during periods of trade depression, which will help to offset the reduced demands of British industry at such periods, and, on the other hand, the greater efficiency which will result from the co-ordination of the country's transport services will enable the community to have its goods conveyed by the most efficient and expeditious means and at the lowest economic cost. Indeed, these recommendations, if implemented without delay by legislation, afford an opportunity for Great Britain to evolve the most efficient and comprehensive system of transport in the world". Alas for these rosy dreams! The coming of war five months later prevented any further progress being made, and the opportunity presented by the recommendations of the Transport Advisory Council for "the orderly planning of the great transport industries of the country" was lost for many years to come.

During 1939 the railway trades unions showed some restiveness, and wage negotiations were practically continuous. Their case was referred to the Railway Staff National Tribunal, and although that body gave a finding against the unions' claims, the companies decided, in view of a slight improvement in traffic, to raise the minimum wage for adult male employees to 45s. per week. In September, under the shadow of the outbreak of war, a further claim was made by the unions, and a further increase was granted.

As the months of 1939 rolled on, and war became more and more certain, preoccupation with emergency measures and air raid precautions absorbed most of the energies of the Company's officers. Many of the major improvement works which had been begun were suspended, including the electrification from Sheffield and Wath to Manchester, on which some £2,500,000 already had been spent. Protection against bombing of signalboxes, control rooms and other key points was carried out as rapidly as possible, as well as the provision of air raid shelters, in accordance with plans which had been in existence for some time past.

Normal passenger services were still being run as scheduled, even including the streamline trains, despite the fact that there was an increasing amount of freight traffic directly concerned with the emergency arrangements. Plans for evacuating the civilian populations from London and other vulnerable centres were drawn up. The L.N.E.R. steamers also were earmarked by the Admiralty for war service. To those who had been through the First World War the return of days which they had never expected to see again seemed a nightmare, but all the staff faced with confidence whatever might lie ahead, determined that there would be no failure on their part, and knowing that they had in their hands first class equipment with which to carry out their appointed tasks.

Actually the railways were taken under Government control, under the Defence Regulations, 1939, on September 1st of that year, two days before war was declared. It was laid down that all net revenue, other than that derived from investments in road transport, would be pooled;

the proportions agreed were 34 per cent. to the London Midland & Scottish Railway, 23 per cent. to the London & North Eastern, 16 per cent. each to the Great Western and Southern, and 11 per cent. to the London Passenger Transport Board. From April, 1939, traffic once again had shown a marked upward trend, and the "square deal" campaign had certainly had a beneficial effect; rather remarkably, therefore, when the 1940 annual meeting was held, Sir Ronald Matthews was able to report that despite the outbreak of war the net revenue for 1939 had climbed back to £9,271,030, permitting the payment to the First and Redeemable Preference stockholders of their dividends in full once again, and ¾ per cent. on the Second Preference shares.

From 1939 onwards the railways never regained their freedom, for Government control continued until they all passed from private ownership into the hands of the nation in January, 1948. The story of the colossal contribution made by the L.N.E.R. to the national war effort has been ably told elsewhere, and it only now remains to recount what happened during the final years of independent London & North Eastern history.

HISTORIC OCCASIONS.
Above: The test run in 1922 with a 20-coach train to prove the ability of Gresley's new Class AI Pacific No. 1471 *Sir Frederick Banbury* to keep the "Flying Scotsman" schedule with a 20-coach train.

Left: AI Pacific No. 4474 *Victor Wild* working the Great Western Railway "Cornish Riviera Express" into Paddington in the 1925 locomotive exchange.

Below: Past and present in 1938: fifty years of "Flying Scotsman" development.

[*British Railways*

Above: Frontier point—Shaftholme Junction, where the former Great Northern Railway made an end-on junction with the North Eastern, and from the formation of the L.N.E.R. the Southern Area joined the North Eastern Area. The line diverging to the left was the L. & Y.R. to Knottingley, which gave G.N.R. trains access to York before the direct Selby line was opened. The train is the up "Flying Scotsman". [*British Railways*

Below: The North Eastern is the only important main line in Great Britain passing over swingbridges. This is Selby bridge, over the River Ouse, and 10 miles further north is Naburn bridge, over the same river. [*W. N. R. Beedle*

Above: The last London & North Eastern locomotive design: Peppercorn Class A1 Pacific No. 60130 *Kestrel* climbing to Stoke Summit with a down Edinburgh express. The first of these engines were not completed until 1948, so that they never bore L.N.E.R. numbers.

[*John Gain*

Below: Another L.N.E.R. frontier point was Carlisle, where L.N.E.R. locomotives took over from the L.M.S.R. through trains from St. Pancras to Edinburgh. A1 Pacific No. 60162 *St. Johnstoun,* the last of the Peppercorn 4–6–2s, leaving Carlisle for Edinburgh by the Waverley route with a stopping train.

[*Eric Treacy*

Above: Viscount Grey of Fallodon, the last Chairman of the North Eastern Railway.

Above: In retirement in his 80th year but still active: Sir Alexander Kaye Butterworth, last General Manager of the North Eastern Railway.

Below: William Whitelaw, former Chairman of the North British and Highland Railways and first Chairman of the London & North Eastern Railway.

Below: Sir Ralph Wedgwood, first Chief General Manager of the London & North Eastern Railway, and in office from 1923 to 1939.   *[British Railways*

XIII

War and the Last Phase—1940-1947

AFTER THEIR effort during the four years of World War I the railways of Britain were in a very run-down state, but by the first year of the grouping, 1923, there had been a recovery to not far short of their pre-war condition. At the end of World War II, however, matters were far worse. Not only had the Second World War lasted half as long again; conditions throughout its duration were far more arduous, shortages of material were far more acute; and maintenance had been starved to a far greater degree than in the earlier agony. Furthermore, as a beleaguered island this country had been subject to severe bombing by the enemy, with the railways as a specially sought-after target. To what might have been regarded the normal traffic there had been added intensive troop and military stores movements, mass evacuation of civilian populations, and additional freight traffic due to diversion of shipping.

Were it not that the railways, and not least among them the L.N.E.R., had built up so high a standard of equipment and maintenance that when the Government assumed control in 1939 they took over the undertakings in a first class condition, railway transport might well have broken down under the strain imposed on it in the ensuing six years. Nevertheless it did not break down. Yet, such was the post-war spirit that at the conclusion of the war, in 1945, no thanks were accorded to the railways for the prudence and good housekeeping that had made their fine war record possible. Rather the reverse; a leading politician of the political party which came to power in 1945 was ungracious enough to refer to the railways as "a poor bag of assets", with the implication that this had been due to the shortcomings of their administration. It can hardly escape comment, however, that this particular politician eventually proved himself not merely to be a poor asset to his party, but also to the nation.

During the war years, as related in Chapter XXVII, both age and stress had taken their toll of the senior officers, and, alas, a number of the promising young men who had qualified through the Traffic Apprenticeship training and were destined for important posts had fallen as war casualties. On their return from the Forces, however, there were sufficient well-trained and enterprising young officers to fill the numerous vacancies, and as the interests of those on active service had been looked after in their absence, their return to their normal vocation was able to proceed with commendable smoothness.

The advent to power in 1945 of a Labour Government clearly heralded changes in the ownership and administration of the railways. At first it was uncertain what form would be taken by the Labour party's doctrine of nationalisation, and the London & North Eastern Railway Board therefore decided on a two-prong line of policy which in its view would be the best for the country, for its undertaking and for its employees. One prong was intended to influence, as far as possible, the scope and form of nationalisation, and its evolution needed consultation and agreement with the other three main line railways. That this policy, when finally agreed, was known as the "Newton Plan" leaves no doubt that its evolution was due in the first instance to the L.N.E.R. Chief General Manager. The other line of policy was domestic, and was aimed at eliminating the ravages of war, and developing the L.N.E.R. system over a period of years on the most modern lines, so that it might be in the forefront of railway progress.

A five-year plan therefore was drawn up, designed both to restore pre-war standards of service and also to introduce progressive improvements based on the latest in design and scientific research. With materials likely to be in short supply for a long time ahead and the retention of control by the Government, it was calculated that £40,000,000 would be needed to overtake arrears of maintenance, and another £50,000,000 for new works needed immediately, apart from the cost of electrification, of new rollng stock, and of longer term developments. During the war the Company had accumulated a Trust Fund of £40,000,000, and it was determined to apply this at once to dealing with maintenance arrears. So rapidly was this work put in hand that despite shortages of materials and labour 579 miles of track were partially or completely renewed during 1946, and over 300 stations and depots were repaired and painted—in the circumstances a fine achievement.

For the new works programme the requirements of the entire system were surveyed, and schemes were drawn up for providing, where most needed, new stations, goods depots, offices, locomotive depots, carriage sheds, marshalling yards, and running and loop lines, together with the modernisation of many existing stations, depots, signalling installations, and hotels and refreshment rooms. Electrification proposals were for completion of the Sheffield and Wath to Manchester scheme, already well advanced, and for the joint London suburban scheme of the Great Eastern Section and the London Passenger Transport Board. Locomotive standardisation was to be pursued systematically, according to a scheme drawn up by Edward Thompson and comprising no more than ten standard classes. The Chief General Manager himself took a hand in the layout of new standard main line coaches, based to some extent on the replies to a questionnaire which had been issued to passengers in 1945. A substantial renewal of the wagon fleet was contemplated, including the construction of new all-steel mineral wagons of 16 tons capacity. Standardisation of such items as signalboxes, platelayers' huts and station name-boards also was put in hand.

A good deal of the work contemplated, including the electrification plans, was begun while the L.N.E.R. was still an independent company, and many other of its proposals were adopted subsequently by the nationalised British Railways. Had there been any disposition in Government circles to abandon doctrinaire theories of nationalisation lock, stock and barrel, and to adopt a scheme on the lines of the Newton Plan whereby public ownership of the assets would have been combined with private enterprise in their exploitation, it might have been of greater advantage to the former L.N.E.R. territories than what actually happened. But this was not to be. With its substantial majority, the Government steam-rollered through the House of Commons the Transport Act of 1947, which transferred to complete public ownership not only the railways, but various other forms of transport as well. So the London & North Eastern Railway came to the end of its history on December 31st, 1947. Some of the major economies effected may be measured by Table 9, which sets out the reduction in mileage and rolling stock during these 25 years.

Table 9

Reduction in Mileage and Rolling Stock during L.N.E.R. 25 Years

	Constituent Companies End of 1922	London & North Eastern Railway End of 1947
Total Mileage, Route	6,674	6,334
Total Mileage, Single Track	17,158	16,890
Locomotives, No.*	7,383	6,445
Passenger Vehicles, No.	20,156	16,451
Freight Vehicles, No.	284,481	241,565
Service Vehicles, No.	15,983	9,331

Not including electric locomotives and motorcoaches; and steam and petrol railcars.

The last annual meeting of the company, with Sir Ronald Matthews in the chair, took place at Grosvenor House, Park Lane, on March 5th, 1948. In many ways the final year had been a difficult one. In the month of March there had been some of the worst snowstorms in living memory, which for two days suspended completely all railway traffic between England and Scotland, and the adverse effects of which were felt until the middle of May. Freight traffic through the year, however, had been well above the pre-war level, the total net ton-miles of 6,750 millions comparing with 5,643 millions in the twelve months up to the outbreak of war. The carriage of coal and coke once again was on the up-grade, but passenger train-miles were 21 per cent. down.

Yet the pooled net revenues of the four railway groups in 1947 had fallen £37,000,000 short of the fixed annual sums payable to them under the control agreement, and the adoption from midsummer of the recommendations of the Court of Enquiry concerning railwaymen's wages and hours had caused a further shortage of £22,000,000, leaving some £59,000,000 in all to be found by the Exchequer. Of this sum, as previously mentioned, the L.N.E.R. share was 23 per cent. The total net revenue of the L.N.E.R. in its final year was £11,520,365, and this permitted the payment in respect of 1947 of the full 4 per cent. on both the First and Second Preference stock and of the full 5 per cent. on the Redeemable Preference stock. The Preferred Ordinary stockholders, after nine consecutive years of receiving no return on their holdings, in this final year were rewarded for their patience with a dividend of 0.81 per cent. though this was hardly much consolation with a stock nominally bearing 5 per cent. interest.

The last Annual Report of the Company underlined the fact that this is an ungrateful world. It contained an addendum reading as follows:

"The resolution proposed by a Stockholder to pay the Directors the total sum of £63,000 as compensation for loss of office was, on being put to the vote, defeated on a show of hands. The Chairman thereupon announced that the dividend on the 5 per cent. Preferred Ordinary stock would be at the rate of 19s. 2d. per annum. After payment of this dividend the undistributed balance of £224 is repayable to the British Transport Commission".

However, the meeting terminated on a happier note. A stockholder, Councillor Wilson, said "I do not think it is fair for us to leave this room without moving a hearty vote of thanks to the Chairman and the Directors, for the last time, for their splendid services to the stockholders". And amid applause he added, "That is unanimous, sir".

XIV

The "Way and Works"

THE FORMATION of the London & North Eastern brought under a single management some engineering works of exceptional note. In particular, its main line from London to Aberdeen passed over five outstanding bridge structures, one of them famous not merely in this country but the world over, the Forth Bridge. Strictly speaking, of course, this was not exclusively L.N.E.R. property. Its construction was financed jointly by the Great Northern, North Eastern and North British Railways, and also by the Midland, a separate Forth Bridge Company being formed for the purpose. After the Grouping, therefore, the bridge was still a joint concern, interest on its debentures and ordinary shares from then on being guaranteed jointly by both railways. With its two 1,710 ft. main spans, its clear height above water of 157 ft. and its great towers rising to 360 ft. above the Firth of Forth, even to-day, three-quarters of a century after its opening, the Forth Bridge can claim to be one of the engineering wonders of the world.

A little further to the north the same main line was carried across the Firth of Tay by the Tay Bridge. For many years after its construction this claimed distinction as being the longest railway bridge in the world, with its 85 lattice girder spans and total length of 11,653 ft.—more than two miles; it has since been beaten in length by the Huey P. Long bridge over the Mississippi and the Oakland Bay Bridge at San Francisco, both in the United States. Then, further south, the North Eastern Railway made some handsome contributions to the list of bridges. There was Robert Stephenson's original High Level Bridge across the Tyne at Newcastle, with its six 125 ft. spans, originally of cast iron, carrying the rails 112 ft. above high water mark, which from its opening in 1850 by Queen Victoria was used by all the East Coast trains until in 1906 the more imposing King Edward Bridge was opened by King Edward VII. This great structure, with two 300 ft. spans, and one each of 231 ft. and 191 ft., has a bridge floor 50 ft. wide, sufficient to accommodate four tracks as compared with the three over the High Level Bridge. From the inauguration of the King Edward Bridge it became possible for East Coast trains to run through Newcastle without the reversal in the Central Station which was necessary when they could use only the High Level Bridge.

This does not exhaust the list of the great bridges. Also on the East Coast main line there is the Royal Border Bridge, another structure opened in 1850 for which Robert Stephenson was responsible, and still to-day, well over a century later, carrying the far greater weight of modern locomotives and trains over its 28 arches which at their maximum are 126 ft. above the bed of the River Tweed.   One bridge of note, in the financing of which the North Eastern Railway had joined with the Sunderland Corporation because it was to carry a road as well as a railway, was the Queen Alexandra Bridge across the River Wear, with a double-deck lattice girder span of 330 ft. flanked by three 200 ft. spans. This was opened in 1909, but even before the end of L.N.E.R. history railway traffic over it had ceased, though road traffic is still as busy as ever.

As to other viaducts, the former North Eastern Railway probably possessed more of them than any other individual railway in the country. In all directions, in the County of Durham in particular, the mineral lines through this extremely hilly region had been carried across the valleys by viaducts, many of very considerable size, and most of them of masonry construction.   There were also some spidery iron or steel structures of note, the most notable of them Belah, on the line across the Pennines from Darlington to Tebay and Penrith, no less than 196 ft. high at its maximum and 1,040 ft. long, and with sixteen 60 ft. lattice girder spans carried on wrought iron trestles.   Immediately beyond Barnard Castle on this line, also, was the viaduct over the profound gorge of the Deepdale river, 161 ft. above the stream.   Unhappily these last two no longer exist, neither does the 152 ft. high Staithes viaduct across the Dale House Valley on the former Saltburn to Scarborough line; both the railways concerned have been closed to traffic and their great bridges have been dismantled.

No other constituent companies of the L.N.E.R. could boast the possession of viaducts of such note as the principal of those which have been described.   Relatively near to London—21 miles out of King's Cross, to be exact—the Great Northern Railway crossed the valley of the Mimram by Welwyn Viaduct, a masonry structure with forty 40 ft. arches, 1,560 ft. length and maximum height of 89 ft.; and in the heart of Nottinghamshire was the Giltbrook Viaduct in the Erewash Valley, not so lofty but 1,772 ft. long and with 46 arches.

On the Great Central Railway the London Extension required a number of substantial masonry viaducts, but probably the most notable viaduct on this system was on the original Manchester, Sheffield & Lincolnshire main line, over Dinting Vale in Lancashire, dating back to 1844.   Carrying the rails at a maximum height of 125 ft. above the stream, the five central arches, each of 125 ft. span, were constructed originally in timber, but later wrought iron plate girders were substituted; and in quite recent years, to carry the much heavier traffic resulting from electrification, five additional piers were built up to carry the centre of each of these spans.   There were also eleven 50 ft brick arches flanking the main spans.   No viaducts or bridges of special note were to be found on the Great Eastern Railway.

One unique feature of the East Coast main line is that in one brief stretch of 11 miles it passes over two swing-bridges, the first spanning the River Aire at Selby and the second the River Ouse at Naburn. Another oddity, of an entirely different kind, has been the existence of three level crossings with other railways made by this main line. First, just north of Newark, the Great Northern Railway crossed on the level the Midland Railway branch from Nottingham to Lincoln. Some 18 miles further north came the crossing on the level at Retford of the Great Central main line from Sheffield to Grimsby, which during the year 1965 was finally abandoned after the latter had been lowered to a dive-under. Then on the North Eastern Railway, a mile north of Darlington, there was the level crossing with the historic Stockton & Darlington line, which had occupied this site for nearly 20 years before the main line from Darlington to Newcastle was opened.

Mention must now be made of the tunnels which came into London & North Eastern ownership in 1923. The Great Central Railway provided the longest of them—the twin tunnels through the backbone of the Pennines between Dunford Bridge and Penistone on the main Sheffield-Manchester line, 3 miles 13 yds. in length. Completed and opened at the end of 1845, Woodhead Tunnel, bored through millstone grit with such accuracy that the headings driven in each direction from the vertical shafts had met with no error greater than 3 in. in the meeting of the centre-lines, was a notable engineering feat for the period. Next in length was the North Eastern Railway Bramhope Tunnel, 2 miles 234 yds. long, between Leeds and Arthington, on the Harrogate line. Catesby Tunnel, 1 mile 1,237 yds. long, between Woodford Halse and Rugby, was one of the principal engineering achievements on the Great Central London Extension.

Then, between 1¼ and 1½ miles in length, the Great Northern Railway had Ponsbourne Tunnel, on the loop line from Wood Green to Stevenage *via* Hertford, and Queensbury Tunnel, between Bradford and Halifax. The only remaining L.N.E.R. tunnels over a mile in length were Bolsover, on the former Lancashire, Derbyshire & East Coast Railway, and Drewton, on the former Hull & Barnsley Railway. Tunnels on both the Great Eastern and North British lines were relatively few and short.

In the matter of stations, as in that of bridges, the North British Railway held the record with their Waverley Station in Edinburgh. That the one-time Edinburgh & Glasgow Railway as far back as 1847 had managed to push its way into the very heart of the city, through what later became the Princes Street Gardens, in face of what a writer in later years described as "the multitude of opposing interests and prejudices", was an amazing feat; in modern times the opposition would probably have made such an entry impossible. Moreover, by the time the Forth Bridge was opened in 1890, traffic had increased to such a degree as to require a considerable enlargement of the station to almost its present size.

The main feature of the reconstruction was the creation of an immense island, with the station offices in the centre, flanked by through main platforms with a maximum length of 1,680 ft. Between them, at both ends of the station, were a series of bay platforms, 15 in all, together with two so-called "Suburban" platforms outside the south wall of the main building, though the latter have frequently been used for main line trains also. As middle crossovers have always made it possible to use the outer ends of the two main platforms separately, Edinburgh Waverley in effect has in effect had a total of 21 platforms, totalling in length 14,305 ft., and with the whole station covering an area of 18 acres. Its nearest competitor on the London & North Eastern Railway was Liverpool Street Station of the Great Eastern Railway; possessing 18 platforms, with a total length of 11,410 ft., this London terminus was more compact than Edinburgh Waverley, for it occupied an area of 16 acres only. But Liverpool Street, still entirely steam-operated up to the end of L.N.E.R. history, was much the busier of the two, handling over 1,200 train movements daily when the G.E.R. handed it over to the larger company.

Next in order of size came Newcastle Central Station of the North Eastern Railway, the only L.N.E.R. station in 1923 that had to handle an electric passenger service. The total length of its 15 platforms was 9,933 ft.; the longest of them measured 1,368 ft., and the entire station covered 17 acres. The N.E.R. had the most reason to be proud of its fine station at York, with its curved all-over roof, 42 ft. in maximum height and of 81 ft. span, which has always been so greatly admired. In 1923 the station was all confined within the main covered area, apart from one through platform, No. 14, outside the west wall; the 14 platforms totalled in length 10,608 ft.; here again the two main through platforms, 1,701 and 1,575 ft. respectively, served by central crossovers, could each accommodate two trains simultaneously.

The North Eastern Railway owned a number of stations of outstanding merit—more, indeed, than those of any other of the constituent companies of the L.N.E.R. Next in order of size after those already mentioned was Hull Paragon, which had been enlarged in 1904 to a total of nine main platforms, with various docks and loading platforms. Darlington Bank Top, looped off the East Coast main line and built on the same principle as Edinburgh Waverley, with one central island accommodating the station buildings and flanked by the down and up through lines, together with terminal bay platforms at both ends, was an imposing structure. The same compliment could be paid to the station at Middlesbrough, which at the time of its opening in 1877 was one of the finest stations in North Eastern England. The North Eastern was also the joint owner with the London & North Western Railway of the capacious Leeds New Station, which from 1923 onwards became joint L.M.S. and L.N.E. property.

By contrast, the Great Northern Railway could lay claim to scarcely any stations of note other than its London terminus at King's Cross. As compared with the pseudo-Gothic flamboyance of St. Pancras terminus next door, the austere frontage of King's Cross, with its two great arches separated by a clock tower 110 ft. high, has always had a dignity all its own, despite the clutter of odd buildings that gradually sprung up in the space between this frontage and the Euston Road. Incidentally, there is reason to believe that the clock itself, still in use, was obtained second-hand from the 1851 Great Exhibition in Hyde Park. The main part of the original station had two platforms on the departure side, separated by four tracks for storing coaches, and four on the arrival side, one of which had inset into it a bay platform, so that it could accommodate two short trains. To this was added later the Suburban station, on the west side, with three platforms, and the platform which served the Moorgate trains, climbing steeply out of the smoky tunnel from the Metropolitan line. Up Moorgate trains stopped, as they still do, at a platform separate from the main station, and in those days known as York Road. With York Road, this made an effective total of 12 platforms.

On the Great Eastern side there was Fenchurch Street terminus, strictly speaking the property of the Blackwall Railway, a line leased to the G.E.R. until the end of the latter company's existence. In its restricted space Fenchurch Street handled all the Midland trains to and from the London, Tilbury & Southend line in addition to part of the G.E.R. suburban service, to and from the Ilford and Loughton lines and also North Woolwich. The Great Eastern's terminal station at Norwich Thorpe also deserves mention, as well as the unique station at Cambridge, where the University influence was so strong that the Great Eastern had never been able to get away from dealing with all its main line trains, both up and down, at a single platform 1,254 ft. long.

Most peaceful of all the London & North Eastern termini in London was the station which the Great Central Railway had built and opened in 1899 to serve its London Extension—Marylebone. By 1922 a sizeable suburban service had developed here, both to and from the High Wycombe direction and also the Metropolitan line to Aylesbury, but at no period of its history could Marylebone be described as a really busy station. In Nottingham the Great Central had combined with the Great Northern Railway to build, in the centre of the city, the fine Victoria Station, little dreaming, no doubt, that less than 70 years later the heavy expenditure so occasioned would be rendered valueless by the station being abandoned under nationalisation, only one pair of lines being left to carry freight traffic passing through. The Sheffield Victoria station, also eventually to be closed, dated back to Manchester, Sheffield and Lincolnshire days; in Manchester the Great Central shared London Road terminus jointly with the London & North Western Railway, and the Central Station as one of the three partners in the Cheshire Lines Committee.

The biggest stations in Scotland used by the North British Railway, other than Edinburgh Waverley, could only be reached by running powers over the lines of its rival—the Caledonian Railway. One was the Caledonian's Perth General Station and the other was the joint

G

Caledonian and Great North of Scotland Aberdeen General. In the former case the length of Caledonian trackage so used was 2 miles only; but in the latter North British trains had to run 38 miles over the Caledonian main line, from Kinnaber Junction, Montrose, before reaching Aberdeen. In Glasgow the N.B.R. had its own terminus at Queen Street High Level, with the through Low Level suburban platforms beneath; the worst handicap of the High Level, apart from its cramped situation, has always been the 1 in 42 exit, largely through tunnel, to Cowlairs, up which trains formerly were assisted by wire ropes from an engine-house at the top of the bank. In the days of the fierce rivalry between the Caledonian and North British Railways it would have caused the former unbounded astonishment, and indeed mortification, could it have been foreseen that eventually all Buchanan Street trains would be transferred to Queen Street, and, still worse, that all trains into and out of the handsome Caledonian Princes Street terminus in Edinburgh would have to seek refuge at Waverley. But this did not happen until well after the end of London & North Eastern history.

One of the first major engineering tasks to be decided on by the London & North Eastern management was to transform the sorting sidings of the former Great Eastern Railway at March in Cambridgeshire into a fully mechanised gravity marshalling yard. A great deal of coal being worked from the Yorkshire and Nottinghamshire pits to London and East Anglia generally had to be dealt with at March, and in addition the introduction of sugar beet as a staple crop in the Eastern Counties and by 1925 the establishment of beet sugar factories, as described in Chapter IX, had helped greatly to increase freight traffic on the Great Eastern Section. The particular interest of the new installation was not merely gravity sorting, but the first application in Great Britain of rail-brakes, to apply automatic retardation of the wagons as they rolled down from the hump into the various sorting sidings.

Hitherto the movement of switches in such yards, and the braking of wagons to prevent undesirable impacts between wagon and wagon in the sidings had been performed by human shunters, whose numbers could now be very substantially reduced. The braking system adopted was the German Fröhlich type, as used in the war-famous Hamm marshalling yard in Germany, with pairs of long brake-beams gripping the wheel rims as the wagons passed, and the intensity of the pressure controlled from the hump cabin, which also operated all the switches electrically. Such methods are now common, but when the new up yard came into operation in 1929, after four years' work in construction, they were novel in Great Britain and attracted considerable attention. The total cost of the yard was £285,000, and so efficient was its operation that in the first year of the new yard it was calculated that the time of transit of wagons through the yard was being reduced by from 12 to 24 hours per unit. In 1933 the mechanised up yard at March was complemented by similar treatment of the down yard.

Meantime there had been various other "Way and Works" developments. A widening of the Great Northern main line had been in progress between Offord and Huntingdon in 1923 and was completed in the following year; its principal feature was a new bridge over the River Ouse. Various stations came in for attention. The cramped and inconvenient two-platform station at Berwick had been replaced in 1927 by a fine new structure embodying a much longer island platform; this meant that there was no longer an independent pair of through lines on the west side of the station, but this caused no inconvenience, and a reduction of the curvature through the station permitted an easing of the speed restriction here. Another new station, opened in 1929, was at Clacton-on-Sea, with an elegant frontage which was an ornament to that town. Of a different kind was an engineering operation which became necessary on the neighbouring branch from Thorpe-le-Soken to Walton-on-the-Naze; from 1926 onwards this line, running along the cliffs, became so threatened by coast erosion that a deviation inland between Frinton-on-Sea and Walton had to be put in hand, and came into use in 1930.

Increased accommodation was becoming urgently necessary at King's Cross, and various useful developments at that station had been carried out. Coupled with the installation of a new 70 ft. turntable adjacent to Gasworks Tunnel, the engine yard between the Suburban station and the line coming up from the Metropolitan had been moved out beyond the latter, and in the space so vacated two new platforms had been added in 1924 to the existing three suburban platforms.

Then, two years later, the four carriage siding lines in the main line station between Platforms 6 and 10 had been replaced by a full length island platform, Nos. 7 and 8. Until then No. 3 arrival platform had been inset into No. 4, as we have seen already, so that both could accommodate relatively short trains only; No. 3 was now abolished, and the outward end of this platform was widened so that No. 4, renumbered 3, could take full length trains. This, incidentally, is the reason why King's Cross to-day has no No. 3 platform, nor, for that matter, any No. 9, which had been a short vehicle loading bay before the new Nos. 7 and 8 platforms were brought into use in 1926. The result of all these changes was to increase the number of full-length platforms in King's Cross Main and Suburban stations to 15, including the down platform from the Metropolitan line and York Road

Widening of existing main lines, to cope with increased traffic, by now was very much in the air. On the Great Eastern Section Romford and its eastern suburb of Gidea Park were developing rapidly, and traffic was much hampered by the fact that the four-tracked section of the Colchester main line extended no further than Romford Junction, just short of Romford Station. As a first stage of improvement, a new four-platform station was built at Romford, and the four tracks were extended to a system of carriage sidings laid out just short of Harold Wood; a new station, comprising two island platforms, was built to serve Gidea Park. The only blot on the Gidea Park scheme was that as the former up main line now became the down main line through the station, the up main line had to be curved around the outside of the up island platform, thereby introducing a speed restriction, if only to 60 m.p.h., at a point where up expresses were normally travelling at high speed immediately after descending Brentwood Bank.

No sooner was this widening completed, in 1931, than a contract was let to extend it for another 6½ miles, to Shenfield. This was a far bigger task, especially the enlargement of the deep cutting between Brentwood Station and Ingrave Summit; new stations also were needed at Harold Wood, Brentwood and Shenfield, the latter with a total of five platforms; and it was also decided that the connection at Shenfield from the down slow line to the Southend branch should reach the latter by a burrowing junction, so keeping the diverging trains clear of the main line. The cost of this major widening operation was estimated at something in the region of £500,000. This was really a stage in the progress towards the electrification of the Great Eastern suburban lines, which had been under consideration for many years, and very seriously from 1923 onwards. On financial grounds this had proved impossible until now, and by reason of war was destined to be delayed another 18 years before the electric dream finally became reality.

Meantime another important widening scheme had been in progress, and had been brought to completion by the summer of 1933. This was over certain sections of the North Eastern main line between York and Northallerton. As yet Skelton Bridge, across the River Ouse 3 miles out of York, remained double track only, but immediately beyond the bridge a widening to four tracks was carried out for 2½ miles to Beningbrough, after which four tracks were already in existence for 5¾ miles to Alne. Beyond here an additional down line was laid in for 5 miles to Pilmoor, and the final stage was a widening to four tracks for 3 miles, continuing the existing four-tracked section beyond Thirsk from Otterington to Northallerton.

The additional down line was dropped just before reaching Northallerton to burrow under the Harrogate-Northallerton spur and join the Harrogate-Stockton line, while a connection was laid in from the latter under both the Harrogate-Northallerton spur and the main line to join the additional up line. These new connections with the low level line from then on permitted a good deal of important freight working to be carried on between the low level line and the high level without fouling the main lines. Attractive new stations were built at Beningbrough and Otterington and new station buildings were provided on the down side at Alne and Raskelf.

Of equal importance with the widening works was the bringing into operation of automatic colour-light signalling throughout from York to Northallerton. As far back as 1905 one of the first automatic signalling installations in Great Britain was installed by the North Eastern Railway between Alne and Thirsk, of the Hall electro-pneumatic type with semaphore signals; these, which had given admirable service, were now replaced by a much more modern all-electric type. One of the outstanding features of the 1933 change-over was the new all-electric signalbox at Thirsk, one of the first in the country with an operating panel of the entrance-exit type—that is, with a large illuminated diagram of the length of line controlled on which a route through it was set up by moving thumb-switches on the diagram at both ends of the desired route. Provided that there was nothing obstructing this route, all the relevant points and signals then moved electrically to the required positions. At the time this also was an installation which attracted a good deal of attention.

In the same year, 1933, electric colour-light signalling was brought into operation at King's Cross terminus. In this case, however, operation was by means of a long row of miniature levers in a frame underneath the illuminated track diagram. All-electric operation at Fenchurch Street terminus followed in 1935. Now that work had begun on the Great Eastern Gidea Park to Shenfield widening, contracts were let for automatic signalling out as far as Shenfield, and also between Bethnal Green Junction and Enfield Town. In the intervening years various other important signalling developments had taken place. As far back as 1925 the signalling of the triangular junctions at both Manningtree and East Gate, Colchester, on the Great Eastern line, had been brought in each case under the control of a single signalbox instead of three boxes. In 1926 the complicated working through Cambridge Station had come under all-electric control.

Other all-electric automatic signalling had been brought into use under L.N.E.R. auspices between Marylebone and Wembley, on the Great Central Section; an interesting installation of electric colour-light signalling with approach lighting between Eryholme and Black Banks, Darlington, on the North Eastern Area; and low-pressure pneumatic signalling between Manchester (London Road) and Guide Bridge on the Great Central Section. As far back as 1909 the progressive North Eastern Railway had brought into use electro-pneumatic signalling through Newcastle Central Station, thereby displacing no fewer than 613 full-length levers in the previous mechanical boxes through this area.

The year 1935 saw the completion of two new marshalling yards of considerable importance. One, foreshadowing the electrification of the Great Central main line over Woodhead Summit between Sheffield and Manchester, was at Mottram; this was located on the steep descent westwards, which made the building of any artificial humps unnecessary. The other was the inward yard at the approach to Hull, North Eastern Region, which had been completely remodelled and mechanised throughout, including Fröhlich wagon retarders of the same type as those which had been installed at March.

In 1936, after the Government had indicated that it was prepared, as described in Chapter XII, to make loans available at $2\frac{1}{2}$ per cent. interest over periods up to 16 years, the London & North Eastern management decided to put in hand some engineering work of considerable importance. The Great Eastern Section of the Southern Area was to come in for special attention. From the earliest days Norwich main line expresses not stopping at Colchester had been compelled to reduce speed to 40 m.p.h. because of the curve through the station; this station was now to be completely rebuilt and extended, and the main line curve eased sufficiently to permit of full speed by non-stopping trains. Between Thorpe-le-Soken and Clacton-on-Sea the single line was to be doubled, and the remaining single-track section of the Felixstowe branch would be doubled also. In addition, the rising importance of the Southend-on-Sea traffic, especially of commuters, dictated a rebuilding and enlargement of Southend Victoria terminus.

On the East Coast main line two tasks of major importance were to be the remodelling of Doncaster and York Stations, including a considerable extension of the platform accommodation at the latter, together with all-electric colour-light signalling and point operation at both. New reception lines for freight trains were to be laid in at various points on the Great Northern main line south of Doncaster. Finally, the electrification of the Great Central main line over Woodhead Summit from Sheffield to Manchester, together with the connection from Wath marshalling yard up the Worsborough incline to Penistone, heavily used by coal trains, was definitely decided on, with overhead conduction at 1,500 volts d.c.

The first contracts for many of these works were let, but many years were to elapse before most of them were completed and brought into use; indeed, the first through electric trains from Sheffield to Manchester did not come into operation until 1954, 18 years later. The reason, of course, was the outbreak of the Second World War in September, 1939, which brought all new work to an abrupt halt.

XV

Pre-Grouping Locomotives

BEFORE WE begin to trace the development of London & North Eastern locomotive power during the twenty-five years' history of that company, it is necessary to examine the variety of locomotive types, set out in Table 9, and the characteristics of their design, that were brought by the constituent companies into the stock of the major system. In certain respects the rolling stock designs of the principal constituents had followed similar lines. In 1898 H. A. Ivatt of the Great Northern Railway had built Britain's first Atlantic or 4-4-2 express passenger locomotive, and had followed this four years later by the enlarged version, with 5 ft. 6 in. diameter boiler, and wide firebox which put to valuable use the space available behind the coupled wheels. This locomotive, No. 251, was to be the standard for Great Northern main line passenger service until the end of the separate existence of that company.

The North Eastern Railway, however, which until the end of last century had depended on 4-4-0 locomotives for its principal express passenger work, had experimented in 1899 by introducing a 4-6-0 design —the first in Great Britain of this wheel arrangement other than a few freight locomotives on the Highland Railway. Then driving wheels of no more than 6ft. 1 in. diameter proved too small for the fast East Coast trains, and a more imposing 6 ft. 8 in. 4-6-0 introduced in 1901 had not proved much more successful. But in 1903 there appeared, from the former Gateshead Works, Wilson Worsdell's first Atlantic express engine, No. 532, like Gresley's No. 251 with a 5 ft. 6in. diameter boiler, and from then on the 4-4-2 wheel arrangement was to become standard for express passenger work on the North Eastern Railway also. But there were some substantial differences between the Great Northern and the North Eastern designs. Worsdell favoured a narrow firebox as compared with Gresley's wide box; and Worsdell's 20 in. by 28 in. cylinders differed radically from the unusually small 18¾ in. by 24 in. cylinders of Ivatt's No. 251. During the remaining years of G.N.R. history few changes were made in the Ivatt Atlantic design other than the incorporation of superheating from 1910 onwards, with an increase to 20 in. in the cylinder diameter; but on the North Eastern Wilson Worsdell's two classes of two-cylinder 4-4-2s, Classes V and VI, were followed in 1911 by Vincent Raven's three-cylinder series of Class Z.

Meantime another of the L.N.E.R. constituent companies had introduced an Atlantic design to take over some of the principal passenger duties from its previous 4–4–0 classes. This was the Great Central Railway, on which John G. Robinson in 1903 turned out of Gorton Works his first Atlantic, No. 192—one of the most handsome locomotive types ever seen on British metals. Like Wilson Worsdell before him, Robinson experimented similarly with both 4–4–2 and 4–6–0 locomotives, but in his case almost identical in every respect other than the number of their coupled axles. Also, like Worsdell, Robinson adhered to the narrow firebox; none of the Atlantics brought into the London & North Eastern stock other than those of the Great Northern Ivatt design were provided with wide fireboxes.

Yet another of the L.N.E.R. constituent companies was eventually to adopt the 4–4–2 wheel arrangement, and this was perhaps the most surprising development of all. In one way it might have been expected that the North British Railway would fall into line with its other two East Coast partners, but in another way it would not be easy to justify this decision. For the North British main lines abounded in lengthy and arduous climbs, and the starts out of many of its principal stations —Hawick, Galashiels, Dundee, Arbroath, Montrose and the Caledonian stations at Stonehaven and Aberdeen used by East Coast trains—had in almost every case to be made up steep gradients. To limit adhesion weight to 40 tons when acceleration from rest and sustained uphill speeds were of such vital importance seemed to cry aloud for six-coupled wheels, but it was claimed that there was so much curvature on the North British main lines that a more flexible wheelbase than that of a 4–6–0 locomotive was essential.

Hence we have W. P. Reid's decision to build a 4–4–2 design, the first of which, No. 868 *Aberdonian*, emerged from the North British Locomotive Company's Hyde Park Works in Glasgow in 1906. So it was that up till 1922, the year before the London & North Eastern Railway came into existence, the Atlantic wheel arrangement had become standard for all the major express passenger work of three of the constituent companies; on the fourth, the Great Central, however, from 1912 onwards Robinson had largely displaced his Atlantics from the fastest duties by his highly efficient "Director" class 4–4–0s, and from 1911 had built a few powerful 4–6–0s also.

A fifth constituent company, the Great Eastern Railway, had been content up till 1911 with James Holden's "Claud Hamilton" 4–4–0s for handling its fairly leisurely schedules, but in 1912, with trains of increasing weight to be handled over main lines with numerous speed restrictions and none-too-easy gradients, a more powerful type appeared from Stratford Works; it was Stephen Holden's 4–6–0 No. 1500. Beset as Stratford was by severe loading gauge and weight restrictions, this proved to be an outstanding design, of the greatest value to the G.E.R. One constituent only remains to be mentioned, and that was the Great North of Scotland Railway. This was unique in that, apart from a few 0–4–4 tanks for local services, it depended entirely on 4–4–0 locomotives for both passenger and freight work.

Above: South Shields electric train running into Newcastle Central over the famous crossing with the East Coast main line at the east end of the station.

Right: Electrically-hauled coal train on the line from Shildon to the Erimus marshalling yard at Middlesbrough.

Below: Bo-Bo electric locomotive designed and built at Doncaster for the Sheffield—Manchester electrification. Though this first example was completed in 1941, owing to delay caused by the war and the boring of a second Woodhead Tunnel these locomotives were not running through until 1954.   [*British Railways*

Above: Interior of the all-electric signalbox at King's Cross terminus, brought into use in 1932.

Below: All-electric signalling at Edinburgh Waverley was installed in two stages, the West End cabin, with 227 miniature levers, in 1936, and that at the East End, seen here, with 207 levers, in 1938.

[*British Railways*]

The operating panel in the Thirsk cabin, one of the first in the country of the entrance-exit type, with all signals and points controlled by the setting on the panel of thumb-switches at the two ends of the desired route.

Above: The all-electric signal cabin at Thirsk, forming a part of the automatic resignalling in 1933 of the main line between York and North-allerton.

Right: One of the first traffic control offices on the L.N.E.R. with visual indications of track occupation, located at King's Cross. This panel shows the main line between Peterborough and Grantham.

[British Railways

Above: Sir Nigel Gresley, Chief Mechanical Engineer 1923 to 1941.

Above: Edward Thompson, Chief Mechanical Engineer, 1941 to 1946.

Below: Arthur H. Peppercorn, Chief Mechanical Engineer, 1946 to 1947.

Below: Sir Landale Train, Chief Civil Engineer, 19 to 1947. [*British Railw*

But before the six constituents had become swallowed up in the London & North Eastern Railway at the beginning of 1923, one major development had taken place in the realm of express passenger power. It was, of course, the emergence from Doncaster Works of the G.N.R. in 1922 of Gresley's magnificent Pacific, No. 1471 *Great Northern*. This was not the first British Pacific, for G. J. Churchward of the Great Western had preceded Gresley by fourteen years with *The Great Bear*; but strangely for so competent a designer, *The Great Bear* could not be counted among Churchward's successes, and as is well known was later converted to a 4–6–0. Not so with *Great Northern*, however; this outstanding design, with modifications suggested by experience in its later versions, was destined to become the standard for heavy express passenger work throughout London & North Eastern history in England and Scotland alike.

Rather belatedly, when the Gresley Pacific plans became known, Sir Vincent Raven put in hand designs for a North Eastern Pacific, but this did not take the rails until 1923. Moreover, whereas Gresley's design had been thought out *de novo*, and was based on the best Pacific practice of that time (in particular the successful K4s 4–6–2s of the American Pennsylvania Railroad), Raven's Pacific was no more than an extended version of his Z class Atlantic.

Direct comparison of the performance of the two types, carried out in 1923, proved the economic superiority of the Gresley design; also the Raven Pacifics suffered a good deal from overheating troubles, and when, following the L.N.E.R.-G.W.R. locomotive exchange of 1925, Gresley began to modify his Pacifics with long-travel valves to permit short cut-off working, a similar alteration to the Raven engines would have necessitated a complete rebuilding of their front-ends. So the history of the N.E.R. Pacifics extended over no more than 13 years. It is difficult to avoid the conclusion that the Raven Pacifics were produced in the hope of proving to the L.N.E.R. directors the superiority of North Eastern over Great Northern designs, and so of securing the control of L.N.E.R. locomotive policy for Darlington rather than Doncaster; but the attempt was doomed to failure.

For heavy freight work three of the major constituents had introduced eight-coupled locomotives. The Great Northern Railway had been the first, with Ivatt's 0–8–0 No. 401 in 1901, though in the matter of time beating only by a very short head Wilson Worsdell's North Eastern 0–8–0 No. 2116 of the same year. The essential difference between these two was that the G.N.R. 0–8–0 had inside cylinders, whereas those of the N.E.R. model were outside. By the end of the following year John G. Robinson of the Great Central also had produced his first 0–8–0, No. 1067. Before many years had passed the increased weight of locomotive front ends, due partly to the addition of superheater headers, and the desire to reduce overhang at the leading end, suggested the addition of a pony truck, and Robinson of the Great Central was the first to introduce a 2–8–0 locomotive, No. 966—a simple and straightforward type destined to be built in very large numbers during and after the First World War for service both in this country and overseas.

This was in 1911, and Gresley, who by now had succeeded Ivatt in charge of Great Northern locomotive affairs, was not far behind, for in 1913 there appeared his first 2-8-0, No. 456. Apart from the 0-8-0 rebuild of the "Decapod" 0-10-0 tank of 1902, the Great Eastern Railway never went beyond the 0-6-0 wheel arrangement for freight service, though its final development, A. J. Hill's superheated No. 1270 series, with the same boiler as the 1500 class 4-6-0s and 20 in. by 28 in. cylinders, was superior in tractive effort to many British 0-8-0s and the most powerful British 0-6-0 type introduced up to that date. The North British Railway never built anything bigger than 0-6-0 types for freight service, and as previously mentioned the Great North of Scotland used 4-4-0s for both passenger and freight trains. Needless to say, the Great Northern, Great Central and North Eastern Railways possessed large numbers of 0-6-0 freight locomotives in addition to their 0-8-0 and 2-8-0 types.

As we have seen, the 4-4-0 locomotives of the Great North of Scotland Railway, with their 6 ft. 1 in. coupled wheels, were in effect the mixed traffic type of that company. All the other constituent companies of the L.N.E.R. group had developed their special mixed traffic locomotive classes. Most of them had fitted some of their 0-6-0 freight engines which had coupled wheels of 5 ft. diameter or over with the continuous brake, so that they could work excursion and other passenger trains not requiring any very fast travel. But in addition new types had been developed specifically for mixed traffic service, and capable if necessary of a good turn of speed. This was really the function of the 6 ft. 1in. 4-6-0s which, as already mentioned, were built in 1899 to Wilson Worsdell's design for East Coast service, before the production of his first Atlantics.

More specific mixed traffic production began on the Great Northern Railway in 1912, with the production by Gresley of his first 2-6-0 design. These were not the first "Moguls" to run on Great Northern metals, for at a time of locomotive shortage in 1899 some typically American engines of this wheel arrangement had been imported from the Baldwin works at Philadelphia. But the G.N. 1912 2-6-0s were of a far more capable type, and introduced a new Great Northern wheel arrangement which was to reach its culmination in the massive K3 Moguls introduced in 1920, with their three cylinders and, for the first time in Great Britain, a parallel boiler of no less than 6 ft. diameter. With 5 ft. 8 in. coupled wheels, these machines soon proved themselves capable of hauling passenger expresses, when required, at quite respectable speeds, up to 70 or even 75 m.p.h. No other constituent company in the L.N.E.R. group, however, followed the Great Northern 2-6-0 lead.

On the North Eastern Railway it was not until twelve years after the appearance in 1899 of Wilson Worsdell's unsuccessful S1 class 4-6-0s, with 6 ft. 1 in. coupled wheels, that Vincent Raven turned out the first of a new series of mixed traffic 4–6–0s, No. 782, a considerably more powerful and competent type, still with 6 ft. 1 in. coupled wheels, but with a better designed front end and a 5 ft. 6 in. diameter boiler. This introduced a lengthy line of similar engines, finishing from 1919 with the seventy three-cylinder 4–6–0s of Class S3, which rendered excellent service all over the N.E.R. and later over the L.N.E.R. The last of this class were not completed until 1924, in the second year of London & North Eastern history. Robinson of the Great Central also was responsible for several 4–6–0 mixed traffic types, though he apparently found difficulty in making up his mind as to coupled wheel diameters, for his 1902 design had 6 ft. 1 in. wheels, that of 1906 5 ft. 4 in., that of 1913 5 ft. 7 in., and his final four-cylinder type of 1921 5 ft. 8 in. drivers. As to the other constituent companies, the Great Eastern depended for mixed traffic work on James Holden's small 5 ft. 8 in. 2–4–0s; the North British had a number of 6 ft. 4–4–0s, but these had been built mainly for service over the most heavily graded lines of that company, such as the West Highland.

The constituents of the L.N.E.R. all possessed tank engines in great variety. These included vast numbers of 0–6–0 shunting tanks, particularly those of the Great Eastern and North Eastern Railways; moreover, the Great Eastern used James Holden's diminutive 0–6–0s, with their 4 ft. 11 in. coupled wheels, extensively on its London suburban services. Ivatt of the Great Northern had experimented unsuccessfully in 1903, when electric competitors were threatening certain London suburban lines, with a large and powerful 0–8–2 type tank, no doubt with such gradients in mind as the 1 in 60 of the High Barnet branch, but these proved too heavy and cumbersome, and eventually were transferred to freight service in the Nottinghamshire coalfield. So Ivatt 4–4–2 tanks continued to handle the Great Northern London suburban services until the advent in 1907 of his 0–6–2 tanks, Gresley's superheated version of which, from 1920 onwards, continued for long afterwards to shoulder this burden.

The Great Eastern's suburban services, other than those which the 0–6–0 tanks worked to and from Chingford and Enfield Town, were entrusted to 2–4–2 and 0–4–4 tanks, and in 1914 a new and more powerful 0–6–2 type, designed by A. J. Hill, had made its *début*. On the Great Central line the working of its limited suburban service into and out of Marylebone had been greatly improved after the substitution, from 1911 onwards, of J. G. Robinson's powerful new 4–6–2 tanks for his 4–4–2s previously in use. The North British Railway depended chiefly on Reid 4–4–2 tanks for its suburban workings round Edinburgh and Glasgow, and the Great North of Scotland on its few 0–4–4 tanks for the Aberdeen local services.

On the North Eastern Railway local passenger services were worked both by William Worsdell's 2–4–2 and Wilson Worsdell's 0–4–4 tanks— the latter on such lengthy runs as the 49¾-mile coastal route between Newcastle, Sunderland, West Hartlepool and Middlesbrough—until the advent, in 1913, of Raven's most handsome three-cylinder 4–4–4 tanks of Class D. These were rebuilt in L.N.E.R. days with the 4–6–2 wheel arrangement, to give greater adhesion; and the same happened to the 4–6–0 inside cylinder tanks which Wilson Worsdell built in 1907 specifically to work the very difficult Salturn-Whitby-Scarborough branch, with gradients in steepness up to 1 in 39. For short-distance freight and mineral working the North Eastern also had developed some powerful types, such as Wilson Worsdell's Class X three-cylinder 4–8–0 tanks for low speed marshalling yard work, and Raven's Class Y three-cylinder 4–6–2 tanks for short-distance mineral workings. Robinson of the Great Central similarly had built at Gorton in 1907 several massive three-cylinder 0–8–4 tanks for service in the large marshalling yard at Wath.

A few words are now needed to compare the differing design characteristics which had been developed by the locomotive departments of the L.N.E.R. constituent companies. Two-cylinder propulsion had been universal up to 1907, apart from experiments with compounding. These compound trials were on the North Eastern with 4–4–0 No. 1619 in 1898, rebuilt by Wilson Worsdell to the designs of his Chief Draughtsman, Walter Smith, with one high pressure and two low pressure cylinders, and unique in that this engine had previously been a two-cylinder compound on the Worsdell-von Borries system. Later, in 1906, two fine four-cylinder compounds on the Smith system had emerged from Gateshead Works; had it not been for the death of Walter Smith very shortly afterwards, there might have been some compounding developments of note on the N.E.R., but this experiment was not carried any further.

In the previous year, 1905, John G. Robinson of the Great Central had turned out two of his Atlantics as three-cylinder compounds, and built two more in 1907, later rebuilding 4–4–2 No. 1090 as a three-cylinder simple for performance comparisons, but this is as far as the G.C.R. experiment went. In 1905 and 1908, also, the Great Northern put into service three four-cylinder compound Atlantics, two of H. G. Ivatt's design and the third built by the Vulcan Foundry on the French de Glehn system, but none of them did as good work as Ivatt's standard Atlantics or the North Eastern and Great Central examples just mentioned, and this experiment also led nowhere.

But when we come to three-cylinder simple propulsion, of course, it is a totally different story. Actually the first such locomotive built by a London & North Eastern constituent company was James Holden's famous and unique "Decapod" 0–10–0 tank on the Great Eastern Railway, but this brilliantly-designed machine never went into active service. Next in the field were the Great Central and North Eastern Railways, with their 0–8–4 and 4–8–0 tanks for marshalling yard work, of 1907 and 1909 respectively. The latter having done well, Worsdell's successor, Raven, decided to provide his new 4–6–2 mineral tanks of 1910 with three cylinders; then followed the more important departure of using the same system in his Z class development of the Worsdell

Atlantics, his first three-cylinder 4–4–2s appearing in 1911. Next came the three-cylinder D class 4–4–4 tanks of 1913, and finally the three-cylinder development of both the S class mixed traffic 4–6–0s and the T class 0–8–0s, the S3 and T3 classes respectively, introduced in 1919. Thus by the end of independent North Eastern history three-cylinder simple propulsion had become standard for all new locomotive construction other than 0–6–0 shunting tanks.

So the N.E.R. ante-dated the G.N.R. in this matter by some nine years, for it was not until 1918 that Gresley's first three-cylinder engine, 2–8–0 No. 461, took the rails. It was followed in 1920 by the first of his highly competent K3 three-cylinder 2–6–0s, No. 1000, and then, two years later, by his three-cylinder Pacific masterpiece, No. 1470 *Great Northern*. With Gresley, as with Raven on the North Eastern, three-cylinder simple propulsion was now well and truly launched, and was later to be applied to most new London & North Eastern designs.

But between these two designers there was one radical difference in the arrangement of the valve-motion for actuating three piston-valves. Raven, like other locomotive engineers, as, for example, Stanier on the London Midland & Scottish Railway and Maunsell on the Southern Railway, favoured a separate valve-motion for each cylinder. Gresley, on the other hand, devised his well-known conjugated motion, with the two outside Walschaerts valve-gears supplying the motion to the inside cylinder piston-valve through the medium of a 2-to-1 lever. The Gresley conjugated motion has always been a bone of contention among locomotive men, chiefly because the whip of the lengthy 2-to-1 lever at high speed has tended to increase the cut-off in the middle cylinder to something well in excess of that in the outside cylinders, which in its turn has led to occasional overheating of the middle big-end. No other railway with three-cylinder simple locomotives has ever adopted this Gresley motion other than on a small scale experimentally, but it would be idle to deny that on the whole it has given admirable service on Great Northern and London & North Eastern locomotives.

As to two-cylinder engines, the Great Eastern, North British (apart from the Reid Atlantics) and Great North of Scotland Railways always favoured inside cylinders; the Great Northern changed to the outside position (apart from tank engines) from the advent of its first 2–6–0 and 2–8–0 types; and the North Eastern similarly after building its first 4–6–0s and 0–8–0s. Robinson of the Great Central seemed unable to make up his mind, applying inside cylinders to some of his 4–6–0s and outside to others, and following his outside-cylinder Atlantics by the inside-cylinder "Director" 4–4–0s. On all the railways coming into the L.N.E.R. group, the traditional methods of valve-setting that had persisted from slide-valve days were still in vogue, with the result that driving for the most part was uneconomically with long cut-offs and partially closed regulators; the lessons of the 1925 locomotive exchange of a Gresley Pacific for a Great Western "Castle" 4–6–0 had yet to be learned and applied.

In the matter of boilers, the Great Northern and North Eastern Railways favoured round-topped fireboxes; the Great Eastern from 1904 onwards had changed over to the Belpaire type of box, which was standard also on the Robinson locomotives of the Great Central; the North British, however, confined the use of the Belpaire box to its Atlantics. Superheating began to infiltrate ino the locomotive stock of the constituent companies from about 1910 onwards, and was being applied almost universally, except to shunting engines, by the time that these independent lines were absorbed at the beginning of 1923 into the London & North Eastern Railway.

Finally there was a contribution made by the North Eastern Railway to the London & North Eastern locomotive stock which was not shared by any other of the constituent companies; it was of electric locomotives and motorcoaches. The locomotives were 13 in number. Of these 12,

Table 10

Steam Locomotives Brought into L.N.E.R. Stock, 1923

Type	Former Owning Railway						Type Total
	G.N.	G.C.	G.E.	N.E.	N.B.	G.N.S.	
4–6–2 tndr.	2	—	—	2	—	—	4
4–6–0 ,,	—	90	70	103	—	—	263
4–4–2 ,,	116	31	—	72	21	—	240
4–4–0 ,,	136	144	169	186	212	100	947
4–2–2 ,,	—	6	—	—	—	—	6
2–4–0 ,,	28	4	100	39	6	—	177
0–6–0 ,,	393	409	440	752	594	—	2,588
2–6–0 ,,	85	—	—	—	—	—	85
0–8–0 ,,	55	89	—	230	—	—	374
2–8–0 ,,	31	148	—	—	—	—	179
Total, tndr.	**846**	**921**	**779**	**1,384**	**833**	**100**	**4,863**
4–6–2 tank	—	21	—	30	—	—	51
2–6–4 ,,	—	20	—	—	—	—	20
0–6–4 ,,	—	9	—	—	—	—	9
0–6–2 ,,	114	202	12	126	78	—	532
0–6–0 ,,	274	67	261	312	44	9	967
4–8–0 ,,	—	—	—	10	—	—	10
0–8–4 ,,	—	4	—	—	—	—	4
0–8–2 ,,	41	—	—	—	—	—	41
0–8–0 ,,	—	1	—	—	—	—	1
4–4–4 ,,	—	—	—	45	—	—	45
4–4–2 ,,	60	52	—	—	52	—	164
2–4–2 ,,	—	49	232	60	—	—	341
4–4–0 ,,	—	—	—	—	3	—	3
0–4–4 ,,	18	6	40	146	30	9	249
2–2–4 ,,	—	—	—	4	—	—	4
2–4–0 ,,	—	2	—	—	—	—	2
0–4–2 ,,	—	—	—	—	—	4	4
0–4–0 ,,	—	2	12	24	35	—	73
Total, tank	**507**	**435**	**557**	**757**	**242**	**22**	**2,520**
Grand total	**1,353**	**1,356**	**1,336**	**2,141**	**1,075**	**122**	**7,383**

of the Bo-Bo wheel arrangement and of 1,000 h.p., had been built just before the outbreak of the First World War to work coal trains from Shildon down to the Erimus yard, between Stockton-on-Tees and Middlesbrough, for use in the Teesside steelworks and for shipment. The system of electrification was 1,500 V d.c., with overhead conduction, and these locomotives, of quite an advanced design for their period, could make four double trips daily, of nearly 150 miles all told, with trains up to 1,400 tons in weight, the gradients being with the load throughout, while against the grade only the empties required working back to Shildon.

The thirteenth electric locomotive was a big 102-ton 2-Co-2 or 4-6-4, built at Darlington in 1922 in anticipation of the electrification of the N.E.R. main line between York and Newcastle, which never, of course, took place. So No. 13, with a one-hour rating of 1,800 h.p., designed to haul a 450-ton passenger train on the level at 65 m.p.h. and to be capable of speeds up to 90 m.p.h., was a white elephant; later electric experience also would have suggested considerable changes in design had the N.E.R. main line electrification ever been carried out. The remaining North Eastern electric stock comprised the 71 motorcoaches and 55 trailers in use in the Tyneside electrified area, which began service in 1904; this was a third-rail electrification, using current at 600 V d.c. The Great Central Railway also possessed 16 electric vehicles, but these were no more than tramcars working between Grimsby and Immingham.

Rolling stock colours had suffered badly by the austerities compelled by the 1914-1918 war, and at the time of the formation of the London & North Eastern Railway the locomotives were only just beginning to have their former liveries restored. Up to the war Great Northern passenger locomotives had been painted in an apple green shade, and those of the North Eastern and Great Central Railways a lighter and darker green respectively; freight locomotives in general were black. Most distinguished of all the colour schemes was the Royal blue of Great Eastern passenger locomotives, tender and tank alike, with their red lining and buffer-beams and much decorative brasswork; here again sober black was the freight livery. The North British Railway also broke away from the prevailing green with a shade known officially as "dark gamboge", though technically there is no such colour; olive green or bronze green was probably a more correct description. On the Great North of Scotland green once again prevailed.

The post-war restoration of these colours was of but brief duration, however, for after the individual railways had lost their identity in the London & North Eastern group a common colour for all locomotives obviously had to be chosen. And not surprisingly, after an exhibition of locomotives in different colours for the choice of the directors, with green as the previous standard on four out of six of the former companies' lines, it was green that was selected for passenger locomotives, the Great Northern apple green. There was some vacillation about what should be done with the other types; freight locomotives, tender and tank alike, were to be black, and at one time it was laid down that all locomotives with driving wheels of 6 ft. in diameter or less should be painted black. But there were various exceptions; for example, the ex-North Eastern S1 and S2 mixed traffic 4–6–0s, with 6 ft. 1 in. coupled wheels, were always black, whereas the Scottish Area were more liberal in the use of green than the new regulations laid down.

XVI

The First Locomotive Years—1923-1924

THE LOCOMOTIVE history of the London & North Eastern Railway revolves chiefly around one name—that of Herbert Nigel Gresley, or, as he became eventually, Sir Nigel Gresley. Chapter VIII has shown that he was chosen by the L.N.E.R. directors to become the Chief Mechanical Engineer of the company, charged with the supreme responsibility for developing its locomotive power, and for the overhaul and repair of its vast collection of rolling stock. The magnitude of this task may be measured by the fact that between them the constituent railways contributed 7,383 steam locomotives, 111 electric locomotives, electric motor coaches and petrol cars, 20,350 coaching vehicles and 307,300 freight vehicles. Table 10 (page 110) sets out the number of the locomotive types so taken over; from this it will be seen that the North Eastern Railway was by far the biggest individual contributor, with 2,141 locomotives; while it reveals also the almost exact equality of the Great Northern, Great Central and Great Eastern stocks—1,353, 1,356 and 1,336 engines respectively.

From now on there came under Gresley's control, in addition to the Doncaster Plant Works of the Great Northern Railway, the North Eastern Works at Darlington, Gateshead, York, Shildon and Springhead (the last-named the Hull Works of the former Hull & Barnsley Railway, which had amalgamated with the N.E.R. in 1922); the Great Central at Gorton and Dukinfield, Manchester; the Great Eastern at Stratford; the North British at Cowlairs, Glasgow; and the Great North of Scotland at Inverurie, north of Aberdeen. Between them these works employed a total staff of about 103,000. The York works concentrated on coachbuilding; that at Shildon on wagons; that at Dukinfield on coaches and wagons; Doncaster, Stratford, Springhead, Cowlairs and Inverurie built all three varieties; while Darlington and Gateshead dealt with locomotives only.

It is hardly to be wondered at that the Chief Mechanical Engineers other than Gresley who were in office up to the time of the Grouping, the majority of them elderly and highly experienced men, had no desire to play second fiddle to another Chief. Thus it was that early in 1923, with the appropriate "golden handshake" in each case, there were a number of resignations. Sir Vincent Raven of the N.E.R., who had had the honour of K.B.E. conferred on him in recognition of his services during the war as Chief Superintendent of the Royal Ordnance Factories

H

at Woolwich, was one of them, and A. C. Stamer, who had been his *locum tenens* at Darlington during Raven's absence from 1915 to 1919, now took charge, as Assistant Chief Mechanical Engineer to Gresley. For one further year Raven remained on call as Technical Adviser.

At the Great Eastern Stratford Works A. J. Hill retired, and C. W. L. Glaze, who had been his Works Manager, now became District Mechanical Engineer, Stratford. John G. Robinson of the Great Central, who was at the retiring age, gave up his office, and R. A. Thom, who had been his assistant at Gorton, was appointed District Mechanical Engineer, Gorton. It may be added that at the time of Gresley's untimely death, in 1941, Robinson wrote a letter to the *Railway Gazette* claiming that on the merits of his designs he had been offered by the L.N.E.R. Directors the post of Chief Mechanical Engineer, and that in declining it he had been personally responsible for recommending Gresley for the post; but by this time Robinson was in the middle 80s, and senility seems to have prompted this communication. For it is in the highest degree improbable that a task of such vital importance should have been offered to a man of 65 years, however good his record might have been.

The North British Railway had never got further than the title of Locomotive Superintendent for its chief mechanical executive, and at the end of 1922 this was W. Chalmers; he remained in office at Cowlairs as Mechanical Engineer, Southern Scottish Area, as also did T. E. Heywood of the Great North of Scotland at Inverurie (Aberdeen) as both Mechanical Engineer and Running Superintendent, Northern Scottish Area. Further changes soon came about. In 1925 Chalmers decided to retire, and R. A. Thom was transferred from Gorton to take over the entire Scottish rolling stock responsibility as Mechanical Engineer, Scotland; he was succeeded at Gorton by T. E. Heywood. By 1927 yet another change had taken place, for Thom was then appointed Mechanical Engineer, Doncaster, while Heywood went back to Scotland as his successor. Other names that had cropped up during this period and were to become much better known in later years were those of O. V. S. Bulleid, appointed as Assistant to the Chief Mechanical Engineer, and Edward Thompson, who in 1927 became Assistant Mechanical Engineer at Stratford.

The vast collection of rolling stock units that had come under Gresley's control was only part of the problem confronting him. The various constituent companies had carried out a certain amount of standardisation, some more and some less; but each company had developed its own standards, and if the economies envisaged by the grouping were to be achieved in the rolling stock realm, future policy must be directed towards systematic reduction in the immense number of individual types of locomotives, carriages and wagons, so reducing the multiplicity of parts to be manufactured and stored, and to the establishment of new standards applicable to the entire system. This obviously was going to be a lengthy process.

At first the building that was in progress at the various works was continued. Stratford carried on with ten "Super-Claud" 4-4-0s of what became L.N.E.R. Class D16/2, ten small 0-6-0 shunting tanks of Class J65, and with 0-6-2 tanks of the Hill design, Class N7. So impressed was Gresley with the last-mentioned type that although Doncaster Works was continuing to build his own superheated modification of the Ivatt 0-6-2 suburban tank (L.N.E.R. Class N2), between 1925 and 1928 the Great Eastern Class N7 had its numbers increased from 22 to 134 by new construction, partly by the outside contractors Beardmore and Robert Stephenson, partly by Gorton Works, and the final 32 at Doncaster, modified by the substitution of round-topped fireboxes for the standard Great Eastern Belpaire type.

The admirable design work of John G. Robinson at Gorton in Great Central days also had a considerable influence on early London & North Eastern locomotive policy. Robinson's two most successful designs had been his 2-8-0 freight locomotive first introduced in 1911, and his express passenger "Director" 4-4-0s of 1913. Both were simple and straightforward types in which the various ratios between boiler and cylinder dimensions seem to have reached the optimum for capable and economical performance. As previously mentioned, out of all possible British types, the Robinson 2-8-0 design had been chosen by the War Department as a standard for overseas service during the 1914-1918 war and had been built in very large numbers. After the war no fewer than 125 of these engines, duly reconditioned, were taken into the L.N.E.R. stock to add to the 148 already owned by the Great Central, many of the new arrivals being allocated to Great Eastern freight service.

Not only so, but the North British directors had cannily stopped the building of new locomotives at Cowlairs after the passing in 1921 of the Railways Act that was to bring about the Grouping, leaving to their successors the cost of making up the leeway. In 1923, therefore, Scotland was urgently in need of new locomotive power, and rather than building additional North British "Scott" 4-4-0s, Gresley decided that the immediate need should be met by a batch of the more powerful Robinson "Director" 4-4-0s. Accordingly in 1924 the firms of Armstrong Whitworth and Kitson shared in supplying 24 of these engines, with slight modifications of the original design, and classified as D11/2, for Scottish use.

If this were not enough, North Eastern requirements for more tank engines to work such services as that between Darlington, Middlesbrough and Saltburn were met by placing an order with Hawthorn Leslie for thirteen Great Central type 4-6-2 tanks of Class A5. There were modifications in appearance of the Robinson designs which did not please the aesthetes, particularly the "flowerpot" chimneys substituted for the massive Great Central type, and in particular the hideous flattened dome covers which disfigured the new 4-6-2 tanks, but such happenings apart that designer may well have felt complimented that up to 1928, five years after his retirement, locomotives of his design were still being built by the London & North Eastern Railway.

At Darlington Works in 1923 three of the Raven Pacifics remained under construction, and were completed. Building also continued of various orders for locomotives of North Eastern types that had been placed before the Grouping, in particular of Class B16 three-cylinder mixed traffic 4–6–0s, of the highly successful three-cylinder freight 0–8–0s of Class Q7, of large-boilered Class J27 0–6–0s and of a few 0–4–0 shunting tanks; but after their completion very few other engines of purely North Eastern design were to emerge from Darlington Works. Finally, as late as 1928, five years after the Grouping, when additional express passenger engines were needed for the Great Eastern Section, it was ten Holden B12 4–6–0s that were put on order with Beyer Peacock. A new design for Great Eastern use was in preparation at this time, and it was only because of the urgency that the order for the older type was given.

In the first years after the Grouping a number of locomotives were exchanged between different areas of the London & North Eastern system for trial purposes. Mention has just been made of the stop on locomotive building by the North British directors in 1921, after the passing of the Railways Act, and this meant that by 1923 Scottish needs for new motive power were urgent. To bridge the gap before the arrival of the new "Director" 4–4–0s, therefore, the Great Northern superheated 4–4–0s of Class D1, Nos. 51 to 65, were sent north of the Border, but however well these machines might have done on Great Northern metals it cannot be said that they were at all popular with their Scottish crews. Also Scotland received a number of Gresley's Class N2 0–6–2 tanks, and Class K2 mixed traffic 2–6–0s. Ivatt Atlantics were experimented with on the Great Central main line, and another engine of this type, No. 1447 (L.N.E.R. No. 4447) was tried in the North Eastern Area.

The last-mentioned locomotive shared in a series of tests conducted in 1924 over the East Coast main line between Newcastle and Edinburgh. The contestants were the Great Northern 4–4–2, with two 20 in. by 24 in. cylinders; Raven's North Eastern 4–4–2 No. 733 with three 16½ in. by 26 in. cylinders; and North British Reid 4–4–2 No. 9878 with two 21 in. by 28 in. cylinders. But the results obtained with these three very dissimilar designs were not very conclusive; only the North Eastern engine was being fired with its normal coal, and it was, moreover, on its own ground, whereas the other two competitors were working over a main line with gradient and other characteristics very different from those of their accustomed routes. The comparative trials in 1923 of Gresley and Raven Pacifics between King's Cross and Doncaster have been mentioned in the previous chapter; the difference in performance in this case was not very marked, but it was in favour of the Gresley design, and had the trials taken place after the redesign of the motion of the A1 Pacifics, permitting short cut-off working (which as previously mentioned would have been impossible with the North Eastern Pacific without a complete rebuilding of the front end) the superiority of the Great Northern engine would have been absolute.

Other transfers some years after the Grouping were of Great Eastern B12 4–6–os as far away from their native heath as the Great North of Scotland Railway—the first 4–6–os ever to work on that system—after some of the weaker underline bridges had been strengthened to carry these heavier loads. Eventually the numerous Great Eastern 0–6–0 tanks found themselves working all over the L.N.E.R. system, and some of Holden's mixed traffic 2–4–os, with their 5 ft. 8 in. coupled wheels, eventually exchanged the comparative flatness of the Eastern Counties for the Darlington to Penrith line of the North Eastern Area, with its 1,370 ft. summit at Stainmore.

Locomotive men are notoriously conservative, and it is not to be imagined that all these strangers were received with acclamation by their recipients. This antipathy came to a head when the first Gresley Pacifics were allocated to the North Eastern Area. They lacked the audible cab-signalling devised by Raven which had been in use for some years on the N.E.R.; the assistance of a steam reversing gear was lacking; the men found the so-called "Gresley knock" (due to the liberal side-play he allowed in his motion) rather irritating; but the worst complaints were about his regulator, which was very stiff to move, and at times needed the fireman's help, in comparison with the Lockyer balanced regulator to which they were accustomed. Eventually a meeting of drivers was convened at York, which Gresley attended in person and at which the aggrieved men were permitted to speak their minds and did so with great freedom. No record remains of the precise upshot of this gathering; no doubt some alterations in design followed, and in due course the men realised that in these fine machines they had something more competent than they had ever handled before.

But the best story of what resulted from one of these locomotive transfers is related in F. A. S. Brown's fascinating book *Nigel Gresley—Locomotive Engineer*. A Great Northern 0–6–2 tank of Class N2 had been sent to Stratford Works for heavy repairs. "The Great Eastern men", he writes, "either set the eccentrics the wrong way, causing a reversal of the motion at the quadrant link, or else the forward and backward eccentric rods were connected to the wrong ends of the link. The precise error is not now too clear but the effect is still remembered. On completion the engine was towed to the yard and steamed. In due course it was placed in full forward gear and the regulator opened when, to the astonishment of all present, the engine ran backwards"

In the first year of the grouping a new scheme of locomotive numbering had to be devised. Most of the constituent companies had been somewhat haphazard in their numbering, giving their new engines numbers more or less at random as withdrawals of older locomotives left numbers vacant; the Great Eastern Railway was the only one that had been more systematic, though with one curious outcome; in 1900 the first "Claud Hamilton" 4–4–0 had received the number 1900 in honour of that year and of its participation in the 1900 Paris Exhibition, but as subsequent engines of this type were built in batches of ten, the numbers ran *backwards*, until with the final batch, of the D16/2 "Super Claud" type, completed at Stratford in 1923, the numbers had got as far back as 1780 to 1789.

In the renumbering North Eastern locomotives retained their original numbers, because the N.E.R. had the largest locomotive stock; those of the Great Northern had 3,000 added to their numbers, of the Great Central 5,000, of the Great Eastern 7,000 and of the North British 9,000; Great North of Scotland numbers were fitted in at the end of the Great Central list. At first there seemed to be some indecision as to whether the Company's initials painted on tender and tank sides should read "L. & N.E.R." or "L.N.E.R.", but the latter soon became standard. The engine numbers were then painted under these initials, in the case of both tender and tank engines, and this was somewhat surprising with the former in view of the fact that not infrequently engines have to exchange tenders when one or the other are under repair. But not until 1928 was the obvious change made; from that time onwards the numbers of tender locomotives were painted on cab sides, and the tender sides carried the company initials only. So the haphazard numbering of the original companies continued on their locomotives, with the addition of the thousands mentioned, until after Gresley's successor took office, when a more systematic plan was inaugurated.

One matter of major importance which Gresley was called on to decide at the beginning of his L.N.E.R. reign was the type of brake to be adopted by the new company for coaching vehicles and continuously braked wagons. The Great Northern, Great Central and Great North of Scotland Railways used the vacuum brake, but the Great Eastern, North Eastern and North British, with the larger stock of locomotives of the two groups, the Westinghouse air brake. One wonders what might have happened had Raven of the N.E.R. rather than Gresley of the G.N.R. become Chief Mechanical Engineer; as matters turned out, it was the latter, and therefore not surprising, perhaps, that the vacuum brake—which it must be admitted was much the more widely used of the two systems throughout the country—won the day.

Not all locomotive engineers have agreed with this preference, and at the present day, with electric and diesel locomotive power and ever increasing speeds, there are many who consider that in common with most other railways in the world we should have been wiser to adopt air-brakes as standard. On the L.N.E.R. the only exception that was made was the suburban area of the Great Eastern Section. with its dense services and frequent stops; throughout L.N.E.R. history Great Eastern suburban engines and passenger stock retained the Westinghouse brake. For some years, also, until vacuum-braked equipment had come into general use, locomotives for service on the Great Eastern, North Eastern and North British lines had to be provided with Westinghouse donkey-pumps and brakes.

XVII

Locomotive Developments under Gresley— 1923-1934

WE COME back now to Gresley and to the locomotive developments that were to take place under his direction. By the beginning of 1923 the work of his two pioneer Pacifics, Nos. 1470 and 1471, had been of such high quality that the Great Northern directors had authorised the building of another ten, which was in progress at Doncaster. The designer, looking well ahead, as he always did, had proclaimed that his new engines would be capable of handling 600-ton trains, and this at a time when 400 tons was regarded as an outsize load for an Ivatt Atlantic. Moreover, he had proved his point by arranging, on September 3rd, 1922, a trial run on which No. 1471 worked a 20-coach train of 610 tons weight over the 105.5 miles from King's Cross to Grantham in 122 minutes—2 minutes only more than the schedule of the "Flying Scotsman" at that time. The 27 miles from Hitchin to Huntingdon had been run at an average of just over 70 m.p.h., and the summit at Stoke had been surmounted at 45 m.p.h.

As soon as the comparative trials of the Gresley and Raven Pacifics in 1923 were over, building of Gresley Pacifics began in earnest, twenty being put in hand at Doncaster, while an order for a further twenty was placed with the North British Locomotive Company. To clear the loading gauges of the former North Eastern and North British Railways, it had been necessary to cut down the boiler mountings and to lower the cab roofs of all the first Pacifics; also, until the Westinghouse brake had been completely replaced by the vacuum brake on the North Eastern and Scottish Areas, the engines intended for service in those Areas had to be provided with Westinghouse pumps and brake equipment.

Something now happened which was destined to have a profound influence on Gresley design policy. It came about in a relatively simple way. Chapter IX has described how, in the British Empire Exhibition at Wembley in 1924, the L.N.E.R. Pacific *Flying Scotsman* was exhibited alongside the new Great Western four-cylinder 4-6-0 *Caerphilly Castle*. The latter, 65 ft. 2 in. in length overall and 126½ tons in weight, was dwarfed in appearance by the 70 ft. 5 in. and 149 tons of the much more massive 4-6-2, and there was some incredulity when the Great Western authorities disputed the London & North Eastern claim to have produced the most powerful express passenger locomotive in Britain.

But this, on the basis of the tractive force formula, the Great Western was certainly entitled to do, for with the help of 225 lb. per sq. in. working pressure the "Castle" 4–6–0 had a nominal tractive effort of 31,625 lb. compared with the 180 lb. Pacific's 29,835 lb. Nevertheless Gresley in his turn could claim that what the tractive force formula fails to take into account—the ability to produce steam—is the true measure of tractive power, and to the onlookers the relative sizes of the two boilers certainly seemed to give *Flying Scotsman* a substantial advantage.

The matter could be decided only by comparative trials of the two types in identical conditions, and, as is well known, this is exactly what happened at the end of April and in early May, 1925. What has not been generally known, however, is how this memorable locomotive exchange was actually arranged, and during the ensuing years even those still living who were in the closest contact with Gresley at the time have been unable to provide any solution of the mystery. There have been all kinds of speculations: that Gresley made a move to challenge the Great Western claim or that the challenge was from the L.N.E.R. Chief General Manager, Sir Ralph Wedgwood, to the G.W.R. General Manager, Sir Felix Pole; alternatively that in view of the interest aroused by the exhibition Sir Felix, who certainly liked the limelight, offered the L.N.E.R. the loan of a "Castle" for test purposes.

In a recent letter O. V. S. Bulleid, who at the time was Assistant to Gresley, cites Sir Nigel as having said in his hearing, "If you cannot think of anything original yourself you ought to be intelligent enough to copy a good thing when you see it," and argues that as Gresley's philosophy was to make use of all improvements of which he became aware, the initiative for the exchange might well have come from him. In his book *Nigel Gresley: Locomotive Engineer* F. A. S. Brown quotes a letter on the subject from Sir William Stanier, at that time Assistant Mechanical Engineer of the Great Western Railway, who said, "I think Gresley was impressed by the free running of the 'Castles' and wanted to try one for himself".

But B. Spencer, who was Technical Assistant to Gresley, takes a different view. In response to a recent enquiry, he wrote: "One thing makes me doubt whether Gresley would have started the contest, and that is the fact that at the time of the tests the Pacifics were burning an abnormal amount of coal per mile." His letter goes on to relate how on the hardest daily assignment, the 11.4 a.m. from Doncaster and the return 5.40 p.m. from King's Cross, both very heavy trains, it was the practice to coal the tender up to its full 8-ton capacity, and after the round trip of 312 miles there was very little left. With the original valve-gear the engines had to be worked with a partially opened regulator and a long cut-off, and the noise at the chimney top was terrific; indeed, it was jokingly said that with a certain driver you could stand on Doncaster platform and hear him when he was passing Bawtry, 8 miles away! "Had I been in Gresley's position and with his knowledge of Great Western design", Spencer concludes, "I don't think I would have issued a challenge to Swindon at that time".

Above: Gresley locomotive development: on the left, Class A3 Pacific (1928); in the centre Class P2 2–8–2 No. 2001 *Cock o' the North* as originally built (1934); on the right Class A4 Pacific No. 2511 *Silver King* (1935). *[British Railways*

Below: Gresley A4 Pacific *Mallard*, which by attaining 126 m.p.h. on July 3rd, 1938, achieved a world record for steam traction. The engine is seen with its British Railways number and livery, as now preserved in the Clapham Railway Exhibition. *[Eric Oldham*

GRESLEY FREIGHT LOCOMOTIVE TYPES. Class J39 0–6–0, for general freight service

Class K3 2–6–0, for mixed freight and passenger service.

Class K4 2–6–0, for the heavily-graded West Highland line.

Below: Class P1 2–8–2, with Pacific boiler and booster to trailing wheels, for heavy main line service. Two only were built of this class. *[British Railways*

Gresley "Hunt" class express passenger 4–4–0, with poppet-valve motion.

Above: Gresley Class V1 3-cylinder 2–6–2 tank engine, for outer suburban work over fairly long distances.

Below: Thompson Class L1 2-cylinder 2–6–4 tank, with larger tank and bunker capacity than the Gresley V1, permitting longer runs without replenishment of supplies.

[*British Railways*

Above: The unsightly transformation by Thompson of Gresley's first Pacific, L.N.E.R. No. 4470, intended to be the forerunner of a new Class A1.

Left: Thompson's first A2 Pacific with 6 ft. 2 in. coupled wheels, No. 500 *Edward Thompson*, later renumbered 60500 and reclassified as A2/3.

Below: No. 1040 *Roedeer*, one of the first of the numerous Thompson Class B1 mixed traffic 4–6–0s, just completed at the Glasgow Works of the North British Locomotive Company. [*British Railway*

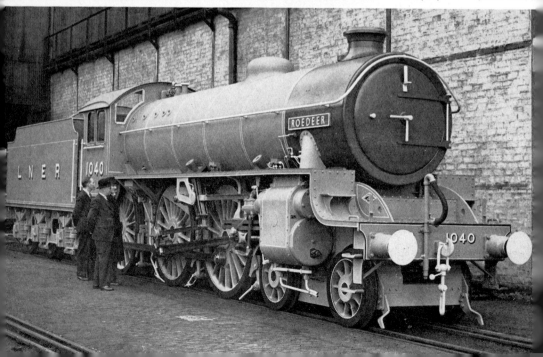

It now proves that Spencer was correct; there was no challenge from Gresley, and, astonishing to relate, the exchange was arranged over the latter's head. It was the result of a meeting on some social occasion, at about the time of the Wembley Exhibition or shortly after, between Sir Felix Pole and Alexander Wilson, who at that time was Divisional Manager of the L.N.E.R. Southern Area at Liverpool Street. Even now it is not clear whether the arrangement was a challenge from either side or a friendly offer from one side or the other of a locomotive for test purposes; suffice it to say that under instructions from their two Managers Chief Locomotive Inspectors Bramwell of the L.N.E.R. Southern Area and Flewellen of the G.W.R. were instructed to make all the arrangements, and not until these were well under way did Gresley become aware of what was afoot—and, moreover, not by being officially informed but by reading a press release in his newspaper.

It is hardly surprising that Sir Nigel was considerably annoyed that the whole thing had been done without his knowledge (and from Sir William Stanier's letter just quoted C. B. Collett, Chief Mechanical Engineer at Swindon, very likely was just as much in the dark), but by now it was too late for the decision to be reversed. Gresley did, however, insist on one change, in which he had his way. The L.N.E.R. Southern Area Locomotive Running Superintendent, W. G. P. Maclure, was a Great Central man and so were most of those in supervisory positions under him, including Chief Locomotive Inspector Bramwell. The change demanded was that the L.N.E.R. arrangements should be in the hands of someone thoroughly conversant with the working of the Gresley Pacifics, and the designer's choice fell on E. D. Trask, at that time Assistant District Locomotive Superintendent at Neasden, who has most kindly provided the explanation of what really happened.

The conditions were that the L.N.E.R. and G.W.R. enginemen should accompany their locomotives, which would be at Old Oak and King's Cross locomotive sheds in time for a week's running over the respective routes prior to the test week proper, Welsh coal would be used on the G.W.R. by the L.N.E.R. Pacific and Yorkshire coal by the G.W.R. "Castle" on the L.N.E.R., and a record would be kept of the weight of coal burned. All speed restrictions would be strictly observed, and pilotmen would, of course, accompany each visiting crew.

The trains selected for the test week were the G.W.R. "Cornish Riviera Express", down and up on alternate days, and in the down direction easily the hardest locomotive assignment on the G.W.R. at that time, and on the L.N.E.R. trains between King's Cross and Doncaster made up to something like the same weight; in this case there would be a return journey on each day, making 312 miles a day as compared with 225½ miles between Paddington and Plymouth. There can be no argument that L.N.E.R. Driver Pibworth and his mate had a far more difficult task than Driver Young on the L.N.E.R.; the easy ups-and-downs of the L.N.E.R. main line bear no comparison with the extraordinary variety of the G.W.R. gradients, ranging from the unbroken even if gradual 70-mile grind from Paddington to Savernake to the sharp climb from Taunton up into the Blackdown Hills, and, finally, the fearsome gradients over the southern slopes of Dartmoor, from Newton Abbot to Plymouth, ranging in steepness to 1 in 42 and even short lengths of 1 in 37 and 36. Moreover, because of its length, in the preliminary week Driver Pibworth had no more than six runs in which to familiarise himself with his G.W.R. course, whereas Driver Young had twelve, six to Doncaster and six back. There were also 19 speed restrictions on the G.W.R. to be strictly observed as compared with 5 only on the L.N.E.R.

So it was that eventually Gresley Pacific No. 4474 *Victor Wild* appeared at Old Oak shed and G.W.R. No. 4079 *Pendennis Castle* at King's Cross. The L.N.E.R. trains were made up to 480-ton loads; the G.W.R. down "Cornish Riviera" used to take a tare load of all but 500 tons out of Paddington, but slip portions detached at Westbury, Taunton and Exeter reduced this to 8 coaches of just over 290 tons on the exacting final stretch. The story of what happened has been told so often that repetition in detail is unnecessary. Though the last thing Gresley wanted, probably, was any undue publicity, it is not surprising that the public regarded this as a sporting contest of the first magnitude. We do not know also what apprehensions Gresley may have had as to the outcome of the tests, but merely to say that the L.N.E.R. operating authorities were surprised would be to put it mildly. For, in the event, whether burning their own Welsh coal between Paddington and Plymouth or the L.N.E.R. Yorkshire product between King's Cross and Doncaster, the "Castles" showed themselves appreciably the more economical of the two types. In this matter, however, the Gresley Pacific was at a disadvantage when burning Welsh coal, for with its relatively low brick arch it was impossible to build up the "haystack" type of fire that permits good combustion with fuel of this description. More than once *Victor Wild* topped Savernake with no more than 125 lb. per sq. in. of steam showing on the pressure gauge.

Also the Pacific wheelbase of 35 ft. 3 in., as compared with the 27 ft. 9 in. of the G.W.R. "Castles", proved most unsuitable for the winding stretches of the Great Western main line, and although *Victor Wild* once or twice was worked up to over 75 and even to 80 m.p.h., 70 m.p.h. was the general limit. Even so at more than one point Pibworth's fireman was thrown off his feet and all loose fittings on the footplate shot in various directions. In the circumstances there was some masterly handling of his engine by Driver Pibworth, who had to make up loss of time resulting from this speed limitation by harder level and uphill work, at the expense of coal, but who kept his end-to-end times and was never further from his intermediate passing times than $2\frac{1}{2}$ min. The competing *Caldicot Castle*, however, made the faster times, gaining no less than 15 min. on its two fastest runs, and at a lower coal consumption.

On its own line the L.N.E.R. had bad luck in that its *Flying Fox* ran hot in the test week, and the substituted *Diamond Jubilee* lost time because of the failure of her sanding gear; yet even apart from these mishaps

Pendennis Castle was making better time and burning less coal, and, more-over, Yorkshire coal rather than the Welsh coal for which her firebox and draughting were designed.   Until 1925 little had been made public about the principles of Swindon locomotive design, and such had been the parochiality of the railways of Britain that there seems to have been little curiosity as to the reasons underlying the fine performance of Swindon locomotives, but now—and even more so after a similar Great Western locomotive exchange took place with the London Midland & Scottish Railway in the following year—it would have been impossible to ignore the lessons learned.

In retrospect, it is astonishing how firmly Gresley had adhered to the traditional methods of valve-setting.   His Pacifics could perform any tasks allotted to them, and from the maintenance point of view were comparatively trouble-free; but one would have thought that the fact of their having to be worked on the harder turns with cut-off up to 45 per cent., and regulators only partly open, with a resultant coal consumption, as we have seen, up to 50 lb. or more to the mile, would have called loudly for some modification of design.   A year before the 1925 exchange Spencer, who had just become Technical Assistant to Gresley, had suggested the redesign of the motion with a long lap, to permit short cut-off working, but when it was found that the change would involve a certain amount of expense, Gresley had dismissed the idea.

Even after the decisive results of the exchange Gresley at first had been disinclined to move, but at last, in 1926, an experiment was made with No. 4477 *Gay Crusader*, and later in the same year the complete modification suggested by Spencer in 1924 was applied to No. 2555 *Centenary*.   The effect was to bring down average coal consumption at one stroke from 50 to 38 lb. per mile—equivalent to a saving of over $1\frac{1}{2}$ tons on a single return journey between Doncaster and London.   From then on all the Pacifics, either when in building or under heavy repair, had the redesigned valve-motion.   The other lesson of the 1925 exchange —the value of a high working pressure—was not applied until 1927. In that year Nos. 2544 *Lemberg* and 4480 *Enterprise* were fitted with boilers carrying 220 lb. instead of 180 lb. pressure, and the 220 lb. similarly became the standard for new Pacific construction, and for the reboilering of the existing stock, which thereby was translated from Class A1 to Class A3.

Meantime there had been other developments.   As his Pacific design had proved, Gresley was familiar with American locomotive practice, and was interested in the early 1920s to note that American locomotive designers were making much use of booster equipment on their loco-motives.   The booster was a small two-cylinder engine at the locomo-tive's rear end which, in conjunction with a pair of wheels of small dia-meter, could give auxiliary power for starting and on steep climbs, but could be cut out by a kind of free-wheeling device as soon as a predeter-mined speed had been attained.   In 1923 Gresley decided to experiment with this equipment, and fitted two 10 in. by 12 in. cylinders to drive the rear pair of wheels of Ivatt Atlantic No. 1419. A steam-operated gear arrangement put the booster engine into mesh with the wheels when the locomotive was starting, boosting the starting tractive effort from 17,300 lb. to 25,800 lb., and the booster could then be cut out completely as speed was attained. No. 1419 gave some convincing demonstrations of the value of the equipment at the actual moment of starting, particularly with a 535-ton test train which was restarted with ease from a stop on the 1 in 105 climb out of King's Cross. But as speed was being attained the drain on the steam supply became greater than the boiler could sustain, and before long the experiment was terminated.

A booster was next applied to a locomotive with a far bigger boiler. For in 1925 there were turned out of Doncaster Works two massive three-cylinder 2–8–2 freight locomotives, Nos. 2393 and 2394, with boilers similar to those carried by the Pacifics, which were the most powerful freight units in the country. With three 20 in. by 26 in. cylinders, 5 ft. 2 in. driving wheels, 180 lb. pressure, and a booster engine driving the 3 ft. 8 in. diameter trailing wheels, these 100-ton monsters could exert a total tractive effort of 47,000 lb., far greater than that of any other contemporary British locomotive. But the irony was that they were *too* powerful! They could handle with ease 100-wagon coal trains of up to 1,600 tons in weight, but such trains could spread themselves over more sections than one where the blocks were short and from the operating point of view were altogether too unwieldy for comfort. With the high capacity wagons of later years such locomotives would have been a valuable asset, but they were before their time.

In the same year, 1925, the London & North Eastern Railway acquired the most powerful steam locomotive that has ever been built for British use. On the Great Central section coal trains from Wath marshalling yard, near Barnsley, to Lancashire by way of Woodhead tunnel had to be worked up the formidable 7-mile Worsborough bank, between Barnsley and Penistone, with two miles as steep as 1 in 40. A train of 1,000 tons required the services of three if not four G.C. 2–8–0 locomotives, and Gresley's idea was to replace two of the bankers with a single unit of the Garratt articulated type. The firm of Beyer Peacock co-operated by building 2–8–8–2 locomotive No. 2395. This 178-ton mammoth, with six 18½ in. by 26 in. cylinders, 4 ft. 8 in. coupled wheels and 180 lb. pressure, could exert a tractive effort of no less than 72,940 lb., well over twice that of a Great Central 2–8–0, and ideal for the hard banking tasks that occupied the engine every working day, though its runs were too short for its maximum potential ever to be developed. Both 2–8–8–2 No. 2395 and one of the new 2–8–2 freight engines, No. 2393, were ready in time to take part in the 1925 Railway Centenary Procession between Stockton and Darlington, described in Chapter IX.

For fairly obvious reasons there was little love lost between Darlington and Doncaster, but by 1924 Darlington Works was beginning to build locomotives of Gresley's design. Reference was made in the last chapter to the introduction of his most powerful development of the Great

Northern Mogul or 2-6-0 type—the three-cylinder Class K3, with parallel boilers of no less than 6 ft. diameter. In 1924 a new series of these was begun at Darlington, but some North Eastern influence was seen in certain changes that were made, in particular the provision of a typical N.E.R. cab with side windows, and a North Eastern type tender, both of which enhanced the appearance of the locomotives considerably.

At this time Gresley also was considering the production of a three-cylinder 2-6-0 with the same 6 ft. boiler as the K3 but coupled wheels of 5 ft. 2 in. only, for slow freight work; but abandoned the idea in favour of some less expensive 0-6-0s. Darlington was therefore given the task of designing and building two new 0-6-0 types, both with 5 ft. 6 in. diameter boilers. One, with 4 ft. 8 in. coupled wheels, Class J38, was intended for service in the Lothian and Fifeshire coalfields in Scotland, and the other, Class J39, with 5 ft. 2 in. wheels, was for mixed traffic use all over the system. The J39 was an outstandingly successful design. These engines were as much at home on excursion or other secondary passenger as on freight trains, and could be whipped up on occasion to 70 m.p.h. or even over. Building of them went on in batches right up to 1941, by which time no fewer than 289 of the class were in service.

By 1927, however, Gresley was firmly set on his three-cylinder course. Building continued, both at Doncaster and by the North British Locomotive Company, of his three-cylinder Class O2 2-8-0s, though at a somewhat reduced rate because of the post-war acquisition of the 125 Great Central 2-8-0s of Class O4. But new three-cylinder designs were now in the offing. In 1927 the first of a new 4-4-0 class, No. 234 *Yorkshire*, emerged from Darlington Works, with three 17 in. by 26 in. cylinders and 6 ft. 8 in. coupled wheels, the most powerful 4-4-0 locomotive on British rails at that time. These engines, Class D49 in the L.N.E.R. books, were known as the "Shire" class, 20 of the first 35 being named after English counties, and 15, intended for service in Scotland, after Scottish counties. They were fitted, needless to say, with the Gresley derived motion for the inside cylinder, but with the three cylinders in line it was possible to mount this motion more advantageously in rear of the cylinders instead of the customary position ahead of them.

Now in 1925 the L.N.E.R. had begun experimenting with poppet-valves of the Lentz type, instead of piston-valves, applied first to Great Eastern 0-6-0 No. 8280, next in 1926 to B12 4-6-0 No. 8516, and in 1927 to six Great Eastern 4-6-0s of the same class. The results were sufficiently encouraging in reducing coal consumption to justify similar equipment for the final series of these 4-6-0s, Nos. 8571 to 8580, built in 1928. At the same time it was decided to build six of the "Shire" 4-4-0s with Lentz poppet-valves, not of the oscillating cam type used on the Great Eastern engines but of the imposed rotary cam type. Comparative tests showed this equipment to be so advantageous that when the final series of 40 three-cylinder 4–4–0s was put in hand in 1932 at Darlington, they were all equipped with the rotary cam Lentz motion, and were distinguished from the "Shires" by being named after famous British hunts. Eventually the class numbered 75 engines.

The Caprotti poppet-valve motion was also under review at this period. Robinson's Great Central four-cylinder 4–6–0s of Class B3 had not shared the success of his 4–4–0 "Directors" and 2–8–0 freight engines, because, despite their much larger boilers, he had still retained fireboxes with no bigger firegrate area than 26 sq. ft. As a result, they were very heavy on coal, and on not a few occasions when working the Pullman trains non-stop between King's Cross and Leeds had run short of steam. In 1929, therefore, Nos. 6166 and 6168 were equipped with Caprotti valves, and as compared with the other four engines of the class showed a 16 per cent. saving in coal. Two of the other four engines of this type, Nos. 6164 and 6167, were rebuilt with an improved form of this motion, but not until 1938. After that the outbreak of war stopped similar treatment of the remaining two.

Other means of getting more efficient performance out of some of the older types were under review at the same time, and in particular the use of exhaust steam to heat the feed water. However competent the Great Eastern B12 4–6–0s might be in carrying out their duties, they were certainly heavy on coal, and in 1927 an experiment was made by fitting Nos. 8505, 8517 and 8523 with French feed-water heaters of the A.C.F.I. type, together with the feed-pumps that were necessary because the ordinary injectors could not handle the heated feed water. The only space available for mounting the heaters was in a very unsightly position between the chimney and the dome, which from the suggestion so given of carrying a *rucksack* earned for the engines so equipped the nickname of "Hikers". The results were so successful that eventually 55 in all of the B12s received this equipment.

Other types with which similar experiments were made were Raven three-cylinder North Eastern Atlantics Nos. 728 and 2206, and Gresley Pacifics Nos. 2576 and 2580; in the latter case, as it was impossible to mount the heaters in the confined space above the boiler barrels, a redesigned form was packed into the upper part of an enlarged smokebox. Feed-water heaters of the Dabeg type were applied to Great Northern Class O2 2–8–0 No. 3500 and North Eastern three-cylinder 4–4–2 No. 2163, but in none of the last-mentioned cases were the savings in coal and water consumption regarded as sufficient to justify the fitting of this equipment on a wider scale.

The year 1928 saw a London & North Eastern locomotive happening that attracted considerable attention. Competition had arisen between the London & North Eastern and London Midland & Scottish Railways as to which of them could advertise the longest non-stop runs with their Anglo-Scottish trains.

By 1928 the L.N.E.R. management had decided to extend the "Flying Scotsman" non-stop run to the entire 392.8 miles between London and Edinburgh, provided that arrangements could be made for changing the engine-crews *en route* without stopping the train. Such was the genesis of Gresley's corridor tenders, the only examples of their kind in the world, massive 25 ft. 10 in. long eight-wheelers which when carrying their full load of 9 tons of coal and 5,000 gallons of water weighed no less than 62½ tons—all but equal to two full-length corridor coaches. At their rear ends each of these tenders was provided with a standard vestibule gangway for connecting with the gangway of the leading coach, and from this a narrow passage along the tender side led to a door opening on to the footplate. The second crew travelled in a compartment till the midway point of the run, when they used the corridor to exchange places with the crew which had worked the train to that point. One can only wonder if the cost of building 20 of these tenders was ever really justified by the prestige of operating, over four months of the year at most, the world's longest non-stop run.

The year 1928 saw the emergence of another new three-cylinder design. At this time the Great Eastern Section was in need of new express passenger motive power, though the shortage had been tided over temporarily by the building of the ten Lentz-valve 4–6–os just mentioned. As to a new design, the problem was that of evolving a locomotive type which would conform to the hampering conditions of the Great Eastern main lines, in particular a very limited loading gauge and weak underline bridgework that severely restricted weight, so much so that the original B12 4–6–os were not allowed to carry more than 44 tons on their three coupled axles.

Now the North British Locomotive Company had had a wide experience in designing locomotives for overseas buyers to conform to all kinds of limitations, and as the Doncaster design staff was heavily committed at that time with other projects Gresley took the most unusual course of asking this firm not only to build but also to design a series of 4–6–0 locomotives suitable for Great Eastern use. The result was the emergence in 1928 of the first ten of the B17 or "Sandringham" class, this being the name of the first example, No. 2800.

As far as possible what were now standard L.N.E.R. details were worked into the design, including Gresley 2-to-1 derived motion for the inside cylinder, but one of his cherished principles, the driving of all three cylinders on the middle coupled axle, had to be abandoned; the middle cylinder drove the leading coupled axle. This had some advantage, however, for as with the "Shire" 4–4–os this made possible the location of the 2-to-1 derived motion in rear of instead of in front of the cylinders. One substantial advantage derived from three-cylinder propulsion was that, with the elimination of hammer-blow so obtained, it became possible to increase to 54 tons the adhesion weight, and so to provide for absorbing the increase from 21,970 lb. to 25,380 lb. in the tractive effort (assisted partly by putting up the working pressure from 180 to 200 lb.) as compared with the Great Eastern B12s.

The design proving successful, building was turned over to Darlington

Works, and continued until the final batch, built by the firm of Robert Stephenson and completed in 1937, brought the total to 73 engines. The last 25 were drafted to the Great Central Section to replace the "Director" 4–4–0s on the London Extension; they were named after prominent football clubs, and carried the shape of a football in relief on the driving splashers below the name. The "Sandringhams" did well on the Great Eastern line, for which they were specifically designed, and outstandingly so on the Great Central.

Gresley and his principal assistant, O. V. S. Bulleid, were both men of adventurous minds; it may never be known to what extent the latter influenced his Chief, though there was ample evidence of Bulleid's inventiveness after he had become a Chief Mechanical Engineer in his own right, from 1937 onwards, of the Southern Railway. However, it was probably Gresley himself who, towards the end of 1927, conceived the idea that compounding might prove successful given a sufficiently high working pressure. So he approached the well-known firm of Yarrow specialists in marine boilers, to obtain the design of a water-tube boiler suitable for mounting on a locomotive chassis. During the following year work was put in hand at Darlington in conditions of some secrecy —which earned for the locomotive the nickname of the "Hush-Hush" engine—on a revolutionary machine with the 4–6–4 wheel arrangement which, carrying the number 10000, took the rails in 1929.

The boiler system comprised an upper water drum, at the highest level permitted by the loading gauge, linked to two pairs of lower water drums by hundreds of arched tubes, round which played the hot gases from the firebox, inside the insulated boiler casing. Nothing in appearance like this strange monster had ever been seen before on British metals. The boiler was designed to generate steam at a pressure of 450 lb. per sq. in., expanded first in two 12 in. by 16 in. high pressure cylinders between the frames (later reduced in diameter to 10 in.), and then in a second stage in two outside low pressure 20 in. by 26 in. cylinders. After seven months of trials, during which a number of design modifications had to be made, No. 10000 was turned into traffic in July 1930, and for a time worked between York, Newcastle and Edinburgh on a turn requiring 420 engine miles daily. The 4–6–4 was also tried on the non-stop "Flying Scotsman" between King's Cross and Edinburgh, and kept time on the very easy schedule of the first years of non-stop running.

But all kinds of troubles were experienced, especially with leaking tubes, which made maintenance an expensive business, and the hoped-for economies in coal consumption were not achieved. So an experiment on which Gresley had set high hopes, and which had aroused widespread interest among locomotive engineers, ended in failure, though it had provided valuable information. And eventually, in 1937, No. 10000 emerged from Doncaster Works rebuilt as a streamlined three-cylinder simple locomotive closely resembling the A4 Pacifics, to which we shall come in the next chapter. She was the only 4–6–4 tender locomotive that has ever run in Great Britain.

During 1927 the derailment at speed of a Southern Railway 2–6–4 tank at Sevenoaks had raised doubts as to the suitability of tank engines for express passenger work. Although trials of one of these engines at high speed round the Offord curves of the Great Northern main line showed that nothing in their design could have caused the accident, but that the condition of the track must have been responsible, other tank engine projects that were in hand at the time were held up, including one of Gresley's for the building of a new type of three-cylinder 2–6–2 tank. However, in 1930 work on these engines was allowed to proceed, and in September of that year the pioneer of a new Class VI, No. 2900, was turned out of Doncaster Works. The first 34 of these locomotives were drafted to Scotland for outer suburban services in the Edinburgh and Glasgow areas. The next batch went to the North Eastern Area, and on such services as the hourly expresses between Newcastle and Middlesbrough did better work than either the Raven 4–4–4s rebuilt as 4–6–2s or the later Great Central type A5 4–6–2 tanks which they replaced. In all, 82 Class VI 2–6–2 tanks were built between 1930 and 1936.

In 1932 there was some recrudescence of booster activity. No. 6171, one of the big three-cylinder 0–8–4 tanks that John G. Robinson had built at Gorton Works in 1907 for service in the marshalling yard at Wath, was provided with a booster to the trailing bogie, the wheels of which were coupled. As the engine might have to work either chimney or bunker first, a booster of a reversing type was fitted. It increased the tractive effort from 34,520 to 46,890 lb., so that this locomotive could now handle more than 60 loaded wagons over the yard hump. The results were so satisfactory that two additional booster-fitted engines of the same type were built at Gorton in 1932.

A rather more curious booster experiment was carried out on Raven three-cylinder Atlantics Nos. 727 and 2171 in the previous year. It consisted in fitting a booster engine to the rear pair of wheels, and then incorporating these into a bogie which also carried the leading end of the tender; the rear end of the latter was carried by another bogie. A boiler of 5 ft. 9 in. diameter replaced the previous 5 ft. 6 in. boiler; the firegrate area was increased from 27 to 30 sq. ft. and the working pressure from 180 to 200 lb. But over a road such as that between Newcastle and Edinburgh, for which these engines were intended, and with express trains either non-stop or calling intermediately only at Berwick, the opportunities for bringing the booster into action were so limited that it is surprising that any such experiment as this was made; boosters can only justify themselves when applied to locomotives required to accelerate from frequent stops, or to give big power output over short periods, as in the work of marshalling yards. These two Atlantics with their boosters and unique articulated tenders did not last for long in this condition.

Mention has been made previously of the rebuilding of the Great Eastern B12 4–6–0s, which began in 1932 directly Edward Thompson

I

had assumed office as Mechanical Engineer (Stratford). No 8579 was the first to be tackled, receiving a 5 ft. 6 in. diameter boiler, and with modified valve-setting, in which Thompson was an expert, the valve-travel being increased from 4½ in. to just over 6 in. Roughly three-quarters of the B12s were rebuilt in the same way during the succeeding years; their coal consumption was appreciably reduced; and they could now put up performances little, if at all, inferior to those of the Class B17 "Sandringham" 4–6–0s. Similar attention was then paid to a number of the "Claud Hamilton" 4–4–0s, beginning with No. 8848, which in its new form came out of Stratford Works in January, 1933, and was followed in February by No. 8900 *Claud Hamilton* itself. These rebuilds possibly looked more businesslike than before, but much of the beauty of the original design had vanished, by the removal of the secondary splashers over the coupled wheels, the loss of much of the former ornamental brassowrk, and the fitting of the severely utilitarian Gresley cast chimney. Next the larger Great Eastern 0–6–0s came in for the same treatment, beginning in 1934.

During these years the building of Gresley Pacifics had gone on steadily, 52 of the original Class A1 having taken the rails between 1922 and 1924, and 27 of the 220 lb. pressure A3 series by the beginning of 1935; also a number of the A1s had been transferred into Class A3 by receiving the higher pressure boilers. Apart from this the only activity other than those already described was the acquisition between 1925 and 1928 of a large number of steam railcars for branch line service. These were of a new type in which small high pressure vertical steam boilers with superheaters and feed-water heaters supplied steam to double-acting cylinders, and with light coach-bodies provided for very economical operation. Between 1925 and 1928 74 railcars of the Sentinel type were obtained from the Metropolitan-Cammell Carriage & Wagon Company, and 11 similar cars from the Clayton Wagon Company. In addition 58 Sentinel locomotives, with boilers and transmissions of the same type, were purchased for shunting service. On the whole the railcars did well; their main disadvantage was that with an average of 60 seats or slightly over they could not cope with peak traffic, such as that at week-ends. Later experiments were made with trailers, which had to be of very light weight in order not to overload the engines, and with a larger two-car articulated unit. The majority of the railcars, which carried names derived from the old stage-coaches, operated in the North Eastern area, and it was shown that their running costs were not more than half those of the N.E.R. push-and-pull "auto-trains" of two coaches with 0–4–4 tank locomotive that they replaced. But railcar maintenance costs were high, and what with their week-end limitations and the progressive loss of branch line traffic to the roads their life was relatively short, though the Sentinel shunters remained in service for quite a lengthy period.

XVIII

Gresley's Final Years—1935-1941

THE EARLY 1930s were years of acute depression in the United States, and during that period some of their influence was being felt in Great Britain also. As we have seen in the last chapter, much locomotive experimenting was in progress on the L.N.E.R., but between 1930 and 1934 no new locomotive type had been evolved. When we come to 1934, however, it is to the beginning of the greatest years of London & North Eastern locomotive history, when Gresley, who two years later was to be honoured with the accolade of knighthood as Sir Nigel Gresley, to receive an honorary degree as Doctor of Science from Manchester University, and to be elected President of the Institution of Mechanical Engineers, was to reach the zenith of his achievements.

Previous chapters have described how American influences had been at work when Gresley's first Pacific design was produced in 1922. Seven years later a European locomotive designer had come to the forefront in the person of André Chapelon, Chief Mechanical Engineer of the Paris-Orléans Railway, who after a good deal of research had rebuilt one of that company's four-cylinder compound 4-6-2 locomotives to give higher thermal efficiency figures than any previously known with steam locomotives. The changes were from the previous high pressure cylinder piston-valves and low pressure cylinder slide-valves to poppet-valves for all four; to steam-pipes of larger cross-section and more direct layout; to the provision of a Nicholson thermic syphon in the firebox to improve circulation and to the addition of an A.C.F.I. feed-water heater; and to a twin blast-pipe and double chimney to improve the draught and facilitate the escape of the exhaust steam—all in all, a kind of internal streamlining. Needless to say, Gresley closely studied Chapelon's work and, moreover, took an early opportunity to visit Paris and make the French designer's acquaintance. But not until 1934 was the fruit of this study seen on British metals.

At this time, with no express locomotives in Scotland more powerful for working the heavily-graded main lines than the unsuitable Reid Atlantics, and the "Shire" and "Director" 4-4-0s, double-heading of the heavier trains was rife, especially between Edinburgh and Aberdeen. A design had been worked out at Doncaster, based partly on the K3 2-6-0 and partly on the two North Eastern Atlantics that had been articulated to their tenders, for a 2-6-4-4 locomotive of what would have been an extraordinary appearance, with 6 ft. 2 in. coupled wheels in place of the 5 ft. 8 in. wheels of the K3, and the 6 ft. diameter boiler raised to the extreme limit permitted by the loading gauge. It was thought that the larger coupled wheels would have permitted higher speeds, and that any tendency to more unsteady running than that of the K3s would be damped down by the articulation. But the articulation would have proved a thorough nuisance in maintenance, and it is hardly surprising that this idea went no further. Instead, the new locomotive for Scotland, when it appeared, proved to be Britain's first and only express passenger 2–8–2 type, with 6 ft. 2 in. coupled wheels.

The Chapelon influence was unmistakable. Although not all the French designer's ideas had been incorporated, No. 2001 had Lentz rotary cam poppet-valves, A.C.F.I. feed-water heater, Kylchap double blast-pipe and double chimney, and large-diameter streamlined steam passages; the three cylinders, 21 in. by 26 in., were the biggest that Gresley had used on any express engine up to that time, other than the original A1 Pacifics, and the 50 sq. ft. firegrate area also was a British record for a passenger engine. The coupled wheels, 6 ft. 2 in., were of the same diameter as those for the projected 2–6–4–4. A partially streamlined casing had been provided for the engine, together with a wedge front for the cab, to reduce air resistance. As a tribute to Scotland, No. 2001 received the name *Cock o' the North*; the second engine of the same type, No. 2002, with piston-valves in place of poppet-valves for comparison purposes, was named *Earl Marischal*. At first *Cock o' the North* was fitted with an infinitely variable valve-motion, but after trouble with the continuous cams, stepped cams had to be fitted, restricting the possible cut-offs to six variations only, from 12 to 75 per cent., and so making difficult any proper precision in handling.

At the end of 1934 No. 2001 underwent tests on the French locomotive testing-plant at Vitry-sur-Seine, and gave some very favourable overall thermal efficiency figures; also on tests on the Paris-Orléans line between Orleans and Tours she developed 2,800 h.p. But the engine never showed up well in Scotland; she was engaged on relatively short runs only and with inexperienced handling was heavy on coal. Eventually *Cock o' the North* was rebuilt as a piston-valve engine with the Gresley conjugated motion. By 1938 four more of these engines, classified as P2, had been turned out, but with the front end wings replaced by a streamlined wedge front derived from a far more famous Gresley class which had been built in the interim. Later Nos. 2001 and 2002 were dealt with similarly.

Gresley had designed his 2–8–2s to be able to handle 550-ton loads between Edinburgh and Aberdeen, which they certainly did with trains such as the "Aberdonian" sleeper; one well-known driver claimed that even with loads of over 600 tons he had never known a P2 refuse to start, not even up such a gradient as the 1 in 68 southbound out of Dundee Tay Bridge station. But the history of the P1 2–8–2s and their 100-wagon freight trains was being repeated in that such enormous Scottish passenger trains made double drawing up necessary at intermediate stops; also it cannot be disputed that the engines suffered from heating trouble, and had a tendency to spread the road on the sharp curves of this Scottish main line. Had Gresley lived we may be sure that the two latter drawbacks might have been cured, for in the United States vastly bigger 4–8–4 locomotives, on such main lines as the Santa Fe, at the same time were working regularly over sharper curves than any between Edinburgh and Aberdeen. But after the designer's death the defects were regarded as justification for a complete rebuilding by his successor, to which we shall refer in the next chapter.

We come now to what undoubtedly was Gresley's masterpiece of design, his streamlined A4 Pacific. Much comment had been aroused after the introduction in 1932 by the German State Railways of their streamlined diesel "Flying Hamburger", booked to cover the 178 miles between Berlin and Hamburg at an average speed of 77.4 m.p.h., which for timekeeping entailed maximum speeds up to 100 m.p.h. over suitable stretches of the route. For the first time in Europe diesel traction was being used for high-speed passenger work. In due course questions were being asked as to why something similar could not be done in Great Britain, and Gresley accordingly obtained from the builders of this German two-car train an estimate of the time which a unit of equal power, seating 140 passengers, and with due observance of all existing speed restrictions, would need to cover the 268.3 miles between King's Cross and Newcastle. The reply given was 4½ hours; and Gresley claimed that this could be bettered by steam power, with the advantage of using British coal rather than imported oil fuel, and with proper restaurant accommodation instead of the German train's cold buffet only.

To prove the point some remarkable trial runs were made. On the first of them, on November 30th, 1934, the A1 Pacific *Flying Scotsman* ran a four-coach train from King's Cross to Leeds, 185.7 miles, in just under 2 hours 32 minutes (a time never since beaten), and returned with six coaches in 2 hours 37½ minutes, which included a top speed of exactly 100 m.p.h. down Stoke bank. Next, on March 5th, 1935, came a six-coach test between King's Cross and Newcastle, on which the A3 Pacific *Papyrus* completed the down journey in 3 hours 57 minutes or 3 hours 50 minutes net, and returned in 3 hours 51½ minutes. On this trial the A3 had shown its ability to cover 300 miles of a single day's round trip at an average speed of 80 m.p.h., with a six-coach train including full restaurant service and substantially more seating than the German diesel streamliner. It was thus obvious that a 4-hour schedule between London and Newcastle would be perfectly feasible. With the encouragement of R. L. Wedgwood, the Chief General Manager, and the approval of the L.N.E.R. Directors, Gresley was then given the "go ahead".

He had in mind a modified Pacific type which would be able to operate such trains with even greater efficiency and competence. So it was that September, 1935, saw the emergence from Doncaster Works of No. 2509 *Silver Link*, pioneer of the A4 class. In honour of the Silver

Jubilee of the reign of King George V and Queen Mary, which was being celebrated in 1935, the new London-Newcastle express was to be called the "Silver Jubilee", and both the train and the four A4s built to haul it were therefore painted in silver-grey. While in general the A4 design followed that of the A3 Pacifics, there were certain significant changes. One was the raising of the boiler pressure from 220 to 250 lb. per sq. in. and the reduction in cylinder diameter from 19 to $18\frac{1}{2}$ in., coupled with an improvement in the layout, size and finish of all the internal steam passages, to ensure the smoothest possible passage of the steam from boiler to cylinders and exhaust. Improvements were effected also in the springing and balancing, to adapt the engines to higher sustained speeds than before.

But the most striking change, of course, was in external appearance. In order to reduce head-end resistance, and at the same time to ensure that at high speed the exhaust steam would be lifted clear of the front windows of the cab, after prolonged experiments a wedge-shaped casing had been devised for the front of the locomotive, continued as a stream-lined casing along both sides to the wedge-fronted cab, and with a very handsome secondary casing, with flat sides and an aerofoil curve above, to cover cylinders and motion. Tests revealed that at "Silver Jubilee" speeds the streamlining caused a reduction of about 100 h.p. in the power output required for timekeeping, equal to a reduction of some 4 lb. of coal per mile, or of 200 tons a year, in the working of this one train alone.

It would be generally agreed that the A4 Pacific was Gresley's finest design achievement. Within three weeks of the emergence of *Silver Link* from Doncaster Works the amazing trial run of September 27th, 1935, had taken place of which the engine smashed every previous British speed record by twice attaining $112\frac{1}{2}$ m.p.h. For the next fortnight, until the second engine of the class had been run in, *Silver Link* worked the new train in both directions without relief, making two 232.3-mile runs at 70.4 m.p.h. daily for five days in each week and without any heating or other trouble—a tribute to the excellence of Doncaster locomotive building. Such was the success of the A4s that late in 1936 building began of additional locomotives of this type, and continued until by 1938 the original four had expanded to a total of 35 engines.

Some were needed to work the two further streamlined trains intro-duced in 1937, the "Coronation" between King's Cross and Edinburgh and the "West Riding Limited" between King's Cross, Leeds and Bradford. The former set a far harder task than the "Silver Jubilee" had done, for as compared with the latter's tare weight of 220 tons, the "Coronation", when made up to its full nine-coach load with obser-vation car, tared 312 tons, which incidentally had to be worked from King's Cross to York at a scheduled average speed of 71.9 m.p.h.—the highest ever required of British steam power. It was with six "Coro-nation" coaches and the dynamometer car that on July 3rd, 1938, on a test run, A4 No. 4468 *Mallard* attained a top speed of 126 m.p.h., which is believed to have been the world's record for steam.

Its attainment was facilitated by the fact that Gresley, following the Chapelon method, had fitted the engine with a Kylchap double blast-pipe and double chimney, which facilitated the escape of the exhaust steam. In view of the advantage so secured, it is surprising that during the designer's lifetime only three other A4s were treated similarly; it was his successors who eventually made this blast arrangement standard Pacific practice. A number of the most outstanding feats of the A4 Pacifics are described in detail in Chapter XX. Seven years after Gresley's death also, his double-chimney A4s achieved for him a post-humous triumph. For in the 1948 large-scale exchange of locomotives for trial purposes that succeeded the nationalisation of the railways, these engines reversed the results of the 1925 L.N.E.R.-G.W.R. exchange by beating the Great Western "King" 4-6-0s both in coal consumption and in timekeeping.

No sooner had the A4 Pacifics begun to make a name for themselves than another new Gresley design made its appearance from Doncaster Works. The previous chapter related how at the end of 1928, to meet the need for a mixed traffic locomotive capable of steady running at higher speeds than were possible with his three-cylinder 5 ft. 8in. K3 2-6-0s, Doncaster had worked out a design for a K3 with 6 ft. 2 in. coupled wheels articulated to its tender in such a way as to form a loco-motive of the 2-6-4-4 wheel arrangement, but that this singular idea had not been pursued. Nearly eight years elapsed before the desired mixed traffic type actually took the rails, and when it did so another wheel arrangement unique among British tender engines was seen to have been introduced, and also a locomotive of considerably greater power than had first been contemplated. The engine was 2-6-2 No. 4771 *Green Arrow*, so named to draw attention to green labels which had recently been introduced by the London & North Eastern Railway in order to expedite the carriage of parcels.

The new type, Class V2, was the most powerful that any British railway had built for mixed traffic duties. It mounted a taper boiler uniform with that of the Pacifics and with the same wide firebox and firegrate area of 41.25 sq. ft. The three cylinders, 18½ in. diameter by 26 in. stroke, were uniform with those of the A4 Pacifics, and drove coupled wheels of 6 ft. 2 in. diameter. Boiler pressure, like that of the A3 Pacifics, was 220 lb. per sq. in., and this gave a tractive effort of 33,730 lb. So successful were the V2s in performance that building continued after their designer's death to a total of 184 units. To the London & North Eastern Railway they gave distinguished service, especially during the Second World War, when the country was in no small degree in-debted to Gresley for the "big engine" policy which he had pursued so consistently.

The V2s shared many passenger duties with the Pacifics, and could be driven on occasion at speeds well over 80 m.p.h.; one was timed, indeed, to attain 93 m.p.h. On another occasion No. 4789 at short notice had to take over the "West Riding Limited" from an A4 Pacific which had failed, and lost no more than 4 minutes on the 163-minute allowance of that train from King's Cross to Leeds. The 2–6–2s regularly worked the heavy "West Riding Pullman" on its mile-a-minute schedule from Doncaster to London, and by contrast were regarded as the most adaptable engines that had ever operated over the difficult Scottish main line between Edinburgh and Aberdeen. It is true that by reason of weight they were permitted to run over 57 per cent. only of the total L.N.E.R. route mileage, and so had nothing like the same general availability as, say, the Stanier Class 5 4–6–0s on the London Midland & Scottish Railway or the later B1 4–6–0s on the L.N.E.R., but even over their more limited mileage there was always plenty of suitable work for the V2s to do. This was another Gresley design of outstanding competence.

By now high speed was very much in the air, and all kinds of ideas were under consideration by Gresley and his staff. One was to streamline some of the Ivatt Atlantics, which in their final form, with 32-element superheaters, were doing fine work on the "Queen of Scots" Pullman and other expresses of moderate weight. Two of the final batch of B17 4–6–0s, Nos. 2859 and 2870, were actually streamlined similarly to the A4 Pacifics, and named *East Anglian* and *City of London*, for the purpose of working the "East Anglian" express, introduced in 1937, over the Great Eastern line between Liverpool Street and Norwich. But this was mainly as a publicity stunt, as a timing of 135 minutes (later 130 minutes) for the 115 miles between the two terminals, with one intermediate stop only, hardly required the assistance of streamlining for its observance.

A much more powerful non-streamlined 4–6–0 design, however, had been prepared at Doncaster, not subject to the severe Great Eastern restrictions which had limited the B17 design. This would have had three $18\frac{1}{2}$ in. by 26 in. cylinders and 6 ft. 8 in. coupled wheels, and a considerably bigger boiler than a B17 4–6–0, with a firegrate of 31.5 sq. ft. area and carrying 220 lb. pressure, and an estimated weight of 84 tons. Such an engine should have proved the equal in performance of any other 4–6–0 type in the country, not excepting the Great Western "Castles" and "Kings", and it is a pity that the class never materialised.

What would have been the Gresley *chef d'oeuvre*, had it ever been built, however, was the monster 4–8–2 which he designed for maximum East Coast express passenger duties. Actually the boiler barrel of this machine, 19 ft. in length, would have been no longer than that of an A3 Pacific; an extremely lengthy smokebox would have brought the smokebox front forward to the normal position above the cylinders. These would have been the customary three, but 21 in. in diameter and of 26 in. stroke, which with 250 lb. pressure would have given a tractive effort of 45,700 lb., considerably greater than that of any other express passenger locomotive in the country.

The crowding together of four 6 ft. 8 in. coupled axles on to a wheel-

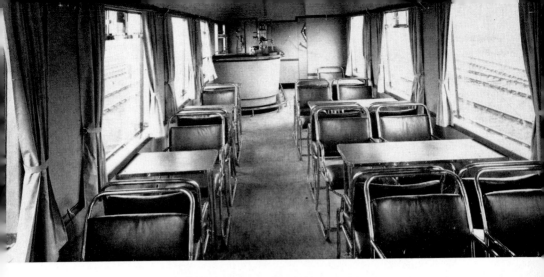

Above: In contrast to the restaurant car below is the simplicity of one of the early buffet cars, bulit in 1932 for use in the new tourist trains.

Right: Luxury in the mid-1930s. First class restaurant car built in 1935 for the "Flying Scotsman" and furnished in the Louis XVI style, with armchair seating and ornamental curtaining.

Below: One of the third class cars with bucket seats which formed part of the tourist trains for half-day excursions.
[*British Railways*

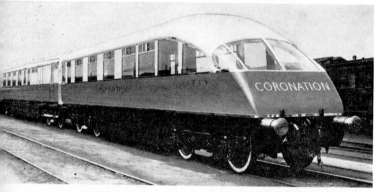

Above: The "Coronation" and "West Riding Limited" streamline trains introduced in 1937 included some of the finest rolling stock ever built for British use. This is a first class open saloon, with rotating armchairs. Note the vista through the aluminium-framed doorways.

Left: Exterior of the "Coronation" beaver-tail observation car.

Below: Interior of the "Coronation" observation car.

[*British Railways*

Above: First class compartment on the "Silver Jubilee" streamline train, introduced in 1935 between King's Cross and Newcastle.

Left: First class restaurant car, "East Anglian", which began to run between Liverpool Street and Norwich in 1937.

Below: The acme of night comfort—first class sleeping compartment on Anglo-Scottish service.   [*British Railways*

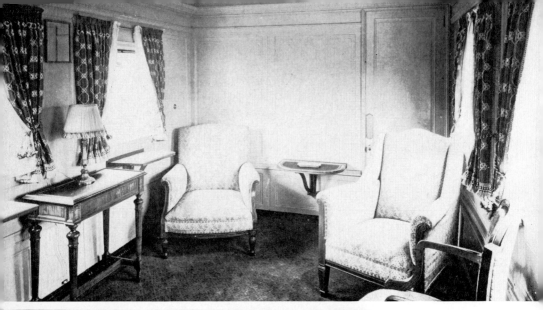

Royal saloon built at York Carriage Works of the N.E.R. in 1908 for the use of Queen Alexandra on her East Coast journeys; a similar saloon was built at Doncaster in 1907 for King Edward VII. These views show two of the saloons and also the dressing room with bath. After the formation of the L.N.E.R. both coaches were reconstructed internally as day saloons, with the bedrooms and bathrooms removed, and still are in use on such Royal journeys as those between Liverpool Street and Sandringham.

[British Railways

base of no more than 21 ft. would have been a fine art, yet even so the total engine wheelbase would have been 42 ft. 3 in., as compared with the 35 ft. 9 in. of a Pacific or the 37 ft. 11 in. of one of the P2 2-8-2s; the weight would have been 115 tons. Engine and tender together would have measured 77 ft. in length overall and would have weighed 173 tons. The aim of using eight-coupled wheels was, of course, additional adhesion; and the performances of the P2 2-8-2s had shown that eight-coupled wheels of no more than 6 ft. 2 in. diameter were no hindrance to the attainment on occasion of speeds as high as 80 m.p.h. But this massive 4-8-2 design also was fated never to take shape.

Designing activity was unceasing during the whole of Gresley's occupation of his office. In 1947 B. Spencer, who had been his personal assistant and with little doubt had influenced his Chief in no small degree, read a paper to the Institution of Locomotive Engineers entitled "The Development of L.N.E.R. Locomotive Design, 1923-1941" in which a number of designs were illustrated that never got beyond the drawing board stage. One, in the final years of Gresley's reign, was a 2-6-4 tank for suburban service which, unusually for Gresley, would have had two cylinders only but a wide firebox and a working pressure of no less than 250 lb. per sq. in. Instead of the 2-6-4, however, a new series of 2-6-2 tanks, Class V3, was put in hand with the working pressure raised from 180 to 200 lb. per sq. in.

Another new design resulted from the need for something more powerful than the two-cylinder K2 2-6-0s to work the very heavily-graded Scottish West Highland line. Despite its curvature Gresley's first plan was for a new version of his Class O2 three-cylinder 2-8-0 freight engine, but with 5 ft. 2 in. in place of 4 ft. 8 in. coupled wheels. To this proposition, however, the Scottish Civil Engineer would not agree. What was produced instead was a new 2-6-0 design, Class K4, with the same cylinders and motion as a K3, but a 5 ft. 6in. diameter boiler instead of 6 ft., and 5 ft. 2in. in place of 5 ft. 8 in. coupled wheels; the K4 also had 200 lb. in place of 180 lb. pressure, though in later years this was reduced to 180 lb. The K4s soon proved themselves capable of handling 300-ton loads up the lengthy 1 in 55-60 climbs of the West Highland line, and made it possible to dispense with a great deal of double-heading in the summer months.

This raised the question of designing a mixed traffic engine which with reduced size and weight would have a wider radius of action than the highly competent V2 class. Eventually a plan was agreed in 1939, but owing to the outbreak of war it was not until 1941 that the only two locomotives built to the new design were completed. They were Nos. 3401 and 3402, Class V4, the first being named *Bantam Cock*. These were V2s in miniature, with cylinders reduced in diameter from $18\frac{1}{2}$ in. to 15 in., coupled wheels from 6 ft. 2in. to 5 ft. 8 in., boilers tapering in diameter from 4 ft. 8 in. to 5 ft. 4 in. as compared with 5 ft. $9\frac{1}{4}$ in. to 6 ft. 5in., and a weight in working order reduced from 93 to $70\frac{1}{2}$ tons. They had the same wide fireboxes as the bigger engines, but with 28.5

sq. ft. firegrate area only as against 41.25 sq. ft.; a notable difference
was that the V4 carried a working pressure of 250 lb. as compared with
the V2's 220 lb.   The tractive effort of *Bantam Cock* was thus 27,420 lb.
For comparison purposes, No. 3402 was fitted with a Nicholson thermic
syphon in the firebox, the first British locomotive to have such equipment.

With its comparatively short and flexible wheelbase, and no more than
48½ tons of the engine's weight concentrated on the coupled wheels, a
V4 could have gone almost anywhere on the London & North Eastern
system, but from the building point of view would have been a very
expensive proposition for the minor duties from which the V2s were
debarred by weight.   And with the Second World War now in progress,
every possible economy had become urgently necessary, so that despite
some quite competent performances by Nos. 3401 and 3402 it can be
no surprise that no further 2–6–2s of this type were built.

In the last year of his life Gresley, with his staff, was concerned in a
design which was not to incorporate steam as its prime mover.   In 1936
the decision had been reached to electrify the busy Sheffield-Manchester
main line of the former Great Central Railway, mainly in the interest
of the heavy coal traffic which had to be worked over the 943 ft. summit
at Dunford, at the eastern end of Woodhead Tunnel.   Considerable
progress had been made with the line equipment before the outbreak of
war in 1939 brought the work to a standstill; but the new locomotives
had been designed, and by 1941 the first of them had been completed;
Doncaster was responsible for the mechanical details, and Metropolitan-
Vickers for the electrical equipment.   This powerful machine, No. 6701,
taking current at 1,500 V. d.c. from overhead conductors, had a one-
hour rating of 1,870 h.p. and a continuous rating of 1,740 h.p.; each axle
was motorised, and the maximum axle-load, out of a total weight of 88
tons, was 22½ tons.   As no part of the Sheffield-Manchester line was
as yet sufficiently advanced with its electrification to have the current
turned on, No. 6701 had to be towed to Manchester to undergo its tests,
which were entirely satisfactory, on the electrified Manchester, South
Junction & Altrincham Joint Line.   In all, 57 Bo-Bo electrics of the
same type as No. 6701 eventually were built.

On February 19th, 1941, both the new V4 2–6–2 *Bantam Cock* and the
electric No. 6701 were exhibited at York to the Directors and to the
technical press, with Sir Nigel Gresley himself present.   But for some
time past his health had been deteriorating, and six weeks later, at his
home, Watton House in Hertfordshire, the great designer died suddenly
from a heart attack.   This was within three months of what would
have been his sixty-fifth birthday, and within six months of completing
30 years of service as Chief Mechanical Engineer in succession of the
Great Northern and London & North Eastern Railways.   Great Britain
has never known a locomotive engineer more highly respected or of
greater ability than Sir Nigel Gresley.

XIX

Thompson and Peppercorn Locomotives— 1941-1947

NEXT IN the line of successtion to Gresley was Edward Thompson, and without delay the L.N.E.R. directors appointed him as Chief Mechanical Engineer. He had begun his career on the North Eastern Railway, and by 1909 had reached the position of Assistant Divisional Locomotive Superintendent at Gateshead; then from 1912 to 1927—apart from the interruption of national service in the First World War—he was engaged on carriage and wagon work, first as Superintendent of that department at Doncaster and then as Manager of the North Eastern Carriage and Wagon Works at York and Shildon. In 1927 he took office as Assistant Mechanical Engineer (Stratford), succeeding C. W. L. Glaze as Mechanical Engineer there in 1930. Next, in 1933, came his appointment as Mechanical Engineer (Darlington) in succession to A. C. Stamer, and finally, in 1938, he had followed R. A. Thom at Doncaster in a position now described as Mechanical Engineer, Southern Area (Western).

Thompson succeeded to the supreme position at a difficult time. By the spring of 1941 many of the engines were being worked harder than ever before, owing to war demands, while the gradual reduction of staff and the increasing difficulty of obtaining materials were having a serious effect on maintenance. As compared with Gresley, who, in collaboration until 1937 with O. V. S. Bulleid had always been the man of ideas, experimentation and new and novel designs, Thompson throughout most of his locomotive life had been concerned with maintenance, and simplicity in design and everything that would play a part in reducing maintenance costs had always been his aim. For this reason he strongly preferred two-cylinder to three-cylinder engines; and such fittings as the Gresley conjugated valve-motion, which lacking its former careful maintenance by 1941 was giving an appreciable amount of trouble, were anathema to him.

So, unhappily, was Gresley himself, and it would appear that the antipathy was mutual, leading to some tense encounters between the two men. In addition, Thompson was steeped in North Eastern traditions; he had married the daughter of Sir Vincent Raven; and but for the grouping in 1923 he would have been next in the line of succession after Stamer for the post of Chief Mechanical Engineer of the North Eastern Railway. As it turned out, in any event he would probably have had to wait until 1933, when Stamer retired, for that position, whereas eight years later, in 1941, he succeeded to the far more responsible post of Chief Mechanical Engineer of the London & North Eastern Railway. But the former frustrations could not be forgotten, especially as by now Thompson had reached 60 years of age, and so had barely five years of service left.

Nevertheless it would have been difficult to forecast, after Gresley's death, that his successor would have adopted such extreme measures to undo the master's work as he actually did. One of the first steps that Thompson took on appointment was to remove from his department to other positions men who had been closely associated with Gresley's work. Among them in particular was B. Spencer, who by now was officially designated Technical Assistant (Locomotive), and who, as previously noted, had had no small share in Gresley's design work. In this case it was not a matter of any personal animosity but merely the burning desire to efface all possible Gresley influence at the earliest possible moment.

Next, Thompson lost no time in preparing for the directors a detailed review of all the recorded locomotive failures which could be attributed to the Gresley derived motion. In the interest of making the outside Walschaerts valve-motions more accessible, and permitting more air to circulate round the motion, he then had cut away from the A4 Pacifics and the three other streamlined locomotives the valances over the coupled wheels which, while it did not improve the appearance of the locomotives concerned, certainly had some justification. The next thing was to set about the production of some new general purpose two-cylinder locomotive designs, in which simplicity of building and ease of maintenance would be the paramount considerations—the opposite extreme, indeed, from Gresley's final V4 *Bantam Cock* design.

At the end of 1942 the firstfruits of this design activity were seen. It was a new general purpose 4–6–0 type of handsome appearance, No. 8301, carrying the name *Springbok*, which had been built at Darlington. With 6 ft. 2 in. coupled wheels, 20 in. by 26 in. cylinders, a 5 ft. 6 in. diameter boiler with a firegrate area of 27.9 sq. ft., and a working pressure of 225 lb. per sq. in., this design was the London & North Eastern counterpart of Stanier's successful Class 5 4–6–0s of the London Midland & Scottish Railway. The principal difference was in the cylinder dimensions, for the L.M.S.R. locomotive had 18½ in. by 28 in. cylinders. When the two types were pitted directly against one another in the 1948 locomotive exchange trials, which succeeded nationalisation, in tractive capacity and overall thermal efficiency there was very little to choose between the two types, the L.M.S.R. engine having only the very slightest advantage.

Piston-valves of 10 in. diameter and with a maximum travel of 6½ in., plus a steam lap of 1⅝ in., helped to produce a free running engine, capable of some quite substantial speeds notwithstanding driving wheels of no more than 6 ft. 2 in. diameter. Building of the B1 4–6–0s continued, with little or no modification of the design, for years after Thompson's retirement, until a total of 410 units had been put in service. With their height above rail of no more than 12 ft. 11 in., their maximum axle-load of 17¾ tons, and a total engine weight of 71¼ tons, they had an almost unlimited radius of action, and soon were at work all over the London & North Eastern system.

Meantime other developments of note were taking place. The last chapter described the introduction of Gresley's outstanding 2–8–2 type, Class P2, for service in Scotland, and detailed some of the troubles experienced with these engines. It is difficult to believe that some of these defects were not curable; and in any event, if by 1941 these machines had been transferred south of the Border they might have proved invaluable in handling outsize wartime loads over the East Coast main line, with lengthy continuous runs (instead of their relatively short spells of duty in Scotland) which would have made much more economical use of their powers, and with little severe curvature to encourage the spreading of the track and overheating of which they had been accused in Scotland. But here was another opportunity for Thompson to show his aversion to Gresley and all his works; and he did not hesitate to seize it. So it was that early in 1943 No. 2005 *Thane of Fife* emerged from Doncaster Works in a totally new guise. In place of the engine's former sleek streamlined outline as a 2–8–2 it had become a 4–6–2 of angular and uncouth appearance.

Gresley's drive of all three cylinders on the second coupled axle had been replaced by a divided drive, with the inside cylinder driving the leading pair of coupled wheels (which had previously been the second pair), and the outside cylinders moved backwards to drive what had now become the middle pair. A leading bogie had been substituted for the former pony truck and leading coupled wheels. Needless to say, the Gresley derived motion had disappeared, and three separate sets of Walschaerts valve-motion substituted. One design improvement was a new type of bogie which Thompson intended to standardise, with the weight of the leading end of the engine transmitted to the bogie frame through the medium of spherical sliding surfaces, lateral movement being controlled by helical springs in place of the former swing links. Redesigned steam passages, 10 in. in place of 9 in. piston-valves, and a double blast-pipe and double chimney, all helped in the free flow of the steam and freedom of exhaust, so that the rebuilt 2–8–2 had now become a particularly speedy type of Pacific.

But its fatal weakness was that the adhesion weight had been reduced from 79 to 66 tons, which cut the adhesion factor from 4.06 to 3.67. As a result, the rebuilt engines—for all six of them received the same treatment—earned an unenviable notoriety for slipping, and when they were returned as Pacifics to Scotland they became so unpopular that eventually all of them had to be transferred to the south and put on to more or less secondary duties. Of all the London & North Eastern Pacifics, these were the first to be scrapped.

Thompson's next conversion aroused more comment even than that of the P2 2–8–2s. For, of all engines to be chosen, the pioneer Gresley

Pacific, No. 4470 *Great Northern*, was taken and transformed into a hideous travesty of the locomotive which had excited such admiration at its first appearance in 1922. As with the rebuilt 2–8–2s, divided drive with three independent Walschaerts motions replaced the Gresley drive of all three cylinders on the middle coupled axle and the conjugated motion for the inside cylinder; to obtain connecting rods of equal length this involved moving the outside cylinders back and lengthening the front end of the engine, smokebox included, to accommodate the inside cylinder and valve-chest, so increasing the engine wheelbase from 35 ft. 9 in. to 38 ft. 5 in. Up to this time No. 4470 had never been rebuilt from Class A1 to Class A3, and so still retained a working pressure of 180 lb. per sq. in.; an A4 boiler with 250 lb. pressure had now been fitted.

What caused the most resentment among Doncaster men was that of all the Pacifics that he might have rebuilt, Thompson had deliberately chosen No. 4470, the engine which had always borne—and still retained —the honoured name *Great Northern*, for this unhappy treatment. The rebuilt No. 4470 was intended to be the prototype of a new standard Class A1, but although it had the advantage of a drop grate and a hopper ashpan, comparative tests showed that it had no advantage in coal consumption over a Gresley A4 Pacific, and was much more inclined to slip on starting than the A4. This was another engine sent to Scotland for trial, but speedily returned south; Gresley had many Scottish admirers, at Edinburgh Haymarket shed in particular, and some of the Thompson innovations were far from welcome north of the Border.

It may be added that when in 1945 the Directors called for a report from Thompson as to what improvements in locomotive performance had been obtained as the result of his changes in Gresley standards, in comparative tests between one of the rebuilt P2 2–8–2s, one of the four 6 ft. 2 in. Pacifics which had been built as remodelled V2 2–6–2s (to which we shall come later), and an A4, the Gresley engine showed a substantially lower coal consumption than its two competitors. The 6 ft. 2 in. 4–6–2s were quicker starters, as was only to be expected with their smaller coupled wheels and maximum cut-off increased from 65 to 75 per cent., but there was little evidence to support other claims that were made in their favour.

It is significant that from now on Thompson made no further serious attempt to modify either the A3 or the A4 Pacifics. Instead, he concentrated on producing a Pacific type with 6 ft. 2in. instead of 6 ft. 8 in. coupled wheels, to succeed the V2 2–6–2s, the last of which had been built in 1944, as the principal main line mixed traffic type of the future. Mention was made in the last paragraph of four V2 2–6–2s remodelled as Pacifics; these were the last of an order for V2s then under construction at Doncaster, Nos. 3696 to 3699, which Thompson fitted with a leading bogie instead of a pony truck, so with the rebuilt P2 2–8–2s now bringing up to ten the total of 6 ft. 2 in. Pacifics in service. With this experience, in 1946 Thompson began work on a series of engines similar to the

A2/2s, including the firebox with 50 sq. ft. of grate, and, for the first time on the L.N.E.R., full size smoke deflectors. The first of the class, No. 500, was turned out in 1946, but the last of the 14 engines did not appear until 1947, after the designer's retirement. No. 500, the first entirely new Pacific of Thompson's design, and the 2,000th engine built at Doncaster, bore the name *Edward Thompson.*

The number carried by the first A2/3 Pacific, 500, brings its reminder that in his last year of office, 1946, Thompson initiated a valuable reform, which was the complete renumbering of the entire L.N.E.R. locomotive stock on systematic lines, instead of the haphazard numbering which had continued, with a few exceptions, from the days of the pre-grouping railways. Pacific and 2–6–2 locomotives were to receive numbers between 1 and 999; 4–6–0 and 2–6–0 engines between 1000 and 1999; 4–4–2, 4–4–0 and 2–4–0 tender engines between 2000 and 2999; 0–8–0 and 2–8–0 freight engines between 3000 and 3999; 0–6–0 tender engines between 4000 and 5999; electric locomotives (now in view because of the pending electrification from Sheffield to Manchester) between 6000 and 6999; 2–6–2, 4–4–2, 2–4–2, 4–4–4 and 0–4–4 tanks between 7000 and 7999; 0–6–0, 0–4–2 and 0–4–0 tanks between 8000 and 8999; and finally freight, marshalling and a few other miscellaneous tank types between 9000 and 9999; leaving the 4–6–4 express passenger engine, No. 10000, as the only one to retain its number.

In 1945 Thompson also laid down a system of future locomotive standardisation which, with no more than two years of his service remaining, he had little hope of seeing carried through. Needless to say, the new standard locomotive classes were to include his A1 Pacific, based on the rebuilding of No. 4470, and his 6 ft. 2 in. mixed traffic Pacific; his B1 4–6–0 and his new L1 2–6–4 tank, to which we shall come in a moment; a 2–8–0 based on the Great Central Robinson 2–8–0 design but with a B1 boiler, cylinders and motion, to be classified as O1; a 2–6–0 class based on a two-cylinder rebuild of the three-cylinder K4 type which Gresley had built for Scottish use; and an 0–8–0 shunting tank based on the rebuilding of some Robinson 0–8–0 freight engines which had been converted to tanks.

It was truly characteristic of Thompson, who carried his vendetta against Gresley to the very end, that no purely Gresley locomotive types were any longer to be regarded as standard. The A3 and A4 Pacifics, V2 2–6–2s, "Shire" and "Hunt" 4–4–0s, V1 and V3 tanks and some others would still be maintained but would be scrapped as soon as they needed new boilers; while the B17 4–6–0s and K3 2–6–0s would be retained, but would all be rebuilt with two instead of three cylinders. It need hardly be added that what would have been a disastrous policy from both the economic and the technical points of view was very soon reversed by Thompson's successor.

Actually the first Thompson rebuild of a Gresley three-cylinder engine had been in 1942, and it was of "Hunt" (D49) class 4–4–0 No. 365 *The Morpeth.* Two 20 in. by 26 in. cylinders were fitted, with Stephenson link motion in place of the Lentz poppet-valves. This could not have been a very successful effort, as no description of the rebuilt engine ever appeared in the technical press, and it was impossible to obtain any details or photographs from official sources. Next, early in 1944, came the first rebuildings of Great Central types, both with B1 boilers, cylinders and motion; two of these conversions were formerly four-cylinder express passenger 4–6–0s which Gresley had rebuilt experimentally in 1929 with Caprotti poppet-valves, to improve their performance, while the other conversion was of a large-boilered Robinson 2–8–0 of Class O4, as the prototype of what was now to be Class O1.

Now one of the standard features of Raven's three-cylinder North Eastern engines had been a massive monobloc casting in one piece of the three cylinders and valve-chests, formed into the shape of a saddle above to support the smokebox. Owing to the difficulty of locating defects in a casting of such size and complexity, failures in service had not been infrequent, and for this reason Gresley, in 1937, had begun rebuilding some of these engines. The changes included separately cast cylinders, and two sets of Walschaerts valve-gear with the conjugated Gresley 2-to-1 motion for the inside cylinder in place of the previous three sets of Stephenson link motion, similarly to the "Shire" 4–4–0s. This deviation from Darlington principles Thompson set about in 1944 to correct by a second rebuilding of the engines concerned, now with three independent sets of Walschaerts motion; 17 of the series in all were dealt with in this way, and thus became transferred from Class B16/2 to Class B16/3.

The next Gresley type to be tackled was the Scottish three-cylinder 2–6–0 series of Class K4. In the spring of 1946 No. 3445 *MacCailin Mor* emerged from Doncaster Works rebuilt with two 20 in. by 26 in. cylinders and a B1 boiler carrying 225 lb. pressure, as compared with the 200 lb. of the original engines. This conversion had a good deal more to recommend it, not merely in the matter of simplification, from the maintenance point of view, but also of standardisation, which Thompson was now steadily introducing. As we have seen, the B1 type boiler was being applied to a number of classes, as also the B1 cylinders and motion; with the rebuilt K4 the pony truck also was interchangeable with that of the O1 2–8–0 freight engines and the L1 2–6–4 tanks.

This conversion, which was definitely a successful one, was intended by Thompson to serve as a 2–6–0 substitute in future construction for the J39 0–6–0s, with a wider radius of action because of less weight on the coupled wheels but a higher tractive effort, 32,080 lb. as compared with 25,660 lb. The same coupled wheel diameter, 5 ft. 2 in., also would permit reasonable speeds in mixed traffic service. So a new Class K1 was introduced, and under Thompson's successor, with very slight modifications of design, 70 more of these engines were built.

The one remaining type for which Thompson was responsible, to which several previous references have been made, was his L1 2–6–4 tank, of which the first example, No. 9000—and the first completely new locomotive type to appear on any independent British railway after the end of the 1939-1945 war—took the rails in the autumn of 1945. In Gresley's time several tentative designs had been prepared for a tank locomotive type with sufficient tank and bunker accommodation for the more lengthy outer suburban runs than the V1 and V3 2–6–2 tanks, but the plans had come to nothing. Once again standardisation was seen in the B1 20 in. by 26 in. cylinders and motion, 5 ft. 2 in. coupled wheels, and pony truck similar to that of the converted 2–8–0 freight engines; also the L1 tanks shared the handsome appearance of the B1 mixed traffic engines.

Thompson's original plan was to build 110 of the L1s, and it is a sufficient tribute to the excellence of their design that 100 actually were built before nationalisation introduced an entirely new set of standards. And so, although Edward Thompson's retirement at midsummer, 1946, closed what had not been the happiest period in London & North Eastern locomotive history, in the short space of five years he had left some substantial achievements to his credit, and chief among them his B1 4–6–0, K1 2–6–0 and L1 2–6–4 tank designs and the very considerable measure of standardisation for which he had been responsible.

His successor was Arthur H. Peppercorn, a Great Northern man to the core, who had begun his service as a premium apprentice at Doncaster in 1905, and apart from war service from 1914 to 1918, and interludes of varying duration in managerial posts at York Carriage and Wagon Works, Stratford and Darlington Locomotive Works, had spent the major part of his life at Doncaster, finally as Assistant Chief Mechanical Engineer to Thompson. Peppercorn was popular in Doncaster Works and lost no time in restoring the happy relations of former days, bringing back those in close contact with Gresley who had been displaced by his predecessor, and in particular the extremely able B. Spencer, who now became his Chief Technical Assistant. Nationalisation by now was immediately in prospect, and Peppercorn had but a short time left for independent action, though actually he remained in office until the end of the second year of nationalisation, 1949.

From the beginning of the Peppercorn *régime* building went on much as before, chiefly of B1 4–6–0s, K1 2–6–0s and L1 2–6–4 tanks, but the construction of Thompson A2/2 Pacifics was brought to an end directly the 14 had been completed which had been begun before the latter's retirement. When the next 6 ft. 2 in. Pacific appeared, at the end of 1947, many changes were seen to have taken place. Divided drive and the three independent sets of Walschaerts motion had been retained, but the outside cylinders had been moved forward, and the bogie had been brought back so that both were again in their customary position central with the smokebox; in this way the engine wheelbase had been shortened from 37 ft. 1 in. to 34 ft. 4 in.

The larger firebox was retained, with its grate area of 50 sq. ft.; but rather curiously Peppercorn had abandoned the double blast-pipe and chimney for the single fittings, though years later the double blast-pipe

K

became standard for all L.N.E.R. Pacifics. The result of these changes externally was to restore the characteristic grace of line of the Doncaster product, greatly welcomed by all lovers of the locomotive. Immediately on appearance No. 525, the last locomotive to be built at Doncaster under L.N.E.R. auspices, received the name *Arthur H. Peppercorn*; it is rather odd to compare this haste with the fact that not until Gresley's one hundredth Pacific had been built at Doncaster, and then only under pressure from the Directors, was A4 No. 4498 honoured by receiving the title *Sir Nigel Gresley*.

The final locomotive class to be described strictly speaking falls outside this record, for the first example of it did not emerge from Doncaster Works until late in 1948, after the London & North Eastern Railway had ceased to exist. But it was definitely an L.N.E.R. design, last of the distinguished line of that Company's Pacific locomotives. More express passenger locomotives with 6 ft. 8 in. coupled wheels were needed to supplement the A3 and A4 Pacifics, and No. 60114 (the new British Railways numbering had now added 60,000 to all L.N.E.R. engine numbers) was Peppercorn's answer. In a measure this was the new Class A1 successor to Thompson's rebuild of Gresley's No. 4470; it would be more correct, however, to describe it as a new version of Peppercorn's 6 ft. 2 in. Class A2, with the larger driving wheels.

No. 60114 differed from the Gresley A4s in having 19 in. in place of $18\frac{1}{2}$ in. diameter cylinders, divided drive with three independent Walschaerts motions in place of all three cylinders driving on the middle coupled axle and the Gresley conjugated motion for the middle piston-valve, and 50 sq. ft. in place of 41.25 sq. ft. firegrate area. This large grate probably accounts for the fact that in some systematic tests with the dynamometer car, one of the new A1s and one of the 6 ft. 2 in. A2s both proved slightly heavier on coal than an A4 though costing less in maintenance, and especially so five of the final batch which were built with roller bearings throughout. Suffice it to say that the new locomotive administration of British Railways after nationalisation thought it worth while to let construction of the Peppercorn A1 Pacifics continue until by the end of 1949, including Thompson's conversion of No. 4470, 50 of the class in all were in service.

That this decision had been thoroughly justified was revealed by J. F. Harrison, a Doncaster man who eventually became Chief Mechanical Engineer of British Railways, when in his 1961 Presidential Address to the Institution of British Railways he revealed that the entire stud of 49 Peppercorn A1 Pacifics had averaged between them just over 200 miles a day for the whole of the twelve to thirteen years that they had been in service—a record equalled by no other British locomotive type. One of the roller-bearing engines had averaged 228 miles for every day since it left Doncaster Works and had completed a million miles of running. Incidentally, the five roller-bearing A1s were averaging 120,000 miles between major overhauls, or 50 per cent. more than the other Pacifics, and with such a record one can only express surprise that no other Pacifics were equipped similarly. Yet although the performance of the Peppercorn engines, as expressed in load haulage, times and speeds, on the average was but little if at all inferior to that of the more celebrated Gresley A4s, it was always the latter which were called upon when record-breaking was in prospect, and which right to the end of their long and honourable history showed themselves capable of speeds of over 100 m.p.h. whenever allowed so to display their powers.

By the time that this Pacific building was at an end, the successors of the London & North Eastern Railway inherited a total of 202 Pacifics, 41 with 6 ft. 2 in. coupled wheels and the remainder 6 ft. 8 in.; the total would have been 203 but for the fact that during the 1939-1945 war No. 4466 *Sir Ralph Wedgwood* was destroyed by a German bomb during a raid on York Station. With 4–6–4 No. 10000 and the 184 V2 2–6–2s, and including the final A1s and A2s completed after nationalisation, the total of high-powered L.N.E.R. locomotives finally rose to 387, and the Company and its successors had every reason to be grateful to Sir Nigel Gresley for the "big engine" policy which he had initiated and largely carried through with such conspicuous success. This policy had also made possible a considerable reduction in the total number of steam locomotives, which, as Table 11 reveals, had fallen from 7,383 to 6,445 between 1923 and 1947.

Table 11

Reduction in L.N.E.R. Steam Locomotive Stock, 1923–1947

Type	Jan. 1 1923	Dec. 31 1947	Type	Jan. 1 1923	Dec. 31 1947
	No.	No.		No.	No.
4–6–4 tender	—	1	4–6–2 tank	51	117
4–6–2 ,,	4	139	2–6–4 ,,	20	22
4–6–0 ,,	263	547	0–6–4 ,,	9	2
4–4–2 ,,	240	53	2–6–2 ,,	—	92
4–4–0 ,,	947	507	0–6–2 ,,	532	619
4–2–2 ,,	6	—	0–6–0 ,,	967	818
2–4–0 ,,	177	18	4–8–0 ,,	10	13
2–6–2 ,,	—	186	0–8–4 ,,	4	6
2–6–0 ,,	85	274	0–8–2 ,,	41	—
0–6–0 ,,	2,588	1,698	0–8–0 ,,	1	13
2–8–0 ,,	179	681	4–4–4 ,,	45	—
0–8–0 ,,	374	246	4–4–2 ,,	164	152
			4–4–0 ,,	3	—
			2–4–2 ,,	341	118
			2–4–0 ,,	2	—
			2–2–4 ,,	4	—
			0–4–4 ,,	249	110
			0–4–2 ,,	4	4
			0–4–0 ,,	73	8
			*2–8–8–2 ,,	—	1
Total, tender	4,863	4,350	Total, tank	2,520	2,095
Grand total				7,383	6,445

*Garratt articulated banking engine No. 2395.

Table 12
Locomotives of London & North Eastern and Constituent Railways that are being preserved

Year of Building	Railway	Wheel Arrangement	No.	Name	Type or Class	Where preserved
1825	Stockton & Darlington	0-4-0	1	Locomotion	—	Darlington Bank Top Stn.
1845	Stockton & Darlington	0-6-0	25	Derwent	—	Darlington Bank Top Stn.
1869	North Eastern	2-2-4 Tank	66	Aerolite	—	York Railway Museum
1870	Great Northern	4-2-2	1	—	8-footer	York Railway Museum
1874	North Eastern	0-6-0	1275	—	Long boiler	York Railway Museum
1875	North Eastern	2-4-0	910	—	Fletcher	York Railway Museum
1885	North Eastern	2-4-0	1463	—	Tennant	York Railway Museum
1893	North Eastern	4-4-0	1621	—	M1	York Railway Museum
1895	Great Eastern	2-4-0	490	—	T26	Clapham Railway Museum
1898	Great Northern	4-4-2	990	Henry Oakley	†C1	York Railway Museum
1902	Great Northern	4-4-2	251	—	—	York Railway Museum
1904	Great Eastern	0-6-0 Tank	87	—	†J67	Clapham Railway Museum
1913	North British	4-4-0	256	Glen Douglas	†D34	Glasgow
1920	Great North of Scotland	4-4-0	49	Gordon Highlander	†D40	Glasgow
1920	Great Central	4-4-0	506	Butler Henderson	†D11	Clapham Railway Museum
1938	London and North Eastern	4-6-2	4468	Mallard	†A4	Clapham Railway Museum
Scheduled for Preservation						
1911	Great Central	2-8-0	*63601	—	†O4	—
1919	North Eastern	0-8-0	*63460	—	T3	—
1936	London and North Eastern	2-6-2	4771	Green Arrow	V2	—
In private ownership and in full running order						
1899	Great Northern	0-6-0 Tank	1247	—	†J11	Keighley (a)
1921	London & North Eastern	0-6-2 Tank	4744	—	N2	Keighley (a)
1923	London & North Eastern	4-6-2	4472	Flying Scotsman	A1	Doncaster (b)
1937	London & North Eastern	2-6-0	3442	The Great Marquess	K4	Leeds (c)

(a) Owned by Keighley & Worth Valley Railway Preservation Society (b) Owned by Alan Pegler (c) Owned by Lord Garnock.
* B.R. numbering; † L.N.E.R. classification.

Brief reference also is necessary to Table 12, which lists all the full-size locomotives of the London & North Eastern Railway and its constituent companies which, as mentioned already in Chapter IX, are being preserved or are scheduled for preservation, in as nearly as possible their original condition and colours.   The original N.E.R. York Railway Museum houses eight of these; the Clapham Museum of British Railways in London four more, including the world-famous Gresley A4 Pacific *Mallard*; and the Scottish Region has two Scottish locomotives in store in Glasgow.   Where the remaining three scheduled for preservation are to be kept is not known at the time of writing.   In addition, there are four *ex*-L.N.E.R. locomotives in private ownership, including the Gresley Pacific *Flying Scotsman*, which during the 1960s has been leading a very active life hauling special trains of railway enthusiasts all over the country.   It is thus all to the good that we are to have these permanent reminders of the past glories of steam in Great Britain.

XX

L.N.E.R. Locomotives at Work

IN THE second half of the Nineteenth Century the Great Northern Railway
established a reputation for speed which had few if any rivals in Great
Britain. Foxwell and Farrer, in their 1889 classic *Express Trains English
and Foreign*, had no doubt about the matter. "The youngest of our
great companies . . . began life with the benefit of other people's experience", they wrote, "and instantly started off on a career of speed whose
brilliance has never since been dimmed. . . . It is the straightforward
dash of the Great Northern and the high standard of excellence maintained in all its services, which have won it the distinguished place it
holds in public estimation. . . . In matters of speed and smartness the
Great Northern has worked like an inspiriting leaven on everything it
has touched". In the first two decades of the Twentieth Century the
G.N.R. to some extent had rested on its laurels, but by the 1930s the
former tradition was being revived by the London & North Eastern
Railway, and by the latter part of the 1930 decade the L.N.E.R. could
claim to have outdistanced all its rivals in Great Britain.

At the beginning of the present century the North Eastern Railway
had introduced into its timetables the fastest scheduled run in the British
Empire—from Darlington to York, 44.1 miles, in 43 min., at 61.5 m.p.h.
By 1923 the Great Western Railway had just beaten this by booking its
"Cheltenham Flyer" over the 77.3 miles from Swindon to Paddington
in 75 min., at 61.8 m.p.h. Within nine years the latter time had come
down to 65 min., and for the first time in history a 70 m.p.h. schedule
—actually 71.4 m.p.h.—had appeared in a British timetable. Three
years later, with the introduction of the "Silver Jubilee", the London
& North Eastern Railway also could boast two 70.4 m.p.h. runs, one
in each direction over the 232.3 miles between King's Cross and Darlington in 198 min., and with the gradients to be surmounted and the speed
restrictions to be observed, these last bookings demanded considerably
harder locomotive work than any 65 min. timing over the practically
level and perfectly aligned course between Swindon and Paddington.

Finally, with the introduction in 1937 of the "Coronation", the blue
riband of speed came back into London & North Eastern hands with
the booking of this flyer over the 188.2 miles from King's Cross to York
in 157 min., at 71.9 m.p.h. These, of course, were individual trains
only out of the numerous expresses in the timetables, but they provided
evidence of the rapidly rising tendency of railway speed in these later

years, in which the L.N.E.R. was taking a leading part. The runs tabulated in this chapter, and about to be described, are selected examples only out of a vast mass of locomotive performance material available; a number also of them have figured in other books and magazine articles, but these are included as showing the maximum potentialities of the various locomotive classes concerned.

First to be dealt with are some runs with engines of the constituent companies, many of which were still in use well into the L.N.E.R. era. In Table 13 is seen a run recorded by R. J. Purves in 1911 on the then "Fastest Train in the British Empire", in which a light six-coach load of 165 tons was hauled by Wilson Worsdell's R class 4–4–0 No. 1672

Table 13

N.E.R. Class R 4–4–0 (L.N.E.R. Class D20)

Engine No. 1672

Load: 6 coaches, 152 tons tare, 165 tons gross.

Dist.		Sched.	Actual	Speeds
miles		min.	m. s.	m.p.h.
0.0	DARLINGTON	0	0 00	—
2.6	Croft Spa	—	3 54	66
5.2	Eryholme	—	6 14	69
6.9	Cowton	—	7 40	—
10.4	Danby Wiske	—	10 33	73
14.1	NORTHALLERTON	14	13 46	70½
17.5	Otterington	—	16 36	73½
21.9	THIRSK	21½	20 04	78
26.1	Sessay	—	23 33	—
28.0	Pilmoor	—	25 09	72
30.7	Raskelf	—	27 23	73½
32.9	Alne	32	29 09	76½
34.4	Tollerton	—	30 20	75
38.6	Beningbrough	—	33 45	74
42.5	Poppleton Junc.	40	37 00	*72½
44.1	YORK	43	39 34	—

*Before shutting off steam.

of the North Eastern Railway, one of the most competent of all locomotive types of this wheel arrangement at that time. An average speed of 72.8 m.p.h. was maintained over the 35 miles between mileposts 37 and 2, and of 75 m.p.h. over the 21.1 miles from Otterington to Beningbrough. So the booked time of 43 min. was cut to 39 min. 34 sec., and for a long time this remained the fastest known run over this particular course.

Table 14 sets out a 4–4–0 locomotive performance of a totally different order, which I recorded in the same year, 1911. The most exacting duty assigned to James Holden's Great Eastern Railway "Claud Hamilton" class locomotives was during the summer months on the "Norfolk Coast Express", in the days when families travelled from London to the coastal resorts by train in such numbers as to justify the running of a daily express which disdained to call at Colchester, Ipswich and even Norwich, and so was booked to cover the 130.1 miles in each direction between Liverpool Street and North Walsham non-stop. Included in the journey were some awkward gradients, such as the ascents of Bethnal Green and Brentwood banks, service slacks round the curves at Stratford, Chelmsford, Colchester and Ipswich, and a snail's pace over the Wensum swing-bridge and sharp curve at Norwich, followed by the steep climb from Whitlingham Junction. For a 50-ton locomotive innocent of any such modern improvements as superheating or long valve-travel, and with a load never less than 12 coaches and at peak periods up to 13, 14 and even 15, this was a tough assignment indeed.

Table 14

G.E.R. "Claud Hamilton" Class 4-4-0

Engine No. 1809

Load : 14 coaches, 371 *tons tare,* 400 *tons gross*

Dist.		Sched.	Actual		Speeds
miles		min.	m	s.	m.p.h.
0.0	NORTH WALSHAM	0	0	00	—
7.3	Wroxham	—	10	04	*45
15.3	*Wensum Junction*	21	21	35	*15
17.2	*Trowse Upper Junction*	—	26	08	—
29.6	Tivetshall	43	43	31	—
35.1	Diss	—	49	25	66
43.5	Finningham	—	59	14	47½
47.2	Haughley	62	63	30	—
49.5	STOWMARKET	64	65	25	74
61.4	IPSWICH	76	76	25	*40
64.9	*Belstead*	—	81	39	31
70.6	MANNINGTREE	88	88	29	67/40½
78.4	COLCHESTER	98	97	20	*55
83.5	Marks Tey	—	103	05	—
91.5	WITHAM	113	111	51	—
100.4	CHELMSFORD	123	121	46	—
109.9	SHENFIELD	134	134	09	—
110.8	*Ingrave*	—	135	39	36
120.1	Chadwell Heath	144	144	20	†76½
			sigs		—
126.1	STRATFORD	151	150	40	*35
129.0	Bethnal Green	—	155	10	*25
130.1	LIVERPOOL STREET	159	157	24	—

Speed restriction.   †At Harold Wood.

Yet the timekeeping was exemplary, as on the run here detailed, with a gross load of no less than 400 tons. A little time was dropped on the uphill stages, such as 7½-mile climb to Finningham, and the 10½ miles from Chelmsford to Ingrave, but was more than recovered on the easier stretches; with top speeds of 74 m.p.h. beyond Stowmarket and 76½ m.p.h. at Harold Wood, Driver Cage had the satisfaction of bringing his train into Liverpool Street just ahead of time, having covered the 130.1 miles in 157 min. 24 sec., or 157 min. net, the latter 2 min. less than the 159 min. allowed. For a 50-ton locomotive to work a 400-ton train over the 96.5 miles from Tivetshall to Stratford at an average speed of 54 m.p.h. was no mean achievement.

Hull Inward Marshalling Yard, showing the hump, king points and four retarders between queen and jack points.

Above: Control cabin at Whitemoor up marshalling yard, which at the time of its opening in 1929 was the biggest of its kind in Europe and the first in Great Britain to be equipped with rail-brakes.

Below: Wagons coming over the hump at the down yard at Whitemoor (near March in Cambridgeshire), completed in 1933. [*British Railways*

NORTH EASTERN RAILWAY WAGON TYPES BROUGHT INTO L.N.E.R. STOCK

From top to bottom:

40-ton quintuple bolster wagon

40-ton double hopper mineral wagon

30-ton hopper wagon for ironstone

20-ton wooden-bodied coal wagon

[*British Railways*]

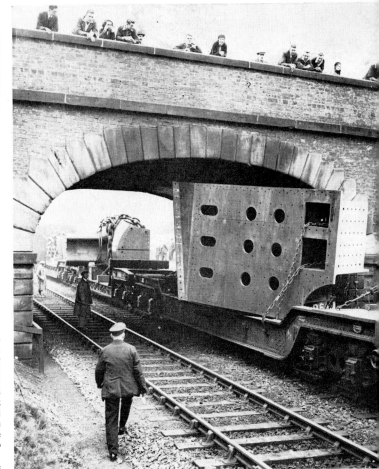

Above: For dealing with exceptional loads—a North Eastern Area wagon set to carry a maximum of 150 tons. The girders at both ends act as cantilevers to take balance weights for the relief of loading on the two central 12-wheel bogies. Total number of wheels, including those of the end trucks, 64.

Right: Handling loads of exceptional size. Eight castings, weighing 625 tons in all, for building into a new Cunard liner, en route from Darlington Forge to Middlesbrough Docks for shipment. The movement took place on a Sunday, and required complete possession of both tracks, with clearance under some bridges of no more than a few inches.

[*British Railways*

Robinson 2–8–0 freight locomotive with train of the former Great Central Railway—a type selected by the War Department for mass building during the First World War, a large number being taken into the L.N.E.R. stock after the war ended.

Above: The first Gresley mixed traffic 2–6–2 of Class VI, No. 4771 *Green Arrow*, on the afternoon "Scotch Goods", timed over certain sections of its journey at more than 50 m.p.h.

Below: The most powerful locomotive ever built for the L.N.E.R., the 2–8–8–2 Garratt, No. 2395 in the L.N.E.R. list, used for banking heavy coal trains up the 1 in 40 Worsborough bank, near Barnsley. This photograph, taken in British Railways days, shows the engine under test up the gradient from Dinting to Woodhead with oil firing instead of coal.

[*British Railways*

It was in 1922, the year before the grouping, that I made the journey set out in Table 15 on what shortly afterwards became known as the "Hook Continental", which a 64-ton 1500 class 4–6–0 had to work over the 68.9 miles from Liverpool Street to Parkeston Quay in 82 min.—another extremely exacting duty, even if of short duration, with a load exceeding 400 tons. I was riding on the footplate of No. 1566 with

Table 15

G.E.R. "1500" Class 4–6–0 (L.N.E.R. Class B12)

Engine No. 1566

Load : 14 coaches, 388 tons tare, 415 tons gross

Dist.		Sched.	Actual		Speeds
miles		min.	m.	s.	m.p.h.
0.0	LIVERPOOL STREET	0	0	00	—
1.1	Bethnal Green	—	3	25	—
4.0	STRATFORD	8	7	50	*40
7.3	Ilford	—	11	55	—
10.0	Chadwell Heath	15	14	50	55
15.0	Harold Wood	—	20	15	55
			sigs.		*35
18.2	Brentwood	—	24	25	33
19.3	Ingrave	—	26	25	33
20.2	SHENFIELD	28	27	40	—
23.6	Ingatestone	—	31	00	71½
29.7	CHELMSFORD	38	36	30	*55
35.9	Hatfield Peverel	—	42	50	—
38.6	WITHAM	48	45	35	66
42.3	Kelvedon	—	49	10	†50
46.6	Marks Tey	—	53	40	‡70½
51.7	COLCHESTER	61	58	25	*50
54.1	Parsons Heath	—	61	10	—
56.0	Ardleigh	—	63	35	—
59.5	MANNINGTREE	70	67	20	67/*30
61.2	Mistley	—	70	15	—
65.1	Wrabness	—	75	20	—
68.9	PARKESTON QUAY	82	80	15	—

*Speed restriction.　　　†At Hill House.　　　‡At Lexden.

Driver Harry Chapman, one of a link of highly competent Parkeston enginemen who regarded it as a point of honour to keep time with this "star" Great Eastern express. Bethnal Green bank, though short, is inclined at 1 in 70; a worse handicap is the 3 miles averaging 1 in 100 past Brentwood to Ingrave summit, in the middle of which a signal check brought speed down to 35 m.p.h. The engine was then opened out to 50 per cent. cut-off with full regulator, which kept the train moving at 33 m.p.h. even up a short strip of 1 in 85 gradient. From Shenfield onwards the average cut-off was about 25 per cent., with the regulator from one-quarter to three-quarters open, according to the gradients; so time was kept with 1½ min. to spare.

In London & North Eastern days, when Edward Thompson was in charge at Stratford Works as Mechanical Engineer, a number of engines of Class B12, as the G.E.R. 1500s were now classified, received new boilers with round-topped fireboxes, and modified valve-setting to permit short cut-off working, which greatly increased their capacity for speed. No. 8535, so improved, was once timed, with a ten-coach train of 305 tons, to climb the 15.3 miles from Ipswich to milepost 84 in 16 min. 44 sec., and to reach 90 m.p.h. on the subsequent descent before being pulled up at Diss because a carriage door had come open. The 26.3 miles to this point had been run in 25 min. 59 sec. From the fresh start, Trowse Upper Junction, 17.9 miles, was passed in 18 min. 12 sec., with a top speed of 84 m.p.h. at Flordon; the equivalent net non-stop time of this run over the 46.3 miles from Ipswich to Norwich could have been no more than 43½ min.

On the Great Central Railway some of the stiffest tasks faced by the Robinson Atlantics were after the formation of the L.N.E.R., and one

Table 16

G.C.R. Robinson 4–4–2 (L.N.E.R. Class C4)

Engine No. 5361

Load to Finmere: 8 coaches, 280/295 tons.

Load to Woodford: 7 coaches, 243/255 tons.

Load to Leicester: 6 coaches, 206/215 tons.

Dist.		Sched.	Actual		Speeds
miles		*min.*	*m.*	*s.*	*m.p.h.*
0.0	MARYLEBONE	0	0	00	—
3.0	Brondesbury	—	6	50	31½/59
5.1	*Neasden Junc.*	9	9	30	*45
7.9	Sudbury	—	13	00	45
9.7	South Harrow	—	15	10	59
11.6	*Northolt Junc.*	17	17	40	*38
13.4	Ruislip	—	20	05	—
16.1	Denham	—	23	10	55
18.8	Gerrards Cross	—	26	15	47½
23.0	Beaconsfield	—	31	35	49/68
27.9	HIGH WYCOMBE	35	36	20	*45
30.1	West Wycombe	—	39	20	46
32.8	Saunderton	—	43	15	41
36.0	PRINCES RISBOROUGH	45	47	20	—
41.4	Haddenham	—	51	50	79
45.4	*Ashendon Junc.*	—	55	15	71½
51.3	*Grendon Junc.*	60	60	50	61½
53.3	Calvert	—	62	45	60/67
59.0	Finmere (slip)	68	68	15	53½/67
63.8	Brackley	—	73	05	60
67.0	Helmdon	—	76	35	55
70.6	Culworth	—	80	05	72½
73.6	WOODFORD (slip)	81	82	40	—
76.0	Charwelton	—	84	55	64½
83.0	Braunston	—	90	30	85
87.7	RUGBY	—	94	30	60/68
94.5	Lutterworth	—	101	05	†55½/67
98.4	Ashby Magna	—	104	45	58½/71½
102.9	Whetstone	—	108	20	80½
107.0	*Goods Junc. North*	—	111	40	—
107.6	LEICESTER	114	112	40	—

*Speed restriction.   †At Shawell.

in particular was the 6.20 p.m. express from Marylebone to Bradford, generally worked as far as Leicester by one of these engines with a crew from Leicester depot, which had a good reputation for timekeeping. As Table 16 shows, this train went out of London with eight coaches, but shed one by slipping at Finmere, and a second at Woodford. On the journey, a little time was dropped on the 1 in 105 climb through the Chilterns, but from Princes Risborough onwards the loss was steadily recouped. The minimum speeds of 53½ and 55 m.p.h. up the long 1 in 176 claims to Finmere and Helmdon were very good, and maximum speeds of 79 m.p.h. at Haddenham, 85 at Braunston and 80½ at Whetstone more than ensured timekeeping. The 71.0 miles from Princes Risborough to Leicester Goods Junction were reeled off at an average speed of 66.2 m.p.h., and Leicester was reached in 112 min. 40 sec., 1½ min. early.

Robinson's "Director" class 4–4–0s, first introduced in 1913, worked interchangeably with the Atlantics, and a typical run with one of the second batch, No. 5502 *Zeebrugge* (L.N.E.R. Class D11) is seen in Table 17. The start out of Marylebone was so vigorous, with a minimum

Table 17

G.C.R. "Director" Class 4–4–0 (L.N.E.R. Class D11)
Engine No. 5502 Zeebrugge
Load: 6 coaches, 204 tons tare, 215 tons gross

Dist.		Sched.	Actual		Speeds
miles		min.	m.	s.	m.p.h.
0.0	MARYLEBONE	0	0	00	—
5.1	Neasden Junc.	9	8	30	67
9.2	HARROW	14	12	35	48
11.4	Pinner	—	14	50	64½
13.7	Northwood	—	17	10	55½/69
17.2	Rickmansworth	23	20	40	*38
19.4	Chorley Wood	—	23	50	40
21.6	Chalfont	29	27	10	39
23.6	AMERSHAM	—	30	10	—
28.8	Great Missenden	36	35	20	72½/49½
33.3	Wendover	—	40	05	70
38.0	AYLESBURY	46	44	15	*45/65
44.1	Quainton Road Junc.	53	50	10	*50
46.8	Grendon Junc.	—	52	55	67
48.8	Calvert	—	54	50	58/65
54.5	Finmere	—	60	30	53/67
59.3	Brackley	—	65	20	61
62.5	Helmdon	—	68	50	54
			p.w.s.		*25
66.1	Culworth	—	73	10	—
69.1	WOODFORD	77	76	10	—
71.5	Charwelton	—	78	45	62
78.5	Braunston	—	84	45	75
83.2	RUGBY	—	88	55	60/68
90.0	Lutterworth	—	95	30	†55/66
93.9	Ashby Magna	—	99	05	—
98.4	Whetstone	—	103	05	75
103.1	LEICESTER	109	107	50	—

*Speed restriction.   †At Shawell.

speed as high as 48 m.p.h. maintained up the 1 in 93-100 to Harrow, that 2¼ min. had been gained by Rickmansworth; the driver was thus able to take matters easily up the 6 miles at 1 in 105 to Amersham, with speed sustained at 40-49 m.p.h. The climbing between Calvert and Helmdon was very similar to that of the Atlantic, but after Woodford, with time again in hand, no higher speed than 75 m.p.h. was reached on the down grades, and even so there was a gain of just over a minute to Leicester. The Great Central never attracted any substantial traffic to its main line, and six-coach loads, such as the 215 gross tons on this run, were a normal formation with the faster trains on the London Extension.

None of the North British main lines, except those from Edinburgh to Berwick and Glasgow respectively, offered much scope for high speed; the East Coast expresses on the Berwick line were, of course, worked by North Eastern locomotives, but the almost dead level line between Edinburgh and Cowlairs, at the crest of the famous Cowlairs bank, seldom tempted N.B.R. drivers to any speed much over 60 m.p.h. Over the other main lines long and severe gradients, even with fairly generous schedules, needed hard steaming, and the Edinburgh-Aberdeen main line, with its starts in both directions out of almost every one of the intermediate stops up steep inclines, has always been one of the most difficult in the country from the locomotive point of view. Thus unspectacular running but exact timekeeping were a general tradition with North British drivers.

A typical run with a Reid Atlantic from Aberdeen southwards to Dundee appears in Table 18. Up to Ferryhill Junction, from the platform end at Aberdeen, the locomotive faces a gradient of 1 in 96; then comes the long climb averaging about 1 in 130 to milepost 234, on which speed varied between 34 m.p.h. on the 1 in 102 at Cove Bay, and 40½ on the final 1 in 160. The conditional stop was called at Stonehaven; after this, on the lengthy climb to Carmont, 35¼ m.p.h. was sustained on the final 1 in 102. The Caledonian line, with its descents to Fordoun and past Marykirk, now offered some scope for speed, but the maximum was no higher than 72½ m.p.h.; this, however, was enough to secure an arrival at Montrose 1½ min. early, conditional stop included. Up the 1 in 88-111 out of Montrose 35 m.p.h. was attained; then, after Arbroath, came a typical piece of North British running, for no higher rate than 60 m.p.h. was reached on the 14 miles of dead level past Carnoustie; even so, however, the Arbroath-Dundee run was completed well inside booked time.

From this rather humdrum North British Atlantic performance we pass to a run by two of the Raven Z class 4–4–2s of the North Eastern Railway, first introduced in 1911. The train concerned was the popular 5.30 p.m. from King's Cross to Newcastle, at the time when H. A. Watson, the N.E.R. General Superintendent, had revived the idea, first tried in summer with the down "Flying Scotsman" as far back as 1903, of cutting out the York stop. In the case of the 5.30 p.m. down, in 1921, this introduced a non-stop run over the 126.8 miles from Grantham to Darlington, for which a not very exhausting time of 142 min. was laid down.   Every day a North Eastern Atlantic worked the same train in the opposite direction over the Great Northern line as far south as Grantham, and waited there to head the 5.30 p.m. from London back to Newcastle, as was the case on the run in Table 19.

Table 18

N.B.R. Reid 4–4–2 (L.N.E.R. Class C8)

Engine No. 9868 Aberdonian.

Load : 278 tons tare, 295 tons gross.

Dist.		Sched.	Actual		Speeds
miles		*min.*	*m.*	*s.*	*m.p.h.*
0.0	ABERDEEN	0	0	00	—
0.6	*Ferryhill Junc.*	2	2	15	39
4.8	Cove Bay	—	9	20	34
7.0	*Milepost* 234	—	13	00	40½
11.6	Muchalls	—	17	55	—
16.2	†STONEHAVEN {	pass	24	15	—
		26	25	10	—
21.6	Carmont	—	36	05	40/35½
23.3	Drumlithie	—	38	25	—
27.3	Fordoun	—	42	05	71½
30.6	Laurencekirk	—	45	05	57
33.8	Marykirk	—	48	20	72½
38.0	*Kinnaber Junc.*	54	52	40	*30
40.7	MONTROSE	58	56	25	—
4.2	*Milepost* 85¾	—	8	40	35
7.5	Inverkeilor	13	12	40	—
10.7	Letham Grange	—	16	35	—
13.6	ARBROATH	21	20	35	—
1.8	Elliott Junc.	—	3	30	49½
6.2	Carnoustie	—	8	55	59
13.1	Broughty Ferry	15	16	05	60
16.3	*Camperdown Junc.*	20	19	35	*20
17.0	DUNDEE	23	21	20	—

Speed restriction.   †Conditional stop.

What possessed Driver Redfern to run so far in advance of time I have no idea, but his 65 min. 5 sec. for the 68.9 miles from Grantham to passing Selby was the fastest that I had recorded up to that time over this section.   The 60.1 miles from Barkston to Templehirst were covered in 53 min. 35 sec., at an average speed of 67.3 m.p.h.   With a normal finish from Selby we should have reached York in 81 min. from Grantham, as compared with the 94 min. allowed this train until the York stop was cut out; but at the approach to York the driver realised that No. 721 was running hot, and that a stop would be necessary to obtain a replacement.   This proved to be No. 2172 of the same type, which then proceeded to cover the 44.1 miles to Darlington in 44 min. 15 sec., 4¾ min. inside schedule time, with speed sustained steadily at 67 to 72½ m.p.h. against the rising tendency of the line across the Great Plain of York, and with a momentary 76½ m.p.h. at Danby Wiske. Putting the two halves of this journey together, the net non-stop time from Grantham to Darlington would have been not more than 125 min. for the 126.8 miles, 17 min. less than the 142 min. scheduled.

This brings us to the performances of the Ivatt Atlantics of the Great Northern Railway. Their designer had laid it down that the measure of a locomotive's ability is its "capacity to boil water", and the 5 ft. 6 in. diameter boiler, with its wide firebox, first fitted to No. 251 in 1902

Table 19

N.E.R. Class Z 4–4–2 (L.N.E.R. Class C7)

Engine: Grantham—York, No. 721

Engine: York—Darlington, No. 2172

Load: 9 coaches, 264 tons tare, 280 tons gross.

Dist.		Sched.	Actual		Speeds
miles		min.	m.	s.	m.p.h.
0.0	GRANTHAM	0	0	00	—
4.2	Barkston South Junc.	—	6	40	69
6.0	Hougham	—	8	10	75
9.9	Claypole	—	11	20	70½
14.6	NEWARK	16	15	15	77½
20.9	Carlton	—	20	20	72½
25.8	Dukeries Junc.	—	24	55	59/61½
28.2	Markham	—	27	20	59
30.0	Gamston	—	29	00	67
33.1	RETFORD	36	32	00	*55
38.4	Ranskill	—	37	00	71½/75
42.2	Bawtry	—	40	10	—
44.0	Pipers Wood	—	41	50	61½
45.8	Rossington	—	43	30	70½/72
50.5	DONCASTER	54	47	30	67
54.7	Shaftholme Junc.	59	51	25	63
57.5	Moss	—	54	10	64
60.5	Balne	—	56	55	68/67
64.3	Templehirst	—	60	15	71½
68.9	SELBY	77	65	05	*30
73.0	Riccall	—	70	40	57½
—		—	sig. stop		*0
82.4	YORK (LOCO. YARD)	†93	‡86	25	—
0.0	YORK (STATION)	†0	‡ 0	00	—
1.6	Poppleton Junc.	3	4	20	—
5.5	Beningbrough	—	9	20	57½
9.7	Tollerton	—	13	25	67
11.2	Alne	14	14	45	68
13.4	Raskelf	—	16	40	69
16.1	Pilmoor	—	19	10	69
18.0	Sessay	—	20	50	70½
22.2	THIRSK	26	24	25	72½
26.5	Otterington	—	28	05	71½
29.9	NORTHALLERTON	34	31	05	70½
33.7	Danby Wiske	—	34	20	76½
37.2	Cowton	—	37	10	69
38.9	Eryholme	42	38	40	69
41.5	Croft Spa	—	40	50	77½
44.1	DARLINGTON	49	44	15	—

*Speed restriction.   †Passing time.   ‡Stopping and starting times.

was exceptionally large for its time.   But as we have seen in Chapter XV
this boiler was mated to cylinders of the unusually limited dimensions
of no more than 18¾ in. diameter and 24 in. stroke, with the result that
in their early days these machines were distinctly sluggish in their
movements.   As with so many other British express passenger types,
however, superheating greatly improved their performance, though
even with cylinders enlarged to 20 in. diameter the tractive effort was
still no more than 17,340 lb., compared with the 19,300 lb. of a North
Eastern Z class Atlantic, with three 16½ in. by 26 in. cylinders.

But it was after Gresley had fitted all the Ivatt Atlantics with 32-ele-
ment superheaters, beginning with No. 1403 in 1919, that their performance was revolutionised.   Table 20 shows what one of them could do
with a relatively light load of seven Pullmans, on the down "Queen
of Scots".   After a normal start, No. 4460 was opened out to some
purpose, maintaining an average speed of 83 m.p.h. over the 30.3 miles
from Stevenage to Huntingdon, with a maximum of 90, and of just
under 78 m.p.h. over the 54.9 miles from Hatfield to Yaxley, with this
290-ton load.

A far more notable achievement was one which I timed personally
in 1936.   By the middle 1930s some of the East Coast expresses had
grown to formations of anything from 15 or 16 coaches upwards; on

Table 20

G.N.R. Ivatt 4–4–2 (L.N.E.R. Class C1)

Engine No. 4460

Load: 7 Pullmans, 275 tons tare, 290 tons gross.

Dist.		Sched.	Actual		Speeds
miles		min.	m.	s.	m.p.h.
0.0	KING'S CROSS	0	0	00	—
2.5	FINSBURY PARK	—	6	27	—
5.0	Wood Green	—	9	44	52
9.2	New Barnet	—	14	45	46½
12.7	Potters Bar	—	19	25	44
17.7	HATFIELD	24	24	19	74
20.3	Welwyn Garden City	—	26	24	67
23.5	*Woolmer Green*	—	29	19	64
28.6	Stevenage	—	33	34	74
31.9	HITCHIN	37	36	05	86
35.7	Three Counties	—	38	38	90
37.0	Arlesey	—	39	32	87
41.1	Biggleswade	—	42	22	88
44.1	Sandy	—	44	46	82
47.5	Tempsford	—	46	52	80½
51.7	St. Neots	—	50	02	77½
56.0	Offord	—	53	14	80½
58.9	HUNTINGDON	59	55	28	74
62.0	*Milepost 62*	—	58	10	64
63.5	Abbots Ripton	—	59	34	66
69.4	Holme	—	63	56	83
72.6	Yaxley	—	66	36	63½
76.4	PETERBOROUGH	†77	†70	34	*20

*Speed restriction.   *†Passing time.*

this run the 1.20 p.m. from King's Cross to Edinburgh was a 17-coach train, with a crowded passenger complement, 546 tons tare in weight and 585 tons gross.   After our A3 Pacific had climbed to Stoke Summit, signs of overheating betrayed themselves, and a change of engine at Grantham became imperative.   The only locomotive immediately available was Ivatt Atlantic No. 4404, which was duly substituted. It took no small effort for the 69-ton 4-4-2, with no more than 40 tons adhesion weight, to get this enormous train on the move, and with nearly 2½ min. dropped on schedule to Newark (Table 21) I anticipated a considerable loss of time.

Table 21

G.N.R. Ivatt 4-4-2 (L.N.E.R. Class C1)

Engine No. 4404

Load : 17 coaches, 546 tons tare, 585 tons gross

Dist.		Sched.	Actual		Speeds
miles		*min.*	*m.*	*s.*	*m.p.h.*
0.0	**GRANTHAM**	0	0	00	—
4.2	*Barkston S. Junc.*	6	8	17	—
9.9	Claypole	—	13	23	74
14.6	**NEWARK**	15	17	23	—
20.9	Carlton-on-Trent	—	23	22	64½
25.8	*Dukeries Junc.*	—	28	30	48
28.2	Markham	—	31	31	48½/77½
33.1	**RETFORD**	35	36	15	*70
36.2	Sutton	—	38	49	72½
38.4	Ranskill	—	40	37	74
42.2	Bawtry	—	43	43	75
44.0	Pipers Wood	—	45	22	61
47.7	*Black Carr Junc.*	—	48	38	72½
50.5	**DONCASTER**	53	51	19	*55
54.7	*Shaftholme Junc.*	58	55	36	62½
57.5	Moss	—	58	15	64
60.5	Balne	—	61	02	65/60
64.3	Templehirst	—	64	42	66
67.5	*Brayton Junc.*	—	67	41	—
68.9	**SELBY**	73	69	17	*30
73.0	Riccall	—	75	18	55
75.6	Escrick	—	78	04	59
78.5	Naburn	—	80	56	60
80.7	*Chaloners Whin Junc.*	—	83	09	—
			sigs		*20
82.7	**YORK**	90	87	40	—

*Speed restriction.

Not so, however.   From Newark onwards there was a steady time recovery, and from Ranskill to Bawtry the 4-4-2 was actually maintaining up to 75 m.p.h. on little easier than level track.   After the Doncaster slack, also, from 64 to 66 m.p.h. was sustained on almost dead level track from Shaftholme Junction to Selby, where an over-cautious slack was made for the curve—30 m.p.h. instead of the permitted 40.   Signals outside York caused a loss of 1½ min.; otherwise the astonishing feat would have been achieved, by a locomotive of such limited dimensions, of working this 585-ton train over the 82.7 miles from Grantham to York in 86 min., 4 min. inside the time allowed for Pacific haulage. It is doubtful if any finer performance has ever been recorded with an engine of this type, and it was all the more remarkable in that the engine-crew, Driver Walker and Fireman Barrick, were North Eastern men from Gateshead depot, and therefore almost complete strangers to an Ivatt Atlantic.

But when we come to the Gresley Pacifics, it is to a range of locomotive performance which includes some well-night legendary feats. The original A1 Pacifics, as we have seen in Chapter XVII, though capable of hard work, were not seen at their best until after the modifications of the valve-motion that followed the 1925 locomotive exchange with the Great Western Railway. What their possibilities then became in the speed realm was made abundantly clear in the trial run from King's Cross to Leeds and back, in November, 1934, referred to in Chapter XVII, which was one of the experiments preceding the introduction in 1935 of the "Silver Jubilee".

On the Leeds run No. 4472 *Flying Scotsman*, with Bill Sparshatt at the regulator, established a still unbeaten record by covering the 185.8 miles from King's Cross to Leeds in 2 hours, 31 min. 56 sec.; for the first time in history the long climb to Stoke Summit was completed with a minimum speed of 81 m.p.h.; and in the first 2 hours from London No. 4472 covered 153¾ miles. True, this was with a light four-coach load of 147 tons; but on the return journey, with six coaches of 208 gross tons weight, the time taken was only just over 5 min. more, and down Stoke bank we had the satisfaction of clocking a top speed of exactly 100 m.p.h. In the one round trip that day, the A1 Pacific had covered 40 miles at 90 m.p.h. and 250 miles at an average of 80 m.p.h.

A year and a half later another A1 Pacific, No. 4473 *Solario*, was responsible for an outstanding performance in very different loading conditions. The train was the summer "Scarborough Flyer", with a gross load of all but 400 tons, and the driver was Duddington, destined to achieve renown in 1938 by attaining the world's highest speed record with steam power. The "Flyer" had left King's Cross 3 min. late, and had been further delayed by an out-of-course stop at Welwyn Garden City to secure a carriage headboard, which an alert signalman had noted to be coming adrift. The express was thus 10½ min. late past Hitchin.

Then followed an astonishing performance, for the A1 Pacific, with 395 tons of train as compared with the 265 tons gross of the "Jubilee", kept the latter's schedule time throughout from Hitchin to Selby; while from Hitchin to York the "Scarborough Flyer" timing was cut by 15½ min., York being reached 5 min. early. The net time for the 188.2 miles from King's Cross to York was 162 min., compared with the 180 min. allowed; over the 50.5 miles from Grantham to Doncaster an average speed of 79.2 m.p.h. was maintained. This run, recorded by the late R. E. Charlewood, is set out in Table 22.

L

Some of the performances put up by the Gresley A1 Pacifics with the vast loads that became general after the outbreak of war in 1939 provided more than ample proof of the designer's claim, when the first of this class appeared in 1922, that they would be able to handle 600-ton trains. I was travelling south one day when the "Flying Scotsman" was made up to 20 coaches, weighing 644 tons tare, and with compartments and corridors so packed with 950 passengers and their luggage

Table 22

L.N.E.R. Class A1† Gresley 4–6–2

Engine No. 4473 Solario

Load : 11 coaches, 371 tons tare, 395 tons gross.

Dist.		Sched.	Actual	Speeds
miles		*min.*	*m. s.*	*m.p.h.*
0.00	KING'S CROSS	0	0 00	—
2.50	FINSBURY PARK	—	6 16	—
4.95	Wood Green	—	9 11	—
12.70	Potters Bar	—	17 37	—
17.70	HATFIELD	22	21 55	77
		—	*sig. stop*	*0
23.50	*Woolmer Green*	—	35 20	51½
28.55	Stevenage	—	40 04	72
31.90	HITCHIN	35	42 38	80½
37.10	Arlesey	—	46 04	91
44.15	Sandy	—	51 02	85½
51.75	St. Neots	—	56 41	76
55.95	Offord	—	59 51	81
58.85	HUNTINGDON	56	62 07	74
62.00	*Milepost* 62	—	64 49	65½
69.35	Holme	—	70 30	83½
		—	*sigs.*	*38
75.00	*Fletton Junc.*	—	75 21	*38
76.35	PETERBOROUGH	73	77 23	*26
79.50	*Werrington Junc.*	—	81 27	60
84.85	Tallington	—	86 18	—
88.65	Essendine	—	89 36	68
92.25	Little Bytham	—	92 47	—
97.10	Corby Glen	—	97 30	60
100.10	*Stoke*	—	100 27	57½
105.45	GRANTHAM	102	104 40	81½
109.70	*Barkston South Junc.*	—	107 49	90
120.10	NEWARK	114	114 56	85
126.30	Carlton	—	119 33	82
133.75	*Markham*	—	125 45	64/84
138.60	RETFORD	132	129 40	*75
143.95	Ranskill	—	133 31	81½
149.50	*Pipers Wood*	—	137 48	71/83½
155.95	DONCASTER	147	142 55	*67
160.20	*Shaftholme Junc.*	151	146 20	—
165.90	Balne	—	150 51	76
173.00	*Brayton Junc.*	—	156 11	—
174.30	SELBY	164	157 53	*34
178.50	Riccall	—	162 31	62
183.95	Naburn	—	167 14	72
186.15	*Chaloners Whin Junc.*	—	169 08	—
188.15	YORK	180	172 06	—

Speed restriction.   †*Original Class A1.*

that the gross weight of the train must have been at least 720 tons. Out of York No. 2576 *The White Knight* passed Arksey, 30.1 miles, in 37 min. 8 sec., including the Selby slack, after which we had attained 59 m.p.h. on the level. Fine work was done thence to Grantham, with 70½ m.p.h. attained at Crow Park and a minimum of 43 m.p.h. up the 1 in 200 past Barkston, which, 46.3 miles from Doncaster, was passed in 54 min. 33 sec. On both these stages time was being gained, but was more than lost by concluding signal stops.

At Grantham No. 2545 *Diamond Jubilee* replaced No. 2576, and after taking 12 min. to climb the 5.4 miles of 1 in 200 to Stoke Summit, attained 74 m.p.h. at Essendine, and passed Werrington Junction, 26.0 miles, in 30 min. 48 sec., only to be stopped once again by signal outside Peterborough. From here to King's Cross, however, there was an actual gain of all but 5 min., the 76.4 miles being run in 89 min. 10 sec., with no lower speeds than 44 and 38 m.p.h. respectively up the 1 in 200 climbs past Abbots Ripton and from Hitchin to Stevenage, and 70 m.p.h. reached at Hatfield and Wood Green. Between them the two A1 Pacifics gained a net total of 16 min., on the eased-out war timings certainly, but in these most onerous load conditions.

The next development of the Gresley Pacific design, in addition to the improved valve-setting which had made possible with the A1s performances of the quality just described, was the fitting of boilers carrying 220 lb. pressure in place of the original 180 lb., to what now became Class A3. With this change the capacity of the Pacifics for sustained high speed was steadily increasing. On the second test run that preceded the introduction of the "Silver Jubilee", A3 4–6–2 No. 2760 *Papyrus* in March, 1935, covered 300 miles out of a total round trip of 536½ miles from London to Newcastle and back at a mean speed of 80 m.p.h., with a six-coach load of 217 tons. On the up journey Driver Sparshatt had the satisfaction of pushing the maximum speed record up to 108 m.p.h., the highest recorded in Great Britain up to that date, again on the descent of the racing stretch southwards from Stoke Summit.

Four years later, on two days in the same week, an A3 Pacific was commandeered at short notice at Newcastle to replace an A4 which had developed a defect when working the up "Coronation" streamliner from Edinburgh. Of the two engines concerned No. 2595 *Trigo* completed the run of 268.3 miles from Newcastle to King's Cross in 229 min., or 225 min. net, while No. 2507 *Singapore* beat this with an actual time of 227½ min. and a net time of 222½ min., the latter entailing an average speed of 72.3 m.p.h. for the whole distance with a 295-ton train.

Table 23 sets out the details of yet another performance with an outsize load, which I recorded in the summer of 1933 when peacetime schedules were being worked to. The train was the 1.13 p.m. from Doncaster to King's Cross, a 19-coach formation of 622 tons tare and 665 tons gross, the working southwards of which was shared by A1 Pacific No. 2549 *Persimmon* to Peterborough, and A3 Pacific No. 2744 *Grand*

Parade thence to King's Cross. Both engines succeeded in recovering part of a 19 min. late start. Specially notable was the time of 23 min. 50 sec. for the climb of 20.0 miles from Newark to Stoke Summit, with a minimum speed of 37½ m.p.h. on the final 1 in 200; then followed a speed of 79 to 80 m.p.h. from Little Bytham to Essendine. So the A1, with a time of 85 min. 11 sec. for the 79.4 miles from Doncaster to Peter-borough, gained all but 6 min. on schedule. The speed of the A3 fell

Table 23

L.N.E.R. Classes A1 & A3 Gresley 4–6–2

Engine, Doncaster—Peterborough, No. 2549 Persimmon (A1).

Engine, Peterborough—King's Cross, No. 2744, Grand Parade (A3).

Load : 19 coaches, 622 tons tare, 660 tons gross.

Dist.		Sched.	Actual		Speeds
miles		min.	m.	s.	m.p.h.
0.0	DONCASTER	0	0	00	—
4.7	Rossington	—	7	53	50
6.5	*Pipers Wood*	—	10	20	44
8.3	Bawtry	—	12	17	64
12.1	Ranskill	—	15	55	60
17.6	RETFORD	20	21	23	55½
22.5	*Markham*	—	27	19	43½
24.9	*Dukeries Junc.*	—	29	57	—
29.8	Carlton	—	34	09	74
35.9	NEWARK	41	39	36	65
40.6	Claypole	—	44	11	60
46.3	*Barkston South Junc.*	—	50	27	44
50.5	GRANTHAM	58	55	52	50
54.0	Great Ponton	—	60	29	—
55.9	*Stoke*	—	63	32	37½
58.9	Corby Glen	—	66	54	—
63.8	Little Bytham	—	70	57	80
67.4	Essendine	—	73	40	79
71.2	Tallington	—	76	41	71½
76.5	*Werrington Junc.*	—	81	15	69
79.6	PETERBOROUGH	91	85	11	—
3.8	Yaxley	—	7	39	—
7.0	Holme	—	11	07	57½
12.9	Abbots Ripton	—	18	01	36½
17.5	HUNTINGDON	22	23	51	64
20.4	Offord	—	26	38	62
24.7	St. Neots	—	30	54	52
28.9	Tempsford	—	35	09	66
32.3	Sandy	—	38	24	60
35.3	Biggleswade	—	41	28	57
39.4	Arlesey	—	45	41	61
44.5	HITCHIN	50	51	09	—
47.8	Stevenage	—	55	33	43
51.4	Knebworth	—	59	44	—
54.4	Welwyn North	—	62	58	—
58.7	HATFIELD	67	66	38	74
63.7	Potters Bar	—	71	19	59
67.2	New Barnet	—	74	37	—
71.4	Wood Green	—	78	02	75
73.9	FINSBURY PARK	—	80	19	—
76.4	KING'S CROSS	87	85	51	—

to 36½ m.p.h. up the 1 in 200 past Abbots Ripton, but the similar climb to Stevenage was surmounted at 43 m.p.h., and the run concluded with speeds of 74 and 75 m.p.h. at Hatfield and Wood Green respectively. Had it not been for the very slow entry needed to No. 5 platform at King's Cross, *Diamond Jubilee* would have completed the run of 76.4 miles from Peterborough in 85 min. or just under; the booked time was 87 min.

Within three weeks of the emergence from Doncaster Works of the first Gresley A4 streamlined Pacific, No. 2509 *Silver Link*, in September, 1935, we were left in no doubt of the speed potentialities of this latest Gresley product. The occasion was the historic inaugural run of September 27th of that year, when *Silver Link*, with the new seven-coach train weighing 220 tons tare and 230 tons gross, crossed the 100 m.p.h. line at the 25th milepost out of King's Cross, and for the next 25 miles, until slowed for the curves at Offord, at no point was travelling at less than 100, and attained a new British maximum speed of 112½ m.p.h. For 43 miles on end speed averaged 100 m.p.h., a record not beaten to this day in Great Britain with any description of motive power. For 70 miles, from Wood Green to Fletton Junction, Peterborough, including 13½ miles in all of 1 in 200 up gradient, an average speed of 91.8 m.p.h. had been maintained.

Eleven months later A4 No. 2512 *Silver Fox* slightly improved on the 112½ m.p.h. record with a speed of 113 m.p.h. down Stoke Bank, hauling an eight-coach load of 270 tons. Yet the A4s were so economical in their fuel consumption that the "Silver Jubilee", with its 70.4 m.p.h. runs in each direction between London and Darlington, consumed no more coal than an average of 39 lb. to the mile.

It was on July 3rd, 1938, that Gresley achieved one of his greatest triumphs in the achievement by one of his A4 Pacifics, not merely of an unchallengeable British speed record, but the highest known speed, backed by fully authenticated figures, ever recorded in any part of the world with steam power. The engine was No. 4468 *Mallard*, which, as mentioned already in Chapter XVIII, had the advantage of the Kylchap double blast-pipe and double exhaust. The record speed was reached with a special eight-coach train of 240 tons during a series of brake trials. In descending Stoke bank, with 40 per cent. cut-off and regulator full open, *Mallard* covered 5 miles consecutively at an average of 120.4 m.p.h., with an absolute maximum over a short distance of 126 m.p.h. The driver responsible for this startling exploit, as previously mentioned, was Duddington of Doncaster.

When the streamlined "Coronation" began to run between London and Edinburgh in July, 1937, it was realised that its haulage would be a far more exacting task than that of the "Silver Jubilee". For instead of the latter's seven coaches of 220 tare tons (later increased to eight of 248 tons), the "Coronation", with its beavertail observation car attached, comprised nine coaches of 312 tons weight, or 325 tons with a normal passenger complement. Moreover, its Pacific was required to work right through over the 393 miles between King's Cross and Edinburgh. Much the hardest timing was over the Southern Area main line, with no more than 157 min. allowed to cover the 188.2 miles from King's Cross to York, demanding an average speed of 71.9 m.p.h.—the fastest booked run in Britain.

The quality of performance so entailed may be deduced from Table 24, which sets out the times and speeds of a typical run—actually that of the opening day. Maximum speed was nominally limited to 90

Table 24

L.N.E.R. Class A4 Gresley 4–6–2

Engine No. 4491, Commonwealth of Australia.

Load : 9 coaches, 312 tons tare, 330 tons gross.

Dist.		Sched.	Actual		Speeds
miles		*min.*	*m.*	*s.*	*m.p.h.*
0.00	KING'S CROSS	0	0	00	—
2.50	FINSBURY PARK	—	5	06	—
4.95	Wood Green	—	7	33	—
12.70	Potters Bar	—	14	37	67
17.70	HATFIELD	18½	18	25	86¼
23.50	*Woolmer Green*	—	22	36	79/90
28.55	Stevenage	—	26	28	*67
31.90	HITCHIN	29½	28	56	88
37.10	Arlesey	—	32	15	94½
44.15	Sandy	—	37	03	90
51.75	St. Neots	—	42	15	83½/90
55.95	Offord	—	45	22	*70
58.85	HUNTINGDON	48½	47	40	80½
62.00	*Milepost 62*	—	50	07	75
69.35	Holme	—	55	07	98
75.00	*Fletton Junc.*	—	59	08	—
76.35	PETERBOROUGH	63½	61	20	*20
79.50	*Werrington Junc.*	—	65	16	—
84.85	Tallington	—	69	23	83½
88.65	Essendine	—	72	04	85
92.25	Little Bytham	—	74	37	82/76½
97.10	Corby Glen	—	78	21	78
100.10	*Stoke*	—	80	48	68
105.45	GRANTHAM	87½	85	17	75
				p.w.s.	*25
109.70	*Barkston South Junc.*	—	89	56	†90
120.10	NEWARK	99½	97	08	*70
126.30	Carlton	—	101	58	85
133.75	*Markham*	—	107	16	76½/88
138.60	RETFORD	114½	110	58	*67
143.95	Ranskill	—	115	08	86½/*65
149.50	*Pipers Wood*	—	119	50	67
155.95	DONCASTER	128½	125	11	*62
160.20	*Shaftholme Junc.*	—	128	42	eased
165.90	Balne	—	133	15	,,
173.00	*Brayton Junc.*	—	138	40	,,
174.30	SELBY	144	140	40	*28
178.50	Riccall	—	145	28	eased
183.95	Naburn	—	150	01	,,
186.15	*Chaloners Whin Junc.*	—	152	13	,,
188.15	YORK	157	155	36	—

Speed restriction.   †At Claypole.

m.p.h., though with both this train and the "Silver Jubilee" the occasional "100" was by no means unknown; on this run, as will be seen, the top speed at Holme was 98 m.p.h. As compared with the almost complete absence of speed restrictions over such a main line, say, as that of the French National Railways from Paris to Dijon, a similar distance, it will be noted that the "Coronation" had to be slowed seven times, in five cases for curves and the other two in order to take water from track troughs, in addition to the permanent way relaying slack at Hougham, north of Grantham. Yet Doncaster, 155.95 miles from King's Cross, was passed in 125 min. 11 sec., or 123¾ min. net—a start-to-pass average speed of 75.6 m.p.h. With more than 3 min. in hand, Driver Dron was then able to ease his hard-worked mount, but even so was into York 1½ min. early, in 155 min. 36 sec. or 154 min. net from London.

The A4 Pacifics could, of course, and did equal and more than equal any of the heavy load performances of their A1 and A3 predecessors. In the middle 1930s and after, the up "Flying Scotsman" was allowed no more than 105½ min. to cover the 105.5 miles from Grantham to King's Cross, with loads which frequently rose to and even exceeded 500 tons. On one journey that I timed No. 4466 *Herring Gull*, with 510 tons, completed the journey in 102 min. 39 sec., running from Little Bytham to Essendine at 90 m.p.h., and, more notable, covering the 30.3 miles from Huntingdon to Stevenage, against the rising tendency of the road, in 26 min. 3 sec., with a minimum speed of 51 m.p.h. up the final 1 in 200. On another occasion No. 4500 *Sir Ronald Matthews*, with a 500-ton Leeds express, almost exactly duplicated the last-mentioned feat, covering the 76.35 miles up from Peterborough start to stop in 73 min. 44 sec.

The magnitude of such loads pales, however, by comparison with those hauled by the A4 and other Gresley Pacifics during the 1939-1945 war. A recorder, Rev. G. C. Stead, travelling behind No. 4901 *Capercaillie* (later renamed *Sir Charles Newton*, one of the four A4s with Kylchap double blast-pipes and double chimneys) in a 20-coach train of 665 tons tare and 730 tons gross, noted the maintenance of an average speed of 75.9 m.p.h. over but little easier than level track from Otterington to Skelton, on the Darlington-York run. But the record of records in loading was on April 5th, 1940, when No. 2509 *Silver Link*, which five years earlier had maintained 100 m.p.h. for 43 miles with a 230-ton train, left King's Cross on the 1 p.m. Edinburgh train at the head of no fewer than 25 coaches, which with a packed complement of passengers and luggage must have scaled at least 850 tons behind the tender. On the wartime schedule No. 2509 dropped 11 min. to Peterborough, but the loss of time from there to Newcastle was no more than 4 min.

Such strenuous wartime loading conditions, coupled with inadequate maintenance, had a serious effect on the Gresley Pacifics, and it was well into the years of nationalisation before they were restored to their normal competence. As late as May, 1959, however, A4 No. 60007,

Sir Nigel Gresley, with Driver Bill Hoole at the regulator and an eight-coach special train of 271 tons tare and 295 tons gross, distinguished itself by attaining 101 m.p.h. at Arlesey, and then by breasting Stoke Summit at 81 m.p.h.—a feat demanding a drawbar horsepower of not less than 2,200.   On the return journey, a top speed of 112 m.p.h. was attained down Stoke bank, and an average of 104 m.p.h. was maintained over the 12.25 miles from Corby Glen to Tallington, even faster than the epic 1938 flight of *Mallard*, because the latter was braked at Essendine.   Later on in the same journey *Sir Nigel Gresley* touched 100 m.p.h. on but little easier than level track at Tempsford—an amazing performance for a locomotive 22 years old, and a "swan song" indeed

Table 25

L.N.E.R. Class V2 Gresley 2–6–2

Engine No. 4817

Load : 9 Pullmans, 362 tons tare, 380 tons gross

Dist.		Sched.	Actual	Speeds
miles		min.	m. s.	m.p.h.
0.0	DONCASTER	0	0 00	—
2.8	*Black Carr Junc.*	—	5 34	—
8.3	Bawtry	—	12 07	65
12.1	Ranskill	—	15 35	—
17.4	RETFORD	19	20 32	65
22.0	*Milepost* 134	—	25 07	54
29.6	Carlton	—	31 29	83½
35.9	NEWARK	36½	36 17	—
46.3	*Barkston South Junc.*	46	45 30	53/60
			sigs.	*50
50.5	GRANTHAM	51	50 18	—
54.0	Great Ponton	—	54 14	53
55.9	*Stoke*	—	56 34	50
58.9	Corby Glen	—	59 24	78
63.8	Little Bytham	—	62 58	93
67.4	Essendine	—	65 19	91
71.2	Tallington	—	67 53	90
76.5	*Werrington Junc.*	—	71 39	*70
79.6	PETERBOROUGH	79	74 34	*20
81.0	*Fletton Junc.*	—	76 35	—
			sigs.	*10
86.6	Holme	—	83 13	—
			sigs.	
94.0	*Milepost 62*	—	93 21	49
97.1	HUNTINGDON	97	96 13	74
104.3	St. Neots	—	102 05	69/72½
111.9	Sandy	—	108 34	69
119.0	Arlesey	—	111 43	68
124.1	HITCHIN	121	119 41	58
127.4	Stevenage	—	123 27	52
132.5	*Woolmer Green*	—	128 55	—
138.3	HATFIELD	135	133 54	77
143.3	Potters Bar	—	138 16	65/73
151.0	Wood Green	—	144 47	—
153.5	FINSBURY PARK	—	147 14	—
			sigs.	*20
156.0	KING'S CROSS	155	151 54	—

*Speed restriction.

L.N.E.R. 4-4-0 LOCO-MOTIVES. *Above:* Former Great Central "Director" class 4-4-0 No. 5511 *Marne* at speed north of Grantham with the down "Queen of Scots" Pullman.

Right: Former Great North of Scotland 4-4-0 No. 62277 (B.R. numbering) crosses the Spey at Carron on the Speyside line.

Below: On the most scenic of all L.N.E.R. routes—the West Highland line in Glen Falloch, with former North British 4-4-0 No. 62496 *Glen Moidart* and train.

W. J. V. Anderson

L.N.E.R. 4-4-2 LOCOMOTIVES. All illustrated on this page were the mainstay of the G.N., N.E. and N.B. express passenger services until the advent of the Gresley Pacifics. *Above:* Former North Eastern Z Class 4-4-2 at Harrogate with the "Harrogate Pullman".

[British Railways

Above: One of the numerous Great Northern Ivatt 4-4-2s, No. 3284, emerging from Stoke Tunnel with the up "West Riding Pullman".

[M. W. Earley

Below: A Reid Atlantic of the North British, No. 9905 *Buccleuch*, leaving Galashiels with a stopping train.

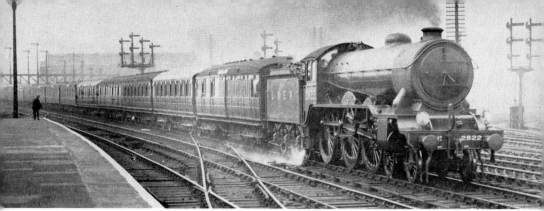

ON THE GREAT EASTERN SECTION. *Above:* The "Day Continental" passing Stratford in charge of L.N.E.R. Class B17 4–6–0 No. 2822 *Alnwick Castle*. Catering on this train was in the three Pullman cars near the rear.
[*G. R. Grigs*

Above: The Summer "Eastern Belle Pullman" excursion train, headed by ex-Great Eastern Class B12 4–6–0 No. 8552.
[*F. R. Hebron*

Below: The "East Anglian", with Class B17 4–6–0 No. 2859 *East Anglian*, one of the only two L.N.E.R. 4–6–0 locomotives ever streamlined.
[*British Railways*

Above: A majestic impression of one of the original Gresley A1 Pacifics, No. 4475 *Flying Fox* leaving Edinburgh Waverley for London with the non-stop "Flying Scotsman", a run of 393 miles.

Below: The most powerful express locomotives ever built for the L.N.E.R. were the Gresley 2–8–2s of Class P2. No. 2004 *Mons Meg* is seen leaving King's Cross with a down express during the running-in period before transfer to the Edinburgh-Aberdeen line. [*British Railways*

for one of the most famous locomotive classes in British history.

It is good to know that of the Gresley Pacifics No. 4472 *Flying Scotsman* has been preserved and kept in first-class condition by Alan Pegler, who has used the engine on railway enthusiasts' excursions in all parts of the country, and that the record-breaking *Mallard* has found a resting-place on public display in the Clapham Museum of British Railways.

Two other Gresley classes require mention. One was his V2 2-6-2s, most versatile of types, equally at home with heavy freight trains and passenger expresses; they were among the first British types to prove that with long-lap long-travel valve-motion and improved front-end design generally, coupled wheels of 6 ft. 2 in. diameter (as compared with the normal express passenger standard of 6 ft. 8 in. or so) are no hindrance to the attainment of high speeds. This is clear in Table 25, in which is set out the performance of No. 4817 at the head of the mile-a-minute "Yorkshire Pullman" from Doncaster to King's Cross—a regular V2 assignment at that time. Down Stoke Bank a maximum speed of 93 m.p.h. was reached, and with this 380-ton train the 2-6-2 had no difficulty in cutting the schedule by 3 min., covering the 156.0 miles in 151 min. 54 sec. With allowance for the three out-of-course delays, the net time was not more than 147 min., a gain of 8 min. on schedule. On many express passenger duties, other than the streamlined trains, the V2s for years were worked almost interchangeably with the Pacifics.

The other express passenger design of note, for the design of which, as we have seen in Chapter XII, the North British Locomotive Company was mainly responsible, was the B17 or "Sandringham" class three-cylinder 4-6-0. It was on the Great Central line that the B17s of the second, or "Football" series (named after well-known clubs) displayed their prowess to the greatest advantage. In Table 26 there is set out a striking up run, timed by Sir James Colyer-Fergusson, from Leicester to Marylebone with a most exceptional load, for the Great Central, of 13 coaches, 437 tons tare and 465 tons gross.

Up the lengthy 1 in 176 out of Leicester speed fell to 42 m.p.h. at Ashby Magna, and there was a minimum of 44 up the similar inclination to Charwelton, so that by Woodford all but 3 min. had been lost. But with top speeds of 79 and 80½ m.p.h. on the two 1 in 176 descents to Calvert 1½ min. were regained to Aylesbury, and one of the hardest efforts of the journey was then seen in a minimum speed of 39 m.p.h. up the 5½ miles at 1 in 116 to milepost 31¼. With another 80 m.p.h. maximum before the Rickmansworth slack, time would have been kept to Marylebone but for the permanent way slowing at Pinner—a first-class piece of work.

The Thompson era produced no improvements in Pacific performance, though some of the changes he introduced certainly cut down maintenance costs. With the experience that had been gained with the V2 2-6-2s of speed possibilities with 6 ft. 2 in. coupled wheels, Thompson's A2 Pacifics all had driving wheels of this diameter, and though some of his engines had an unenviable record for slipping, they were certainly speedy. Sir James Colyer-Fergusson once timed No. 60502 *Earl Maris-chal* (one of the six Gresley P2 2–8–2s converted by Thompson to the Pacific wheel arrangement) with a 220-ton train, to pass Milepost 1, at the approach to York, in 34 min. 46 sec. for the 43.1 miles from Darlington, having averaged 88.7 m.p.h. for 32½ miles of but little easier than level track and reached a maximum of 95 m.p.h. on the dead level.   Major R. A. Colville also timed No. 60524 *Herringbone*, with a much heavier

Table 26

L.N.E.R. "Sandringham" 4–6–0 (Class B17)

Engine No. 2848 Arsenal

Load: 13 *coaches,* 437 *tons tare,* 465 *tons gross.*

Dist.		Sched.	Actual	Speeds
miles		*min.*	*m. s.*	*m.p.h.*
0.0	LEICESTER	0	0 00	—
4.7	Whetstone	—	7 45	50
9.2	Ashby Magna	—	13 55	42
13.1	Lutterworth	—	18 59	†73½
19.9	RUGBY	—	25 12	63
24.6	Braunston	—	29 23	70
27.9	*Staverton Road*	—	32 42	—
31.6	Charwelton	—	37 17	44
34.0	WOODFORD	37	39 53	69½
37.0	Culworth	—	42 40	60
40.6	Helmdon	—	45 58	—
43.8	Brackley	—	48 46	79
48.6	Finmere	—	52 37	69
54.3	Calvert	—	57 03	80½/72
56.3	*Grendon Junc.*	56	58 45	*63
59.0	Quainton Road	59	61 14	71
65.2	AYLESBURY	65	66 37	69
67.4	Stoke Mandeville	—	68 49	—
69.8	Wendover	—	71 54	—
71.9	*Milepost 31½*	—	75 05	39
74.3	Great Missenden	76	77 37	71
79.5	Amersham	—	82 33	55
81.5	Chalfont	83	84 26	80
85.9	RICKMANSWORTH	87½	88 11	*42/48
89.4	Northwood	—	92 45	46/60
			p.w.s.	*30
93.9	HARROW	97	98 47	—
98.0	*Neasden South Junc.*	101½	103 12	68
100.1	Brondesbury	—	105 21	49
103.1	MARYLEBONE	109	110 06	—

Speed restriction.   †Beyond Shawell.

eleven-coach train of 380 tons, to run from York to Darlington, 44.1 miles, against the rising tendency of the road in 36 min. 29 sec. start to stop, touching 90 m.p.h. on the level at Thirsk, and covering the 41 miles between mileposts 2 and 43 at an average of 82.5 m.p.h.

Thompson's most successful design, however, was his simple and straightforward B1 4–6–0, the London & North Eastern counterpart of the London Midland & Scottish Stanier Class 5 4–6–0.   Table 27 sets out a performance of No. 61116 from Leicester to Marylebone with a substantial eleven-coach load of 395 tons, which makes an interesting comparison with the work of the B17 class 4–6–0 in Table 26, except that in the run now being described there were four intermediate stops. Even allowing for a load lighter by 70 tons, the work of the B1 up the initial 1 in 176 was certainly superior, with its minimum speed of 51 m.p.h. after Ashby Magna; also the attained speed of $42\frac{1}{2}$ m.p.h. up the 1 in 116 to milepost $31\frac{1}{2}$ was from a dead start out of Aylesbury, as

Table 27

L.N.E.R. Class B1 Thompson 4–6–0

Engine No. 61116

Load: 11 *coaches,* 371 *tons tare,* 395 *tons gross.*

Dist.		Sched.	Actual		Speeds
miles		*min.*	*m.*	*s.*	*m.p.h.*
0.0	LEICESTER	0	0	00	—
4.7	Whetstone	—	7	04	57
9.2	Ashby Magna	—	12	03	53
11.6	*Milepost* 114$\frac{1}{2}$	—	14	50	51
13.1	Lutterworth	—	16	17	70/67
16.3	*Shawell*	—	19	05	76
19.9	RUGBY	25	22	33	—
4.7	Braunston	—	6	20	68
			p.w.s.		*23
8.0	*Staverton Road*	—	9	46	—
11.7	Charwelton	—	16	37	35$\frac{1}{2}$/53$\frac{1}{2}$
14.1	WOODFORD HALSE	20	19	58	—
1.8	*Culworth Junc.*	2$\frac{1}{2}$	3	29	54/50$\frac{1}{2}$
6.6	Helmdon	—	8	32	66
9.8	Brackley	—	11	22	79
14.6	Finmere	—	15	18	69$\frac{1}{2}$/81
20.3	Calvert	—	19	40	73$\frac{1}{2}$
22.2	*Grendon Junc.*	20$\frac{1}{2}$	21	23	*53
25.0	Quainton Road	23$\frac{1}{2}$	24	23	57/69$\frac{1}{2}$
31.1	AYLESBURY	34$\frac{1}{2}$	30	30	—
2.2	Stoke Mandeville	—	5	34	38
4.6	Wendover	—	9	12	40$\frac{1}{4}$
6.7	*Milepost* 31$\frac{1}{2}$	—	12	10	42$\frac{1}{2}$/61$\frac{1}{2}$
			p.w.s.		*25
9.1	Great Missenden	16	14	53	54$\frac{1}{4}$
14.3	Amersham	—	21	45	49
16.4	Chalfont	24	23	51	65
18.6	Chorley Wood	—	25	47	71
20.7	RICKMANSWORTH	30	28	13	*34
			p.w.s.		*23
22.8	Moor Park	—	31	56	—
24.2	Northwood	—	34	18	39$\frac{1}{4}$
26.5	Pinner	—	36	53	61$\frac{1}{2}$
			sigs.		—
28.7	HARROW	44	40	27	—
2.3	*Milepost* 199	—	3	34	63$\frac{1}{4}$
			sigs.		*33
4.1	*Neasden S. Junc.*	5$\frac{1}{2}$	6	32	—
			sigs.		—
9.2	MARYLEBONE	15	17	30	—

compared with the B17's 39 m.p.h. after passing Aylesbury at 69 m.p.h. So No. 61116 gained time on every stage, a particularly smart effort being to cover the 31.1 miles from Woodford to Aylesbury in 30 min. 30 sec. start to stop.

The last L.N.E.R. express passenger designs were those of Peppercorn, of which building continued well into the years of nationalisation. A typical example of the work of one of his Class A2 Pacifics, with 6 ft. 2 in. coupled wheels, is seen in Table 28; the run was recorded by Ronald I.

Table 28

L.N.E.R. Class A2 Peppercorn 4–6–2

Engine No. 60527, Sun Chariot.

Load: 11 coaches, 381 tons tare, 400 tons gross.

Dist.		Sched.	Actual		Speeds
miles		min.	m.	s.	m.p.h.
0.00	ABERDEEN	0	0	00	—
0.65	Ferryhill Junc.	—	3	01	16½
4.80	Cove Bay	9	9	32	47
7.10	Milepost 234	—	12	17	53
10.40	Newtonhill	—	15	19	63
11.55	Muchalls	—	16	22	68
13.40	Milepost 227½	—	18	18	59/69½
16.15	STONEHAVEN	25	21	07	—
1.00	Milepost 223¾	—	3	31	31
2.55	Dunnottar	—	5	55	41/47
5.50	Carmont	—	9	36	44½
7.15	Drumlithie	—	11	26	56
11.10	Fordoun	—	14	56	68
14.40	LAURENCEKIRK	19	17	57	64
15.50	Milepost 209¼	—	19	04	63
17.60	Marykirk	—	20	45	72½
19.75	Craigo	—	22	26	78½
21.85	Kinnaber Junc.	29	25	24	*15/53½
24.75	MONTROSE	33	29	27	—
2.05	Usan	—	6	11	28½
4.00	Milepost 26¾	—	9	28	39½
7.45	Inverkeilor	13	13	02	71/63
8.75	Cauldcots	—	14	13	67/58
10.65	Letham Grange	—	16	00	63½/61
13.10	St. Vigeans Junc.	19	18	42	—
			p.w.s.		*15
13.65	ARBROATH	20	20	26	—
1.40	Elliott Junc.	—	3	32	18½
4.35	Easthaven	—	6	27	64¼
6.15	Carnoustie	—	8	03	69
7.75	Barry Links	—	9	23	71
10.70	Monifieth	—	11	54	70
13.05	BROUGHTY FERRY	—	13	57	69
			sigs.		*10
16.30	Camperdown Junc.	—	18	59	*15
17.05	DUNDEE	22	21	25	—

*Speed restriction.

Nelson. No. 60527 *Sun Chariot* had to work an eleven-coach train of 400 tons from Aberdeen to Dundee, and the run provides an interesting contrast with that of the North British Atlantic, hauling 295 tons, set out in Table 18. With a load 35 per cent. heavier, the 4–6–2's speed up the long climb past Cove Bay was never lower than 47 m.p.h., compared with the 4–4–2's 34 m.p.h., and Stonehaven was reached in 21 min. 7 sec. as compared with 24 min. 15 sec. For most of the climb out of Stonehaven the 4–6–2 was maintaining 41 to 47 m.p.h., whereas the best the 4–4–2 could manage was 35½ to 40 m.p.h. From Stonehaven to Montrose the respective times were 29 min. 27 sec. and 31 min. 15 sec. (with the Pacific reducing speed far more severely than the Atlantic over Kinnaber Junction). Up from Montrose the 4–6–2 attained 39 m.p.h. as compared with 35 m.p.h., and finally, on the dead level between Arbroath and Dundee *Sun Chariot's* 71 m.p.h. was well ahead of *Aberdonian's* 60 m.p.h. Such were the increases in speed over this difficult Scottish main line in a little over a quarter of a century.

Lastly we have the Peppercorn A1 Pacifics, in which the 6 ft. 8 in. coupled wheel diameter was reverted to. These proved themselves to be pretty well the equal of the Gresley A4s in speed capacity, though slightly higher in coal consumption, but the latter was balanced by reduced maintenance costs, due in part to the use of three separate sets of Walschaerts valve-motion for the three cylinders, as against the Gresley derived motion for the inside cylinder. No better example of Peppercorn A1 speed capacity could be given than that set out in Table 29. This run also was recorded by Ronald I. Nelson on a day on which the diesel hauling the southbound "Talisman" had failed at York, and had had to be replaced at a moment's notice by A1 4–6–2 No. 60140 *Balmoral*. The nine-coach 325-ton train left York 26 min. after the time at which it was due to pass that station.

With a load almost exactly equal to that of the pre-war "Coronation" streamliner with observation car attached, *Balmoral*, in the capable hands of Driver Turner, ran throughout in "Coronation" times, notwithstanding the severe signal and permanent way checks at Bawtry, outside Peterborough, near Huntingdon and Sandy and at New Southgate. Indeed, but for the aggravating signal stop at Belle Isle, the King's Cross arrival would have been on time, the entire 26 min. arrears of the "Talisman" schedule then in operation having been recovered. High lights of the performance were the minima of 68, 68, 71 and 73 m.p.h. at the summit of the climbs to Peascliffe Tunnel, Stoke Summit, Abbots Ripton and Stevenage respectively, and the top speed of 100½ m.p.h. at Essendine. The net time for the 188.15 miles from York to King's Cross was 158 min., 4 min. less than the pre-war "Coronation" allowance, and with a lower speed down from Potters Bar than those habitually run by the pre-war flyer. Throughout its 25-year history, the London & North Eastern Railway had every reason to be proud of the performances of its most capable locomotives.

Table 29
L.N.E.R. Class A1 Peppercorn 4-6-2
Engine No. 60140, Balmoral
Load : 9 coaches, 308 tons tare, 325 tons gross

Dist.		Sched.	Actual	Speeds
miles		min.	m. s.	m.p.h.
0.00	YORK	‡0	§0 00	—
2.00	Chaloners Whin Junc.	—	4 17	45
9.65	Riccall	—	11 10	77
13.85	SELBY	14½	14 52	*40
18.40	Templehirst	—	19 17	73
22.25	Balne	(†4)	22 20	77½/85
27.95	Shaftholme Junc.	31	26 30	82
32.20	DONCASTER	36	30 03	*56
36.80	Rossington	—	34 20	69½
38.65	Milepost 149¼	—	35 55	66
			sigs.	*20/*45
44.20	Ranskill	—	42 53	61/73½
49.55	RETFORD	52	47 28	*65/69
54.40	Milepost 133¾	—	51 48	66
61.85	Carlton	—	57 08	92½/*77
68.05	NEWARK	68	61 35	79/80½
72.80	Claypole	(†4)	65 11	79
78.45	Barkston South Junc.	81	69 34	74/68
82.70	GRANTHAM	85	73 07	70½/72
88.05	Stoke	90	77 41	68
91.05	Corby Glen	—	80 01	85½
95.90	Little Bytham	—	83 10	99
99.50	Essendine	98	85 20	100½
103.30	Tallington	(†2)	87 42	95
108.65	Werrington Junc.	106	91 30	*70
			sigs.	*10
111.80	PETERBOROUGH	111	95 45	—
113.15	Fletton Junc.	—	98 12	48½
115.55	Yaxley	—	100 34	69
118.80	Holme	—	103 08	78
120.80	Connington South	—	104 37	81
124.65	Abbots Ripton	—	107 38	71
			p.w.s.	*20
129.30	HUNTINGDON	128	113 50	68½
132.20	Offord	—	116 17	74/77
136.40	St. Neots	—	119 34	76
140.65	Tempsford	—	122 40	86½
			p.w.s.	*30
144.00	Sandy	139	126 21	47
147.00	Biggleswade	—	129 10	74
151.05	Arlesey	—	132 25	80½/83
156.25	HITCHIN	149	136 13	77
159.60	Stevenage	(†2)	138 52	73/80
163.10	Knebworth	158	141 37	78
164.65	Woolmer Green	(†2)	142 46	79
167.85	Welwyn Garden City		145 03	90
170.45	HATFIELD	166	146 51	*75
173.70	Brookmans Park	(†1)	149 25	74
175.45	Potters Bar	172	150 53	72½
179.00	New Barnet	(†4)	153 54	69
			p.w.s.	*25
183.20	Wood Green	—	159 15	64
185.65	FINSBURY PARK	186	161 49	—
		(†2)	sig. stop	*0
188.15	KING'S CROSS	193	169 12	—

*Speed restriction.   †Recovery time (min.).   ‡Passing time.
§From dead start 26 min. after scheduled passing time.

XXI

Electrification

ON THE formation of the London & North Eastern Railway in 1923, its only electrified lines were those on North Tyneside, between Newcastle Tynemouth, Whitley Bay and Monkseaton, by two different routes, brought into use in 1904, and between Shildon marshalling yard and the Erimus yard, Newport, just west of Middlesbrough, electrically operated from 1915 onwards. The former were suburban passenger lines, with third-rail conduction at 600 volts d.c.; the latter was a mineral line, bringing coal from the Durham pits down to the Tees for shipment and also for the Tees-side steelworks, and the second British electrified line to use overhead conduction, at 1,500 volts d.c. Before the end of London & North Eastern history, the North Tyneside electrification had been complemented by the equipment in the same manner of the South Tyneside line from Newcastle to South Shields, completed in 1938.

Meantime the London & North Eastern had co-operated with the London Midland & Scottish Railway in electrifying the suburban Manchester, South Junction & Altrincham line (formerly the joint property of the London & North Western and Great Central Railways) on the overhead system, also using current at 1,500 volts d.c., and this had been electrically worked from 1931 onwards. As yet, therefore, L.N.E.R. electrification experience was no more than limited; but by 1936 a plan of major importance was in view.

As far back as 1923 serious consideration had been given by the London & North Eastern management to the long-desired electrification of the London suburban lines, of both the Great Eastern and Great Northern sections, but the needed finance was not available. Ten years later the London Passenger Transport Board was formed, to take over all the London tube and underground lines and their surface extensions, and to enter into pooling arrangements with the main line companies with which connections already existed, or might be made in future. By now the continued growth of the eastern suburbs of London was creating an insistent demand for additional transport facilities, which, it was realised, could be most logically met by an extension of the former Central London Railway eastwards from Liverpool Street, and a link up with the Great Eastern line at Stratford and beyond.

With the promised assistance of a substantial loan from the Government, therefore, the L.N.E.R. and the L.P.T.B. worked out the ambitious scheme mentioned already in Chapter XII. The Central tube would be extended to come to the surface in a completely reconstructed Stratford Station, where there would be cross-platform exchange with the L.N.E.R. suburban trains. The tube trains would then dive again into tunnel under Stratford Locomotive Works, surface through the L.N.E.R. Leyton and Leytonstone Stations, and then take to tunnel yet again on a circular course eastwards through Wanstead and Gants Hill to come out finally into the open at Newbury Park. From here the L.P.T.B. would take over and electrify the former Great Eastern Woodford & Ilford line, and in addition the whole of the Loughton and Ongar branch from Leyton onwards would become part of the L.P.T.B. system. Needless to say this far-reaching plan, which was linked up with the Great Eastern electrification from Liverpool Street and Fenchurch Street to Shenfield, required Parliamentary sanction, which was duly obtained in 1936.

Apart from the enormous benefit of electrification to the teeming eastern suburbs of London, the removal from the two terminals just mentioned of the trains to and from the Loughton and Ongar line would greatly ease the problem of operation, especially over the flat junctions between Bow Junction and Stratford. It would also free what had been known as the "Local" lines between Liverpool Street and Stratford to serve in future as the Colchester main line, with the Gidea Park and Shenfield electrics starting out of the East Side at Liverpool Street, and running over the former "Fast" lines from there. But it would be necessary at some point short of Ilford to get these trains back to their normal north side of the four-track lines, in order to give access to the Ilford carriage sheds and the Gidea Park carriage sidings without fouling the main lines. This made necessary the construction of a fly-over, for which a suitable site was available between Manor Park and Ilford.

With this costly development in view, the London & North Eastern management could not simultaneously face the electrification of its Great Northern suburban lines, which in any event was not so urgent as those of the Great Eastern section. But by agreement with the London Passenger Transport Board, the latter was to extend its Northern tube from Archway through Highgate to join the Great Northern High Barnet branch at East Finchley, from which point the line to High Barnet, with the Mill Hill branch, would be taken over by the L.P.T.B. and electrified. This was the first of the new electrification plans to come to fruition. By the spring of 1939 the first Northern tube trains were running into a rebuilt East Finchley Station, now with four platforms, and April, 1940, saw electric trains for the first time at High Barnet. The system adopted, needless to say, was the standard L.P.T.B. fourth-rail electrification at 600 volts d.c.

What of the other great electrification projects? By the autumn of 1939 war had broken out, and apart from the Northern tube extension just mentioned, all new work had been brought to a complete standstill. Already some £2,500,000 had been spent on the Sheffield-Manchester electrification, but as yet it had not been realised that before its completion a new Woodhead Tunnel would need to be bored, adding some £4,250,000 to the cost of the work and delaying the opening throughout of the electrified route until 1954. Well before this date electric trains had begun to run from Liverpool Street to Shenfield and from the Central tube to Fairlop and Epping, but even these inaugurations were not until September, 1949, some 13 years after the plans had been authorised and work had been begun. By this time the London & North Eastern Railway as such had ceased to exist, and these works and many others had been brought to completion under the auspices of British Railways.

M

XXII

The Evolution of Coaching Stock—1923-1947

THE MANY thousands of passenger coaches brought by the constituent companies into the control of the London & North Eastern Railway on the formation of the new group were as varied in character as the locomotives, if not more so. A high standard was set by the carriages which had been built jointly by the Great Northern, North Eastern and North British Railways for operating the through trains of the East Coast Route, lettered "E.C.J.S.", for East Coast Joint Stock. As far back as 1896 Doncaster Works had turned out the first two trains of palatial 12-wheel coaches which in various ways were to set a standard for future E.C.J.S. construction, very American in style, with clerestory roofs, bow ends, short Pullman vestibules and Gould automatic couplers. Shortly afterwards the Great Northern Railway was building similar trains for its London-Leeds service.

In the years before his appointment as Locomotive Engineer of the G.N.R. Gresley had been Manager of the Carriage and Wagon Works at Doncaster, where his influence was seen first on the emergence in 1907 of a new corridor train for the King's Cross-Sheffield-Manchester service. One important change was the substitution for the clerestory of the high elliptical roof, eventually standardised also by all the constituent companies which previously had specialised in the former type. The new Great Northern roof sloped downwards towards the coach ends, as the clerestory roofs had done; the bow ends, Pullman vestibules and automatic couplers—practices not followed by any British railways other than the North Eastern at that time or for long afterwards—were retained.

In the same year, 1907, the North Eastern Railway had built at York some singularly ugly flat-sided coaches for the joint Great Northern and North Eastern services between London and Newcastle, but so greatly did Gresley's new trains commend themselves that his design was adopted forthwith as standard for all future East Coast Joint Stock construction also. With his compound-bolster bogie, first introduced in 1908, Gresley had produced coaches of which the exemplary smoothness of riding at high speed could find few, if any, rivals on other railways; and apart from modifications in interior furnishing and *décor* a standard had been set which was to remain without change practically to the end of London & North Eastern history.

A highly original feature of Gresley coach design had been evolved in 1907. It was the taking of earlier 6-wheel coaches in pairs, mounting the outer ends of the two bodies on bogies, and carrying the two inner ends on a bogie-supported casting; the articulated unit so formed gave far better riding than the previous 6-wheel coaches had done, and the central supporting casting performed the function of a hinge, so that the lengthy twin vehicle could traverse curves easily. From the first articulation of existing coaches it had been but a step to the building of new articulated trains, beginning with eight-coach suburban trains each composed of four twin sets, then of similar trains of two quadruplets apiece, next of triplet restaurant car sets comprising a central kitchen car flanked by open first and third class restaurants, and finally in 1921 of a complete five-coach restaurant car train, mounted on six bogies only, for the London-Leeds service.

The advantages of articulation were smooth riding and a slight reduction in train length and weight as compared with individual coaches; the disadvantages were that the formation of an articulated train could never be varied, so that in the event of a defect developing in one of the coaches, such as a hot axle-box, the whole articulated set had to be taken out of action. This no doubt explains why no other railway company, apart from the building by the London Midland & Scottish and Great Western Railways of one or two experimental articulated sets, had ever followed Gresley in this matter. Another Gresley innovation, first introduced in the London-Leeds articulated train of 1921, was the installation of electric cooking, so making it possible for the first time to dispense with all gas cylinders.

From the opening of its London Extension in 1899 the Great Central Railway had been very advanced in its main line coach design; one slogan which it used to attract passengers to the new service was "Every Express Train Vestibuled and with Buffet Car Attached"; this was at a time when restaurant car accommodation on British trains was still very limited, and buffet cars were non-existent. Handsome new trains had been built to work to and from London, and their number had been increased as the service had expanded. By the last years before the grouping Great Central coaches, with their vertical panelling, had developed very distinctive characteristics, both externally and internally, under John G. Robinson. One feature, never copied elsewhere, was his fitting to his coach-ends of massive castings, with tooth-shaped projections running horizontally across the width of the coach, designed to engage with one another in the event of a derailment, and so to prevent one coach body over-riding the next. But it is questionable if the addition of these heavy fittings would have proved more effectual in preventing telescoping than the Great Northern and East Coast Joint buckeye couplers have done in more than one accident, when complete trains so formed have been kept in line.

The Great Eastern Railway had been relatively late in introducing corridor stock. Its first three-car restaurant sets, introduced in 1899, had been isolated from the remaining vehicles in their trains, and not until 1904 did the first complete G.E.R. corridor train emerge from Stratford Works, to act as the Hook of Holland boat train between Liverpool Street and Parkeston Quay. Two years later a similar train began service between Harwich and York, with through coaches to and from Birmingham, Manchester and Liverpool; and a third corridor train had been completed in 1907 for the summer "Norfolk Coast Express". After that the building of corridor stock began in earnest, and by 1922 all the principal Great Eastern main line trains were so formed, with the majority of them restaurant car-equipped. Incidentally, Stratford Works of the G.E.R. was the first to devise the sliding upper glass panels of coach windows which are now standard practice for all British corridor stock, and which provide for draught-free ventilation. Windows of this type were first fitted to Great Eastern restaurant cars in 1912. Some exceptional main line coaching vehicles which the G.E.R. brought into the London & North Eastern pool were the Pullman cars which had been introduced in 1920 by the Great Eastern's American General Manager, Sir Henry Thornton, and which led to later L.N.E.R. Pullman developments on a considerable scale, as described in Chapter XXIV.

The stock used by the G.E.R. for its London suburban services was Spartan to a degree; the problem of its vast commuter and workmen's traffic was that of packing a maximum number of passengers into a minimum of space. In 1899 James Holden, then Locomotive Superintendent, had designed and built the first British coaches to seat six passengers a-side; new 27 ft. 4-wheel coaches provided seats for 60 in five compartments, and a 15-coach train seated no fewer than 828. After a good deal of this stock had been built, Holden took the older five-a-side suburban coaches, sliced the bodies in half down the centre, and ingeniously inserted strips which widened the seating to six-a-side. Not until 1911 did the first Great Eastern bogie suburban coaches appear, made up into eight-coach trains; later on some 500 of the former 4-wheel vehicles were mounted in pairs on 54 ft. frames and converted to bogie vehicles. But to the end space was still as precious as ever, and apart from the change from flat to elliptical roofs with the new 1911 trains, giving a little more spaciousness in the compartments, the seating still remained as tight a fit as before.

For so important a constituent of the L.N.E.R. group, the North Eastern Railway was remarkable in that up to the end of 1922 it had built less corridor stock for its own internal use than any of its associates. Along its main trunk route, of course, it was part owner of the stock used on all the East Coast trains, and the joint Great Northern and North Eastern services, such as the nightly Newcastle sleeper and the 8.0 a.m. from Newcastle to King's Cross with its return working at 5.30 p.m. from London. But corridor North Eastern trains were confined to those built for the through service between Newcastle and Liverpool Exchange and the daily express from Leeds to Glasgow and back—the present "North Briton". The latter had the distinction of running the greatest daily distance—555 miles—of any complete train set in the country, closely followed by the 536½ miles of the 8.0 a.m. from Newcastle to London and its return express.   Before the 1914-1918 war the North Eastern Railway also for a time provided a set of corridor coaches for working between King's Cross and Scarborough.

Local and cross-country N.E.R. trains were usually four-coach formations which included one semi-corridor composite with lavatory accommodation and the remainder non-corridor stock.   But these compartment coaches set a high standard of comfort; their clerestory roofs were standard practice until elliptical-roofed coaches began to appear about 1912.   Incidentally, the North Eastern Railway was joint owner of some coaching stock other than that already mentioned; this was the two sets of postal vehicles which worked nightly between Newcastle and Bristol, lettered "M. & N.E.J.P.S.", for Midland & North Eastern Joint Postal Service.

The North British Railway similarly was joint owner with the Midland of the stock used in the through Midland services to and from St. Pancras, the West of England and Lancashire.   This included restaurant and sleeping cars and ordinary corridor coaches, all lettered "M. & N.B."; like the postal vehicles just mentioned, these became the joint property of the London & North Eastern and London Midland & Scottish Railways after the grouping had taken place.   The North British had begun to build corridor coaches for its own use as early as 1901, including vehicles without end gangways for the lengthy journeys over the West Highland line.   But nothing outstanding in comfort appeared until the N.B.R. had been challenged by its great rival, the Caledonian Railway, with the latter's "Grampian Corridor" train sets of 12-wheel stock for the service between both Glasgow and Edinburgh and Aberdeen.   The North British reply in 1905 and 1906 had been some handsome new block trains of corridor stock to work between the same cities on accelerated timings.

The N.B.R. had no restaurant cars of its own until a comparatively late date.   The day trains brought East Coast Joint cars into Edinburgh, and also Midland & North British cars from Carlisle.   One or two East Coast cars were taken over eventually for the Edinburgh-Aberdeen route, but not until 1920 did the North British become possessed of six massive dining cars of all-steel construction, weighing no less than 46 to 50 tons apiece—the heaviest coaches in the entire country at that time. But much rather primitive N.B.R. passenger stock, both 6-wheel and 8-wheel, was still in service until the formation of the London & North Eastern Railway.

For a small and by no means wealthy company, the Great North of Scotland had established quite a high standard with its passenger rolling stock, including some handsome composite bogie lavatory coaches with internal corridors but no end vestibules, first turned out of Inverurie Works in 1908; but G.N.S.R. enterprise never extended quite as far as restaurant car construction, although in 1922 this company borrowed from the North British a car to work between Aberdeen and Inverness. Such, then, was the varied collection of passenger rolling stock which came under the jurisdiction of H. N. Gresley on his appointment in 1923 as Chief Mechanical Engineer of the London & North Eastern Railway.

One of the first matters to be decided was what should be the standard L.N.E.R. coach livery. Great Northern and East Coast Joint stock had always had a varnished teak finish. The Great Central, having painted its first stock for the London Extension with light grey upper panels and dark brown lower, in later years also had adopted varnished teak, but the Great Eastern, after keeping to varnished teak exteriors for many years, in 1919 had decided to change to maroon red, which was also the colour of North Eastern and North British stock. The Great North of Scotland coaches were rather more gay with crimson lower panels but white upper panels. The total of L.N.E.R. rolling stock was therefore fairly evenly divided in colour between varnished teak and crimson; it was probably the East Coast Joint livery that finally settled for varnished teak as the standard L.N.E.R. colour. In later years, when steel exterior panelling replaced wood, this led to the rather ludicrous but unavoidable practice of painting steel sheets to resemble varnished timber!

As soon as the new London & North Eastern Railway administration had settled down, a carriage-building programme of considerable magnitude was announced at the beginning of 1924. Most important were to be four new trains for the Anglo-Scottish day trains and a fifth for the Continental boat service between Liverpool Street and Parkeston Quay. Some 700 new suburban coaches were to be built, bringing the total estimated expenditure on new coaching stock to £1,700,000; and 500 of the older 4-wheel suburban coaches would be scrapped. Electric lighting and steam-heating from now on were to be standard for all types of stock, as also articulation for suburban trains and for restaurant car sets, and electric cooking in restaurant car kitchens.

By the inauguration of the winter timetable in October, 1924, the new "Flying Scotsman" trains were ready, each composed of eleven coaches and weighing 370 tons. The triplet restaurant car set comprised central kitchen car flanked by first and third class open restaurants, and with all-electric kitchen equipment. One interesting feature was that four composite coaches in each set—three of which ran through beyond Edinburgh to Glasgow, Perth and Aberdeen—all included first class *coupés*, or "honeymoon compartments", as they have sometimes been called. The other two set trains, for the midday departures from King's Cross and Edinburgh, were in service by November, 1924.

On April 1st, 1925, the handsome new eleven-coach Hook Continental boat train made its *début*—the first complete train of standard L.N.E.R. main line 61 ft. 6 in. bow-ended coaching stock with automatic buck-eye couplers to run on Great Eastern metals. An innovation for the comfort of first-class passengers was the provision of loose cushions and hassocks. The internal *décor* of this stock was a complete change from former

G.E.R. standards which,in first class compartments particularly, included all kinds of fancy mouldings and Lincrusta panelling, fussy in appearance and well adapted to harbouring dust and dirt. From his years as Carriage & Wagon Superintendent at Doncaster, Gresley's tendencies had been in the opposite direction, towards the simplicity of finish which was to become universal in later years.

In 1908 he had been responsible for building at Doncaster some sets of elliptical-roofed coaches, well provided with lavatories but not with corridors or end vestibules, for intermediate main line and long-distance branch services. Trains of this type now began to appear on the Great Eastern line, working between Liverpool Street and Southend and elsewhere, and also on the outer suburban services of the Great Central line between Marylebone and both Aylesbury and High Wycombe In the same year, 1925, new stock having become urgently necessary to replace the Holden 4-wheelers on the Great Eastern London inner suburban services, the G.E. line made its first acquaintance with Gresley articulated trains.

These were not in quadruplet sets, as with the Great Northern trains, but quintuplets—five coach-bodies carried on six bogies. To have fitted this stock with the Gresley compound bolster bogie would have been too expensive, and a simpler single bolster bogie was therefore devised, with satisfactory results. Some of the early Great Eastern experience was not too happy, however, as with trains carrying a number of standing passengers in the rush hours the deflection of the coach frames at times became sufficiently severe to prevent the doors from opening. However, some frame strengthening soon cured this trouble. Two quintuplets coupled accommodated 872 seated passengers in a tare weight of no more than 214 tons—a most economical ratio of four passengers to the ton of coach weight.

The next development of note came about in 1928. For long past third class passengers had been agitating for more comfort on their night journeys, between London and Scotland in particular, and at last they received some satisfaction. It was by the building at York of a batch of what were called third class sleeping cars, though actually the counterparts of the Continental *couchette* coaches of to-day. They were vehicles with seven compartments, in each of which the normal seats provided lying down accommodation for two passengers at night, when upper berths, folded into the compartment walls in the daytime, provided sleeping accommodation for two further passengers. That is to say, these cars could serve as ordinary passenger coaches in the daytime and as sleeping cars at night. A modest supplementary charge of 7s. was exacted for their use, and this covered the provision of pillows and blankets. The cushioning was superior to that of ordinary compartments, and there were various other fittings devised for night comfort.

Not many years passed before it was realised that, with these cars definitely allocated to night trains only, the folding out of action of the upper berths became unnecessary, and from then on third class sleepers were built with four fixed berths in each compartment. The London & North Eastern Railway was not alone in this development; on the night on which they began to run, September 24th, 1928, third class sleeping cars were introduced also by the London Midland & Scottish and Great Western Railways.

In the same year, when summer non-stop running between King's Cross and Edinburgh first came into operation, it was thought that with passengers confined to the inside of a train for more than eight hours, with no opportunity of stretching their legs otherwise than in the corridor, some specialised interior furnishing might be an asset. Two new articulated triplet restaurant car sets were therefore built, in the equipment of which a well-known specialist in furnishing, Sir Charles Allom, was called into consultation. The first class restaurant car interiors certainly broke away entirely from British traditions. The furnishing was in the Louis Quatorze style, with loose chairs, wall colourings in delicate tones, curtaining to match, and lighting concealed behind luminous pelmets. The third class cars were less elaborate, but also original in their design and *décor*. This was the beginning of a number of experiments in amenities for passengers by the "Flying Scotsman". In 1928 the train carried a newsboy dispensing papers and magazines. May, 1929, saw the introduction of a coach with a hairdressing compartment, which continued in service, summer and winter alike, for nine years. In the year 1932 another coach made its appearance with a small cocktail bar, which six years later was to blossom out into a full-length buffet-lounge car.

Meantime further developments were taking place. In 1927 and 1928 the first coaches appeared—a series of centre-gangway thirds—in which steel panelling replaced the traditional wooden exterior panels. By 1931 the fact that Continental main line coaches almost invariably were provided only with end doors, rather than doors to each compartment, led to the building of the first coaches of this type by the L.N.E.R.; these soon were included in the formation of the "Flying Scotsman" and other important trains. With this change it became possible to fit each compartment with the wide picture windows which up till then had been possible only in restaurant cars and centre corridor stock. Also a great improvement in the comfort of third class main line corridor coaches was the beginning made in 1932 to fit the compartments with folding arm-rests, so arranging for them normally to seat three instead of four a-side. In 1932 the experiment was tried of equipping the 1.20 p.m. from King's Cross and the 2.5 p.m. from Edinburgh with wireless receivers, so permitting passengers with headphones—hired from the train staffs—to listen to broadcast programmes and to records played in the intervals on a record-player in the train. This facility lasted for about three years, until the novelty had worn off.

The same year saw the introduction of some Doncaster-built first class sleeping cars in which for the first time a showerbath compartment was included. Although not fully air-conditioned, these cars were equipped with pressure ventilation, which soon became standard for all the L.N.E.R. sleeping car stock.

Attention was also directed in 1932 to the service between King's Cross and Cambridge, and it was decided to put on a series of new fast corridor trains, provided with refreshment facilities. The buffet accommodation at first was of the simplest kind, two bays of an open third class coach being replaced by a bar counter, with facilities for serving hot as well as cold drinks, but not for cooking. However, the "Beer Trains", as they were dubbed irreverently by the Cambridge undergraduate population, soon became so popular that this type of buffet proved quite inadequate. Later in the same year, therefore, new buffet cars were put in service with much longer bar counters, a gas grill, a range of tables throughout the rest of the car with tubular steel chairs, and some attractive *décor*, which developed into a general pattern for future buffet car construction.

In 1933 excursion traffic was increasing to such a degree as to justify the building of special stock to accommodate it. So it was that the summer of that year saw the introduction of some new "tourist trains" of very high carrying capacity in relation to their tare weight. Each train comprised twelve vehicles, entirely of open stock apart from the two buffet cars. The formation was of brake third, twin articulated third, buffet car, two twin articulated thirds, buffet car, twin articulated third and third brake, 677 ft. in length and with a tare weight of 338 tons. A total of 600 passengers could be accommodated in each train, in bucket seats arranged two abreast on each side of the centre gangways. Each coach was entered though centre doors only, and was without any partition throughout its length, so giving a very spacious appearance. The buffet cars were provided with kitchens, counters for stand-up service, and tables seating 24 passengers. Chromium-plated fittings throughout replaced the usual brass.

An experiment was tried with exterior panelling of plywood, for the reduction of weight, but experience proved that this did not stand up well to wear, and eventually steel panelling had to be substituted. A cheerful external livery of apple-green lower and cream upper panels was adopted. It was for a limited period only that these trains remained in their completely assembled original form; in later years they were split up, the bucket-seat coaches being included in many ordinary express trains, while the buffet cars found a wide use on various parts of the system.

We come now to 1935, and to the startling vision of silver-grey and stainless steel that first burst upon the public view on September 27th of that year. This was the "Silver Jubilee", Britain's first fully stream-lined train. The wedge-fronted streamlined locomotives for its haulage have been described already in Chapter XVIII; it is with the train that we are now concerned. This was a seven-car set, comprising articulated twin brake third, triplet articulated restaurant car set, and articulated twin first and brake, the whole weighing 220 tons. Such was the popularity of this four-hour service between King's Cross and Newcastle that by February, 1938, the leading twin-coach had been converted to a triplet, raising the tare weight of the set to 248 tons, and the passenger accommodation from 198 to 240 seats.

The most noticeable exterior features of the train were the deep valances between the bogies of each coach, and the flat rubber sheets joining each coach side to the next, in order, with the locomotive stream-lining, to reduce air resistance to a minimum. The coach side-panels were covered with Rexine of a silver-grey shade. Internally the stan-dard of comfort in both classes was above the normal, especially the armchair seats in the first class restaurant and the open section of the adjoining first class coach, and the two a-side seating only in the first class compartments. Pressure ventilation made double windows possible, and helped to quieten the running. Some new methods of suspension caused some very lively sensations on the memorable trial trip, when an average speed of 100 m.p.h. was maintained for 43 miles on end, but blocks of rubber, triangular in shape, inserted between the bogie bolsters and the side stops, damped down the lateral vibrations, and from then on the train ran with commendable steadiness at the highest speeds.

Mention has just been made of the excellent patronage which made it necessary in 1938 to provide an additional coach; it also proved that the public wanted speed and was prepared to pay extra for it. So the London & North Eastern directors, looking round for fresh fields to conquer in the streamline realm, decided next to introduce a similar train between King's Cross and Edinburgh in celebration of the Corona-tion of King George VI, and to call the train the "Coronation". Two coach sets were required this time, and on their appearance in July 1937 proved to be totally different from anything seen previously on British metals, the "Silver Jubilee" included. Externally the coaches, with their deep valances and rubber sheeting between each pair, resembled those of the "Jubilee", but not in their finish, which was unique; the new stock had a brilliant exterior similar to that of a motorcar body, in two shades of blue, light Marlborough blue above and dark Garter blue below. The four streamlined A4 locomotives specially built for this service were painted blue also. Window-frames, exterior mouldings and fittings were all of stainless steel.

The formation of the train comprised four articulated coaches, a brake third, kitchen third, open first, kitchen third brake—two kitchens were thus included, so that all passengers might be served with meals at their seats—and finally, at the rear, an observation car. This last, a remarkable example of the coach-builder's art, had a rear end of beaver-tail shape, rounded off at both corners, with the object of eliminating the vacuum-producing effect of a square coach-end at speed, and so in effect streamlining the tail as well as the head of the train. The number of seats in each train, excluding the observation car, was 216—48 first and 168 third—and the total tare weight 312 tons, so that from the haulage point of view this was to provide a very considerably harder task than the 220-ton "Silver Jubilee".   In the winter months, however, the observation car was not attached, most of the journey being after dark, and the weight then dropped to 279 tons.

Each train was of open stock throughout, and the first class cars were of a highly original design, with swivelling armchairs in alcoves, and tables of oval shape, so that passengers could rotate their chairs towards the windows during meals, or at other times towards the gangway if they so desired.   Separating each pair of alcoves were doorways framed with aluminium architraves, which presented a charming vista through the whole length of the twin cars.   Each alcove had a two-toned green finish in restful colours, the two halves being separated by a curved aluminium fret, which was also seen in the third class cars.   There were various other decorative details which marked this stock out as the finest ever built for British use, other than Royal train vehicles.   Double windows throughout ensured quiet running, and forced draught ventilation could change the air in each coach completely every three minutes.

In anticipation of the success of the "Coronation", and with every reason, by the time it went into service another similar train had been put in hand at Doncaster Works to run as the "West Riding Limited" between King's Cross, Leeds and Bradford, which began to operate in September, 1937.   A fourth set of these coaches also was built as a stand-by, for use on any of the three streamlined workings in the event of the normal train set being out of action for maintenance or repair.   Also in September, 1937, there went into service between Liverpool Street and Norwich a new "East Anglian" train, of six coaches but without the streamlined valances and rubber coach connections and with varnished teak exterior finish.   This again had two kitchen cars and was of open stock throughout, the third class furnishing being very similar to that of the streamline trains, but the first class cars seated three passengers abreast and though extremely comfortable were rather less lavish in their equipment than those of the "Coronation" and "West Riding Limited".

In 1938, however, the Great Eastern line drew level with the Great Northern and East Coast lines by coming into possession of a brand new "Hook Continental" train, of which the equipment was almost identical with that of the "Coronation", including the first class swivelling chairs and alcoves.   Two first class Pullman cars continued to be attached to the rear of the "Hook Continental", but the train itself undoubtedly offered superior first class accommodation, and without the payment of any supplement.   The eleven coaches of the new train accommodated 84 first and 240 second class passengers, and with the two Pullmans made up a total tare weight of 484 tons—a formidable proposition for the B17 "Sandringham" 4–6–0s which by now had to haul it over a by no means easy road.

The year 1938 saw the introduction of yet another pair of new trains for the "Flying Scotsman".   The most interesting feature of these 14-coach sets was the inclusion of a full length buffet car, additional to the triplet restaurant cars; the former had a buffet counter of substantial length, but its opposite end was occupied by a charming little lounge compartment, to which the refreshments could be carried, furnished with tables for two, separated from the corridor by a glass partition. The hairdressing saloons in the previous trains did not reappear, but a new amenity for ladies was a lounge and retiring room, fitted with dressing tables and with a maid in attendance. Such had been the operating cost of increased luxury, that whereas the eleven-coach "Flying Scotsman" trains introduced in 1924 had weighed 370 tons, and the timetable of that year required the A1 Pacifics of that date to do nothing harder than, for example, to maintain an average speed of 52.7 m.p.h. between London and Grantham, by 1938, fourteen years later, the weight of the new 14-coach trains had risen to 503 tons, which the A4 Pacifics had to bring up from Grantham to King's Cross at a scheduled average of 60 m.p.h.

One important development of 1937 concerned the method of cooking in restaurant cars, which by this time on the L.N.E.R. had become almost exclusively electric. The majority of the terminals or sidings from which the cars worked had been equipped with electric points, so that the battery supply of electricity generated from the dynamos while the train was running might be supplemented before starting, but on some runs such points were not available. In 1937, therefore, a car was turned out with an anthracite fire to heat the cooking range, ovens and water, and electric equipment for the grills, hot cupboard, coffee machine, refrigerator and other purposes. This car was tried first on the cross-country Harwich-Liverpool boat train, which finished its day with a Liverpool-Hull run, and did the same in reverse on the day following, and proved such an improvement on electric equipment alone that by the end of 1937 eight similar cars had been turned out for other cross-country routes, such as Newcastle-Bournemouth. Later this became standard L.N.E.R. kitchen car practice.

Over the remaining eight years of London & North Eastern history relatively little remains to be recorded as to passenger rolling stock development. The outbreak of war in 1939 brought new rolling stock construction largely to a stand, apart from the building and equipment of hospital trains, and the adaptation of existing vehicles to serve in this way. The streamline trains were dispersed to various safe hiding places, but on the conclusion of the war unhappily not to return to high speed service, for neither the tracks nor the locomotives were in any condition to resume such fast running. In view of rolling stock shortage these trains had to be split up, and their constituent parts dispersed in all directions, in some cases to perform quite humdrum duties.

It was not until after the L.N.E.R. had ceased to exist that several of the beautiful "Coronation" and "West Riding Limited" twin firsts found some more suitable occupation, one as part of the "Master Cutler" between Marylebone and Sheffield, and, later and still more appropriately, two in the high speed "Talisman" trains between King's

Cross and Edinburgh. The passenger coaches of the "Silver Jubilee", less the restaurant cars, were drafted to the "Fife Coast Express" between Glasgow and St. Andrews; the restaurant cars, and all the kitchen twins from the "Coronation" and "West Riding Limited" sets, were much in demand because of the shortage of such vehicles when restaurant car service was restored after the war.

When coach building was resumed it was, of course, after Gresley's death, and even without his driving force the necessity for economy would have restricted any ideas for radical changes in design or equipment. However, when new corridor coaches were turned out in 1945 it was seen that there had been no reduction in the previous general standards of comfort. One alteration in the corridor stock was to move the doors and entrance lobbies from the coach ends to central positions; in the first class coaches this change split the compartments into three groups of two apiece; in the thirds there was a group of three compartments in the centre, flanked by two groups of two with the cross passages between. The idea was to facilitate entry and exit, but this type of construction continued for a relatively limited time only.

By November, 1945, the "Hook Continental" had been restored to service, with its 1938 stock complete, at first three times a week, but a year later once more daily; in October, 1946, the "East Anglian" train reappeared. In November, 1946, also, the "Yorkshire Pullman" recommenced running. But the London & North Eastern coach-building enterprise which had achieved such distinction was now at an end.

XXIII

The Evolution of Wagon Stock—1923-1947

TO THE vast total of wagons brought into the London & North Eastern stock in 1923—just over 291,000 all told or 307,300 including service vehicles—the North Eastern Railway, with its territory including numberless coalmines, and the great iron, steel, shipbuilding and chemical industries of Teesside, Wearside and Tyneside, made, as might be expected, by far the biggest contribution. Another reason is that alone among British railways (other than those serving the Yorkshire coalfields) the N.E.R. was responsible for providing its own wagons for coal traffic; there were no wagons of private owners in use, wagon hire charges being incorporated in the rate for carriage. So it was that the N.E.R. total of 130,360 wagons and 4,256 service vehicles was greater than that of any other British railway, except the Midland, which had about a thousand more. But the Midland total of mineral wagons was less than one-third that of the North Eastern vehicles of this type; it was the movement of coal in North-East England, particularly from the pits down to the sea for shipment, that accounted for this preponderance.

Next biggest wagon-owner in the L.N.E.R. group was the North British Railway, also greatly concerned in the carriage of coal, with an aggregate of 55,806 wagons and 3,164 service vehicles; the Great Northern, with 38,706 of the former and 2,870 of the latter, just beat the Great Central, with 35,330 and 2,963 respectively. The mainly agricultural traffic of the Eastern Counties accounted for a considerably smaller Great Eastern contribution, and that of the Great North of Scotland was but a fraction of the stocks of its bigger and more influential partners.

The North Eastern mineral wagons had been developed into various types, to suit the different methods of discharging. At the ironworks and steelworks, and at many of the station depots, coal and ore were dropped from raised gantries into dumps below, and this called for hopper wagons with bottom doors. But shipping coal was a different matter. Whereas at some ports, such as Tyne Dock and Blyth, the staiths required bottom door discharge, at other ports round the North East coast, emptying in some cases was through side or end doors, and other wagons were lifted by special coaling plants and tipped bodily for the purpose. A beginning had been made, also, in building locomotive coaling plants of the same type. Most of the hopper wagons for bottom discharge had been designed with floors sloping downwards from the two ends to the centre, to speed up the emptying. In order to reduce train lengths and the ratio of tare to loaded weight, the North Eastern had been increasing its wagon capacities more rapidly than most other railways in the country, and far more than the private owners; as early as 1902, when 10 to 12 tons load was the maximum for the majority of 4-wheel wagons, the N.E.R. was building its first wagons on four wheels with as much as 20 tons capacity.

In the same year came the first introduction of bogie double-hopper wagons to carry 30 tons, but in this the N.E.R. were not alone, for the Great Northern Railway also purchased in 1902 from Hurst Nelson & Co. some all-steel bogie wagons of the same capacity. These were not built on any extensive scale by either company, however, as the sharply curved siding tracks of most collieries could not cope with wagons of such length. Four years later there appeared on the Great Northern some 30-ton wagons intended mainly for brick traffic, with wooden bodies which reduced their tare weight to 14½ tons, as compared with the 17 tons of the all-steel type. All these Great Northern bogie wagons were fitted with the vacuum brake, and it became a custom to marshal two or three of them at the head of lengthy freight trains, in order to provide the locomotives with additional braking power. In 1902, also, the Great Eastern Railway had built its first all-steel wagons, 4-wheelers to carry 10 tons, but with a tare weight of only just over 5½ tons. By contrast, as late as June 1906 the *Locomotive Magazine* illustrated a diminutive and very primitive type of coal wagon still extensively in use on the North British Railway which weighed 5 to 5¼ tons, but could carry no more than 6 tons of the mineral.

Several of the constituent companies possessed wagons of types suitable for carrying unusual loads. The North Eastern, which could boast a variety of wagon types probably more extensive than any other railway in the country, had to transport a considerable quantity of steel products from the works in Teesside and at Consett. Thousands of short 4-wheel bolster wagons were in use, marshalled in sets of two or three, according to the length of the loads, to carry steel rails and sections. Early in the first decade of the century, however, 40 ft. bogie wagons had been introduced for such loads, in this case chiefly of long steel plates. Both the North Eastern and the Great Northern also had built 40 ft. wagons with deep wells between the bogies for carrying large and heavy castings and machinery. In 1921 Gresley of the Great Northern had gone further, and to cope with the rapidly increasing brick traffic from the Peterborough area had designed a bogie brick wagon of sufficient capacity to accommodate 20,000 bricks, with a total weight of 50 tons. This was a wooden-bodied vehicle on diamond-framed bogies which weighed 17 tons, and which therefore gave a load to tare ratio of only just under 3 to 1—an almost record figure.

By 1922 most of the other constituent companies in the L.N.E.R. group had acquired a good proportion of modern wagon stock, both open, covered, and of special types, but a good deal of leeway in construction from the 1914-1918 war period still remained to be made up.

So it was that the 1924 programme envisaged the building of no fewer than 11,830 goods vehicles and 300 brake-vans, at an estimated cost of £2,400,000. Of these 11,750 wagons were to be built in the Company's shops, but 80 refrigerator wagons and the 300 brake-vans were to be put out to contract. Soon after assuming control, therefore, Gresley had to set about building, not only large numbers of wagons of existing types that had been standardised, but others for carrying special types of load.

In these initial orders coal wagons of increased capacity took a prominent place. By 1929 various new classes of bogie wagon were coming into service, including one type 63 ft. in length, capable of carrying 40 tons of 60 ft. steel rails, which previously had to be accommodated on a string of four single-bolster 4-wheelers. These new 63 ft. wagons were of two types, one with five bolsters and the other with seven, and weighed about 23 tons. Another new type was also 63 ft. in length, and had a deep well capable of taking steel plates up to 40 ft. in length, and also up to 13 ft. 6 in. wide; such plates could not be laid flat, of course, within loading gauge limits, but the wagon was provided with a series of diagonal trestles in order to carry wider plates at an angle of 45 deg. Other new bogie wagon types were a 55 ft. trolley wagon with a deep well; a 39 ft. 10 in. coal wagon of 40 tons capacity with double hopper doors weighing no more than 18 tons; and a 40 ft. 5 in. box wagon with an even lighter weight of 15 tons. Also containers, for loading on 4-wheel flat wagons, by now were coming into use, so giving door-to-door transit.

At the end of March, 1930, when the Sheffield Rotary Club was being addressed by W. M. Gracie, Assistant Goods Manager of the Southern Area, the opportunity was taken to assemble for the inspection of members a train of all the latest types of L.N.E.R. freight vehicle types, appropriately headed by 2-8-8-2 Garratt locomotive No. 2395, the most powerful in Great Britain. In the train the *pièce de résistance* was Britain's largest and highest capacity wagon set. This imposing assemblage comprised a central wagon carried on four 6-wheel bogies, 83 ft. 2 in. in length overall, flanked by two 60 tons capacity 12-wheel flat wagons each 36 ft. 6 in. long, and outside them two 20-ton 4-wheel well wagons. The centre wagon was provided with a deep well for the accommodation of an outsize load, such as an electric stator, and if this load did not exceed 110 tons, the flanking wagons were not needed. But loads up to 150 tons could be dealt with safely by mounting hog-backed cantilever girders on the two 36 ft. 6 in. wagons, with the counter-balance weights at their outer ends dropped into the wells of the outer 4-wheel wagons, and their inner ends helping to support the load. The entire assembly measured 226 ft. overall, had 56 wheels, and weighed 221 tons, so that if the full load were being carried, the total weight imposed on the track was no less than 370 tons. Obviously, however, the occasions on which this mammoth has been loaded to full capacity have been but few.

An extraordinary type of vehicle was turned out of Stratford Works in 1929. With the increasing speed of freight trains complaints were being made by guards of the rough riding of the standard 4-wheel brake vans, most of which had a wheelbase of 12 ft. or thereabouts. These vans had to be weighted with cast iron, in order that they might be heavy enough for their brake-power to be effective when working on unbraked freight trains, but the new van, though mounted on a standard steel underframe, had a superstructure of reinforced concrete, heavy enough to permit the balance weights to be dispensed with. The guards, however, were full of complaints; their feet got so cold, and the van suffered so much from condensation on the walls, that some of them refused to ride in it. Experiments were tried by spraying the walls with cork and fitting a wooden floor, but although the reinforced concrete body stood up well in traffic, the experiment was not carried any further.

In 1929, Gresley tackled the problem of unsteady riding in another way by building 20-ton brakevans with their wheelbase lengthened from 12 to 16 ft. Bodies of the normal length were fitted, leaving platforms at both ends between the body and the buffer-beams. This experiment was completely successful, and the design became standard for all future L.N.E.R. brakevan construction, and in later years for the whole country. As to the concrete experiment, consideration was given in 1940, after the outbreak of war, to building wagons with concrete bodies, in order to economise in timber or steel, but this was decided against because of the increase in tare weight which would have been involved.

Container traffic was now developing on a considerable scale all over the country, the door-to-door service so offered greatly appealing to manufacturers. Some of the earliest containers were loaded into ordinary open wagons, but in 1930 a start was made in the construction of special 4-wheel flat wagons for this purpose, fitted with chocks at different spacings to hold containers of varying sizes, with the assistance of chains, securely in position. Later on container flats were built with chocks which could be adjusted to any length of container, and the chains acquired shock absorbers so that the containers might be protected as far as possible from excessive vibration.

With the likelihood of war in view, some more of the immense wagons for outsize loads were turned out, one on four 4-wheel bogies to carry 100 tons, and another on four 6-wheel bogies to carry 120 tons, 10 tons more than the 110-tonner of 1929. Then in 1939 there was built a well wagon on six fixed axles, three at each end, to carry a load of 50 tons. Bigger plate wagons of the trestle type also were turned out suitable for loads up to 50 tons. When Gresley's untimely death came about, in 1941, he had been successful in reducing the stock of wagons and service vehicles from 307,300 to 270,000, but with a greater aggregate carrying capacity, despite the reduction in numbers. Considerable progress also had been made in adapting wagons to fast freight service by fitting them with vacuum brakes; the L.N.E.R. by now owned some 50,000 continuously braked wagons.

N

Little else needs to be recorded in this chapter. The post-war leeway needing to be made up in wagon construction ruled out any experiments in new types; indeed, the various London & North Eastern wagon works were so heavily pressed, in 1947, that an order was placed with Ashford Works of the Southern Railway for 1,500 16-ton all-steel coal wagons, both side-door and end-door types. For this work a special shop was set aside, and a new method of assembly was devised with the wagons during construction moving round the shop on their own wheels for the bodies, partly welded and partly riveted, to be built up in stages. It should be added that the welding of wagon frames had been first tried in 1932 at the Great Central wagon works at Dukinfield, and had proved completely successful, especially in reducing tare weight. The practice was extended later to coach underframes. Nationalisation had been under way for between ten and fifteen years before other major freight developments such as the Liner Trains came into the picture.

XXIV

Passenger Train Services—1923-1947

AT THE time of the formation of the London & North Eastern Railway in 1923, the passenger train services of its constituent companies were just recovering from the effects of the 1914-1918 war. This recovery had been slow; an analysis based on the fastest times between London and various provincial cities and towns in 1922 showed that those over the East Coast Route were 20 per cent. slower, of the Great Northern Railway 26.1 per cent. slower, and of the Great Eastern Railway 26.5 per cent. slower than before the outbreak of war in 1914. The Great Central Railway, however, which had contrived to keep some quite fast services in operation during the war, even including the restaurant cars that had disappeared on other lines, could show an average deceleration no greater than 8.5 per cent., well below that of any other British railway. There was still operating, for example, such an express as the 3.15 p.m. from Marylebone to Manchester, non-stop to Leicester, 103 miles, in 114 minutes, and after a stop at Nottingham reaching Sheffield in 3 hours 22 minutes.

By 1922 the East Coast deficiency had shrunk from 20.0 to 7.1 per cent., the Great Northern from 26.1 to 8.5 per cent., the Great Eastern from 26.5 to 3.2 per cent., and the Great Central from 8.5 to 1.9 per cent., and there was now much speculation as to what effect the fusion of the individual railways into one company would have on these figures. There need have been no fears. In the very first summer of London & North Eastern history some massive accelerations took place. The best time from King's Cross to Edinburgh, by a night express, came down at one stroke from 8 hours 25 minutes to 7¾ hours, and to Aberdeen from 11 hours 52 minutes to 11 hours 10 minutes; and although these times soon had to be eased because of the growing weight of the night trains, other accelerations were to be an advance indication of steadily faster train services.

The coming into operation of the "Harrogate Pullman", of which more in a moment, pared the best London-Leeds time from 3 hours 55 minutes to 3 hours 25 minutes; Bradford was 21 minutes nearer at 3 hours 54 minutes, Harrogate 25 minutes nearer at 4 hours, and Hull 29 minutes nearer at 3 hours 53 minutes. Great Central main line expresses by now were back practically to their full pre-war speed, and on the Great Eastern the very tight 82-minute schedule of the Hook of Holland boat train between Liverpool Street and Parkeston Quay again was in opera-

N*

tion, together with various fast summer services, such as the 2½-hour Yarmouth non-stops, though the remainder of the Great Eastern main line trains continued to maintain their somewhat lethargic journeys.

One train service development shortly before the Grouping had been the subject of widespread publicity, though not adding very materially to travel facilities. It had been, by the co-operation of the North British, North Eastern, Great Central and Great Western Railways, a through service between Aberdeen and Penzance. Actually for most of its history the passenger accommodation that covered the entire 785 miles was no more than a single coach, alternately of North British and Great Western stock; on the westbound journey passengers could change into a sleeping car from Swindon onwards, and going north they could have similar sleeping accommodation from York northwards. Between York and Swindon the through coach was attached to a four-coach train which included a buffet car, with several parcels vans, expanded in summer to whatever longer formation the traffic required.

The through journey occupied a total of about 21 hours, and though the number of passengers taking through tickets must have been infinitesimal, the train performed useful service intermediately, giving passengers from such Midland towns as Sheffield, Nottingham and Leicester comfortable through service both to the West of England and the North of Scotland. The through working began in October, 1921, and continued up to the outbreak of war in 1939, with the only alteration that in later years the coach was diverted from Aberdeen to Glasgow as its Scottish starting-point and destination.

We come now to the principal train service developments from 1923 onwards. One which was of no small importance took place in that year. During his period of office as General Manager of the Great Eastern Railway, the American Sir Henry Thornton, accustomed to Pullman travel in his own country, had considered that Pullman cars ought to find more extensive use in Great Britain than over the relatively short runs of the London Brighton & South Coast and South Eastern & Chatham Railways to which by his time they were confined. He therefore reached an agreement with the Pullman Car Company to operate cars over the G.E.R., on the Continental trains between Liverpool Street and Parkeston Quay and over the main lines in various other directions. The cars in the Continental trains prospered, but Eastern Counties travellers in general did not take kindly to the payment of supplementary fares, and by 1922 such of the other Great Eastern Pullman services that still remained were languishing for want of patronage. The agreement with the Pullman Car Company still had a number of years to run, and something had to be done to make the cars more profitable.

By the summer of 1923 a solution of the problem had been found. An experiment began by marshalling six of the cars (which up till then had been run singly) into an all-Pullman express to operate between King's Cross, Leeds, Harrogate and Newcastle, called the "Harrogate Pullman". The schedules were so arranged that departures from both

King's Cross and Harrogate were at 11.15 a.m., which meant that the up train, calling intermediately at Darlington and Ripon, had to leave Newcastle at 9.20 a.m., while the down "Harrogate Pullman" was into Newcastle by 5.0 p.m. The non-stop booking of 3 hours 25 minutes between King's Cross and Leeds equalled the fastest that had been scheduled between the two cities up to that time; to and from Harrogate the time taken was 4 hours each way.

The experiment proving successful, the decision was reached to try a second all-Pullman service, which began to operate in June 1924. This was between King's Cross and Sheffield, but not at first by the direct route *via* Retford; instead, leaving London at 11.5 a.m., 10 minutes ahead of the "Harrogate Pullman", the new train left the main line at Grantham to run non-stop to Nottingham Victoria, taking 2 hours 23 minutes for the 128¾ miles, and then continuing over the Great Central main line to reach Sheffield at 2.20 p.m. After a layover of 2½ hours here, the return journey was begun at 4.45 p.m., and with the same Nottingham stop only the London arrival was at 8.0 p.m.

This development had a less happy outcome, however. No more than a month later the working was completely altered, the train beginning its day at Sheffield at 10.30 a.m., and returning at 6.5 p.m., with the same Nottingham call. But the Midland city still refused to be attracted, and the next step, in April, 1925, was to base the train on Manchester, with a start from the Central station at 9.50 a.m. and from Sheffield at 11.3 a.m., and a non-stop run over the 161¼ miles from there *via* Retford to King's Cross, reached at 2.0 p.m. The return non-stop 6.5 p.m. working to Sheffield recalled a Great Northern experiment in the even faster time of 2 hours 50 minutes twenty years earlier; the 1925 Pullman train finished its day in Manchester at 10.12 p.m. But, like Nottingham, both Sheffield and Manchester appeared to take little interest in Pullman luxury, and by September, 1925, yet another plan was inaugurated.

This was to run the short-lived "Sheffield Pullman" instead to Leeds and Bradford as the "West Riding Pullman", leaving King's Cross at 11.10 a.m.; the "Harrogate Pullman", at 11.20 a.m., now avoided Leeds altogether by taking the Knottingley and Church Fenton route, non-stop over the 198¾ miles between London and Harrogate in 3 hours 43 minutes. This brought the latter train, which meantime had been extended to Edinburgh, into the Scottish capital by 7.35 p.m., an acceleration of 20 minutes. With a similar routing on the up journey, King's Cross was reached at 4.45 p.m. For the return working of the "West Riding Pullman", the Leeds cars were worked empty from Leeds to Harrogate, to form a new up service at 11.15 a.m. *via* Leeds, where the Bradford cars were attached; leaving Leeds at 11.50 a.m., the train reached King's Cross at 3.15 p.m. From now on, therefore, Harrogate enjoyed two daily Pullman workings to London, but one only in the reverse direction; and four complete Pullman trains were needed to operate the service.

So matters continued until May, 1928, when a change was made which, apart from acceleration, was to be permanent. A new and handsome train of seven all-steel Pullmans was built for the London-Harrogate-Edinburgh service, and the "Harrogate Pullman", from now on extended from Edinburgh to Glasgow, was renamed the "Queen of Scots". The former 11.15 a.m. departure from London was reverted to, also the Leeds route, with reversal at Leeds Central as before; Glasgow was reached at 8.45 p.m., after a journey of 450¾ miles. The down "Yorkshire Pullman" was altered from the same date to leave King's Cross at 4.45 p.m. instead of 11.10 a.m., and from now on Leeds and Bradford had both morning and evening Pullman trains to and from London. In 1935 it was decided that Hull also should enjoy Pullman service, and in the fastest time ever scheduled between Hull and London —3½ hours each way—and this involved stopping the main train at Doncaster in order to attach and detach the Hull cars. It also made necessary a mile-a-minute timing of this heavy train over the 156 miles between Doncaster and King's Cross—155 minutes up and 156 minutes down.

The only remaining L.N.E.R. Pullman services throughout the year were those of the Great Eastern Continental boat trains between Liverpool Street and Parkeston Quay, to which two first class cars were still attached. But from 1923 onwards a complete train of first and third class cars was kept assembled for special Great Eastern workings. It was used to and from Newmarket in the race weeks and on Sundays it became the "Clacton Belle", giving London patrons a day at that resort. From this beginning there developed the excursion trips in summer of the "Eastern Belle Pullman Limited" from Liverpool Street on different days to Cromer, Sheringham, Yarmouth, Lowestoft, Walton-on-the-Naze, Hunstanton and Skegness at quite cheap fares and at high speed—a much appreciated facility.

Meantime there had been other important happenings. Competition between the East and West Coast routes from London to Scotland, which had been more or less quiescent after the "Races" from London to Edinburgh and Aberdeen in 1888 and 1895, had begun to revive with the formation of the London & North Eastern and London Midland & Scottish Railways. From 1895 onwards it had been agreed between the two sides that the minimum journey times of the day trains between London and both Edinburgh and Glasgow should not be cut below 8½ hours, and notwithstanding the rising tide of acceleration elsewhere in the country this hampering agreement was still being observed. Competition in prestige therefore had to take other forms. In the summer of 1927 the L.M.S.R. introduced an entirely new train for its 10 a.m. service from Euston to Edinburgh and Glasgow, and the corresponding return working, calling it the "Royal Scot" and with no publicly advertised stops intermediately. For changing engines a stop was made at Carnforth, and there was a second stop at Symington in Scotland to detach the Edinburgh section. To beat the L.M.S.R. 236¼-mile Euston-Carnforth non-stop run the L.N.E.R. decided from the same date to run the first section of the "Flying Scotsman" non-stop over the $268\frac{1}{4}$ miles between King's Cross and Newcastle.

By 1928 the L.M.S.R. was in possession of its new "Royal Scot" 4-6-0 locomotives, and began to run the "Royal Scot" train non-stop over the 301 miles between Euston and Kingmoor, 2 miles north of Carlisle, to which point the engine-changing was now transferred. This move the L.N.E.R. decided to counter by breaking a world record. This was the inauguration of the longest regular non-stop run in the world by booking the "Flying Scotsman" without any intermediate stop over the $392\frac{3}{4}$ miles between King's Cross and Edinburgh. And as engine-crews could not be expected to man their locomotives for over 8 hours continuously, this development required the production by H. N. Gresley, the Chief Mechanical Engineer, of the unique corridor tenders described in Chapter XVII, to make it possible for a second engine-crew to replace the first at the midway point on the journey.

To add to the attraction, from the date of introduction of the non-stop schedule, in May, 1928, a brand new pair of trains made their appearance, including cocktail bar, hairdressing compartment, and retiring room for ladies. But it was slightly ludicrous that, owing to the East-West Coast minimum time agreement, the non-stop "Flying Scotsman" had to be allowed the same $8\frac{1}{4}$ hours between London and Edinburgh as the second portion which followed it, making the intermediate stops at Grantham, York, Newcastle and Berwick, *plus* Darlington on the up run. At last, in 1932, a more realistic view of the situation had to be taken, and the speeds of the Anglo-Scottish day trains brought more into line with the general standard of speed elsewhere. With the L.N.E.R. and L.M.S.R. authorities agreeing to keep each other informed as to their plans, therefore, acceleration at last began.

In May, 1932, 25 minutes were cut from the all-the-year-round timing of the "Flying Scotsman", bringing it down to 7 hours 50 minutes with the usual intermediate stops; and when the non-stop running was resumed for the summer season in July of that year, 45 minutes were slashed at one stroke from the schedule, which now became $7\frac{1}{2}$ hours. In 1936 this was reduced to $7\frac{1}{4}$ hours and in 1937 to 7 hours; while by the time the Second World War began the year-round timing of the main "Flying Scotsman" train also had come down to 7 hours 20 minutes. The new set of stock which had been introduced in 1938, with a minimum weight of 504 tare tons, and a total which, with extra vehicles, passengers and luggage might amount to 600 tons, made the working of this train one of the most onerous locomotive assignments in the country. The "Flying Scotsman", of course, was not the only train thus speeded up; the afternoon service between London and Edinburgh and the "Queen of Scots" Pullman had shared in the acceleration from 1932 onwards, though not in so great a degree as their more famous companion.

Before the outbreak of war in 1939, there had been other express train developments of first-class importance over the East Coast main line. As described in earlier chapters, the first twenty-five years of the reign of King George V were celebrated by the introduction of the "Silver Jubilee", Britain's first fully streamlined train. From September 30th, 1935, Newcastle was brought within 4 hours of London by this express, which left the Tyneside city at 10 a.m., called only at Darlington, and had a 70.4 m.p.h. schedule from there to King's Cross, 232¼ miles in 198 minutes, arriving at 2.0 p.m. Its Tyneside and Teesside patrons then had 3½ hours for the transaction of their affairs in the capital, and at 5.30 p.m. were starting homewards, to reach Darlington at 8.48 p.m. (with a smart connection for Middlesbrough) and Newcastle at 9.30 p.m. A small supplementary fare of 5s. first and 3s. third class proved no deterrent to patronage, and the "Silver Jubilee" was soon running filled to capacity; indeed, had the precaution not been taken of reserving a seat, the would-be traveller would not infrequently find himself left behind. As soon as the "Silver Jubilee" began to run, the popular 5.30 p.m. from King's Cross to Newcastle had its starting time altered to 5.45 p.m., and acquired a through portion for Hull, to detach which an additional stop was made at Doncaster.

Streamline service did not stop short at the "Silver Jubilee". Such had been the success of this experiment that the London & North Eastern management was soon looking round for fresh fields to conquer, and what better than a high speed service between London and Edinburgh? Moreover, such an introduction would serve to celebrate a Coronation, for King George V had passed away in 1936, and his son was to be crowned as King George VI in 1937. So two new trains, outstanding examples of coach construction and equipment, as described in Chapter XXII, were completed in readiness for the introduction of the "Coronation" streamlined express in July, 1937. The down train, leaving King's Cross at 4.0 p.m., wrested the speed supremacy from the Great Western Railway's "Cheltenham Flyer" by being booked over the 188¼ miles from King's Cross to York in 157 minutes, at 71.9 m.p.h. start to stop; the next stop was Edinburgh, reached in 6 hours from London— 2¼ hours less than the 8¼ hours which had persisted as the minimum time for a day train until a mere five years earlier.

The up "Coronation", starting from the Scottish capital at 4.30 p.m., called only at Newcastle, now giving the Tyneside city both morning and evening 4-hour flyers to London, and reached King's Cross at 10.30 p.m. After a short time, it was realised that even though Novocastrians had the 5.30 p.m. "Silver Jubilee" to provide them with an evening 4-hour service from London, Newcastle was too important a city for the down "Coronation" to miss, and as Gresley's streamlined A4 Pacifics had a little in hand north of York on this extremely fast schedule, a stop at Newcastle was added to that at York without any increase of overall journey time.

The economic value of streamline service by now was fully realised, and the winter timetable of 1937-1938 saw the introduction of a third streamline train, with coaching stock similar to that of the "Coronation". This was the "West Riding Limited", which for the first time brought

Leeds within less than 2¾ hours of London daily, and Bradford within 3 hours 5 minutes. Leaving Bradford Exchange at 11.10 a.m., the new train was worked by two 0-6-2 tank engines to Leeds Central, reversing there, and restarting at 11.33 a.m. for London. The 2 hours 42 minutes allowed for the 185¾ miles to King's Cross non-stop was not beaten or even equalled after the war until 1966, when modern 3,300 h.p. "Deltic" diesels made possible a time of 2 hours 40 minutes each way daily. The mid-morning start of the up "West Riding Limited" conflicted with the up working of the Harrogate portion of the "Yorkshire Pullman", and the latter was therefore diverted to run *via* York to Doncaster, thus giving York its first regular Pullman service. In the down direction the "West Riding Limited" left King's Cross at the relatively late hour of 7.10 p.m., being due in Leeds at 9.53 and Bradford at 10.15 p.m.

Yet another train with some pretensions to being described as streamlined, though not claiming any streamline speed, was the "East Anglian", also beginning to run in the autumn of 1937 between Liverpool Street and Norwich. As described in Chapter XXII, this was a six-coach formation, with interior equipment somewhat similar to that of the "Coronation" but not quite so lavish. Two 4-6-0 locomotives of the B17 type were streamlined for its working, but the demand made on their tractive power was no more than moderate; the timing initially fixed for the 115 miles, including a 4-minute stop at Ipswich, was 2¼ hours. In the down direction departure from Liverpool Street was at 6.40 p.m., and in the up the train left Norwich at 11.55 a.m. A year later the schedule was cut to 2 hours 10 minutes, and the Ipswich-Norwich booking came down to 48 minutes for the 46¼ miles, requiring a start-to-stop average of 57.9 m.p.h., the fastest known until then over Great Eastern metals.

A new express of note which appeared for the first time in the summer timetable of 1925 was the "Scarborough Flier"—it will be noted that the L.N.E.R. preferred the word "Flier" to the more common "Flyer" —leaving King's Cross at 11.50 a.m. and running the 188¼ miles to York without any intermediate stop. At first it carried as far as York a portion for Glasgow, and later on through coaches to Whitby; the overall time from London to the popular Yorkshire resort was 4½ hours. Eight years later the London-Scarborough time was cut to 4 hours 10 minutes, and in 1935 to 3 hours 55 minutes; this meant that in no more than two years the allowance from King's Cross to York had come down from 3½ to 3 hours, raising the start-to-stop speed to 62.9 m.p.h.

Over these years the Great Central main line trains which were strongly in competition with the L.M.S.R. Midland service, especially between London and Sheffield, were being gradually speeded up. In 1929, for example, 33 minutes were pared from the timing of the 7.30 a.m. from Sheffield to London, bringing the train into Marylebone by 10.40 a.m.; at the same time the 4.45 p.m. from Marylebone was accelerated to reach Sheffield at 8.2 p.m. New corridor stock was introduced on all the principal trains at the same time. A further general smartening of Great Central services took place in 1932.

In the same year Cambridge came under review. The route used by most passengers between London and Cambridge was the Great Eastern one, from and to Liverpool Street, but the difficult exit from the terminus, with its severe speed restrictions, and the congestion north of Tottenham due to the heavy freight traffic, were a considerable handicap to any material speed-up of the Great Eastern trains. The former Great Northern route from and to King's Cross was a little longer—58½ as compared with 55¾ miles—but it had greater speed possibilities, and gave the opportunity for improving the service at several important stations intermediately. So in 1932 an entirely new series of trains was put into operation, five each way daily between King's Cross and Cambridge, calling at Welwyn Garden City, Hitchin and Letchworth—hence the name "Garden Cities and Cambridge Buffet Expresses"—each provided with a buffet car, and with the third class compartments furnished with armrests (a comparative novelty at that time) and therefore seating three a-side only.

The new service was an immediate success. It began with three-coach trains which in a very short time had doubled in length and at times grew to formations of nine or ten vehicles, no small problem of haulage on the tight times laid down. At first the overall times were fixed at 82 minutes down and 77 minutes up, but by 1933 these had been cut to 75 and 72 minutes only, faster than the best Great Eastern times. In the course of time Royston stops were introduced into some of the schedules, and since the war the importance of what has now become the satellite town of Stevenage has compelled stops there also; but the overall times of these trains to-day are considerably longer than in the heyday of the service.

Before the outbreak of war in 1939, however, the Great Eastern Section had discovered that it could after all run much faster trains than previously between Liverpool Street and Cambridge. Three new non-stop trains in each direction were put on, at 11.10 a.m., 1.40 and 4.12 p.m. down and 11.50 a.m., 2.20 and 8.30 p.m. up, each taking no more than 65 minutes for the 55¾ miles—the fastest daily service Cambridge has ever enjoyed to and from London. Buffet cars were run in each train. The North Eastern Area also was steadily improving its internal services; one 1937 development of note was that the non-corridor train sets which since 1913 had worked the hourly even-interval service begun in that year between Newcastle, Sunderland, West Hartlepool, Stockton-on-Tees and Middlesbrough were replaced by corridor trains with buffet cars. A similar transformation took place of the services between Newcastle and Carlisle; and also between Leeds and Scarborough.

Further north, the Scottish Area, now with the use of Gresley's magnificent Class P2 2-8-2 express engines, as well as his Pacifics and 2-6-2s, had been steadily improving its coastal service between Edinburgh and Aberdeen. For the first time since the abortive attempt of the North

Various exchanges of locomotives between the different lines took place after the Grouping. *Above:* Great Central 4–4–2 No. 6083 working a former Great Northern "Cambridge Buffet Express" past New Southgate. [*C. L. Turner*

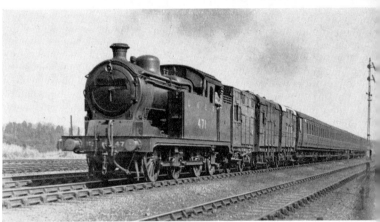

Right: Great Eastern Class N7 0–6–2 tank No. 471 near New Southgate with a Great Northern suburban train to Hatfield. [*F. R. Hebron*

Below: One of the numerous Great Northern Class N2 0–6–2 tanks with a Gresley articulated suburban train.

[*British Railways*

Above: The S.S. *Arnhem*, first of the ships built for the Harwich–Hook service in replacement of those lost during the 1939–1945 war.

Left: One of the Harwich–Zeebrugge train-ferries backing into her berth at Harwich.

Below: A comfortable lounge on the S.S. *Duke of York*, transferred after the war from the Heysham–Belfast to the Harwich–Hook service.

[*British Railways*

Above: A scene of activity at No. 12 Quay of the King George Dock, Hull. Steel is being loaded for export.

Below: Parkeston Quay West, the extension opened in 1934 mainly for the use of Dutch and Danish ships to the Hook of Holland and Esbjerg respectively. At the quay is the Danish M.V. *Kronprinsesse Ingrid.*

Left: Sir Ronald Matthews, L.N.E.R. Chairman from 1938 until the end of the Company's history in 1947.

Right: Sir Charles Newton, Chief General Manager from 1939 until the middle of 1947.

Below: A remarkable record was that of Miss Pearl Wadham, who as Personal Secretary acted as "cox" to a "crew" of no fewer than eight successive G.E.R. General Managers and L.N.E.R. Southern Area Divisional General Managers at Liverpool Street —from left to right Sir Henry Thornton, S. A. Parnwell, Alexander Wilson, G. F. Thurston, Sir Charles Newton, H. H. Mauldin, George Mills and Sir Michael Barrington-Ward.

[*British Railways*

British Railway in 1905 to meet Caledonian competition by introducing 3-hour schedules between the Scottish capital and the Granite City, which very soon had to be eased out, 3-hour trains reappeared in 1937, one, northbound, at 5.15 p.m. from Edinburgh, connecting with the down non-stop "Flying Scotsman", and giving a 10¼ hour service from London to Aberdeen, and the other, southbound, at 9.0 a.m. from Aberdeen. But the fastest Aberdeen-London service was that which connected with the 4.30 p.m. "Coronation" from Edinburgh; passengers leaving Aberdeen at 12.45 p.m. could now be into King's Cross 9¾ hours later. Further, an excellent service also was being provided between Edinburgh and Glasgow, not as yet on an even-interval basis, but with trains roughly at hourly intervals, almost all with restaurant car facilities, and most taking between 60 and 65 minutes for the journey.

And then, in 1939, the heavy hand of war came down and changed everything. At the start of the First World War, in 1914, curtailments and decelerations of train services came about gradually over the years of war, but from September, 1939, in expectation of early bombing raids, the changes were immediate and very drastic. As the months of the so-called "phoney war" dragged on, some improvements were made, but after the autumn of 1940, when Britain herself came into the "front line", and raids, shortage of staff and materials, and consequent deterioration in maintenance began increasingly to take effect, matters steadily worsened. The "Flying Scotsman" and the "Aberdonian" still proudly retained their names, but finally it took all but 9 hours to reach Edinburgh, and the up journey time declined to 9 hours 7 minutes. Restaurant cars had disappeared, and with military personnel added to the ordinary travellers trains had become enormously weighty; indeed, as mentioned already in Chapter XX, there are records of loads up to 25 bogie coaches, with a gross weight of something like 850 tons, being imposed on the Gresley Pacifics during this period.

After the war had dragged on to its end, in 1945, train service recovery was a far slower business than it had been after the 1914-1918 war. By October, 1945, however, the first restaurant cars reappeared, and a year later full restaurant car service was once again in operation over all the L.N.E.R. main lines. October and November, 1946, saw the restoration of the "Yorkshire Pullman" and the "East Anglian", while in 1947 the 7.30 a.m. from Sheffield to Marylebone and the return 6.15 p.m. became a new named service, the "Master Cutler". But the last year of London & North Eastern history also saw a recession, due to shortage of motive power for freight workings and also of coal, which led to a temporary suspension of certain trains. The difficulty was less on the London & North Eastern Railway than on some of the other lines; for a time, indeed, the Great Western Railway withdrew even as famous a train as the "Cornish Riviera Express".

In the summer of 1947 a test was carried out between King's Cross and Edinburgh with the Gresley streamlined Pacific *Silver Fox* and a six-coach train which included the dynamometer car, in order to ascertain whether the track had been restored to a condition suitable for the restoration of higher speeds.   The 4–6–2 achieved some point-to-point times which up to that date were certainly unprecedented, in particular 70 minutes for the 80 miles from York to Newcastle and 68 minutes in the reverse direction, while the highlight was a top speed of 102 m.p.h. on the descent from Stoke Summit towards Peterborough.   This trial prompted some speculation as to whether the "Silver Jubilee" and the "Coronation" were to be restored to service, but when in September, 1948—the first year of nationalisation—a new fast train did appear, it turned out to be the "Tees-Tyne Pullman" between King's Cross and Newcastle, at 9.30 a.m. up and 5.30 p.m. down.   For the time being, however, its overall time of 5 hours 20 minutes was far longer than the 4 hours of the former "Silver Jubilee".

From the start the popularity of this new all-Pullman service was sufficient to ensure that it would be permanent, and with the "Queen of Scots" also back in operation from July, 1948, three Pullman trains were now working once again over former L.N.E.R. metals.   By degrees the timing of the "Tees-Tyne" was cut down, but not until after the advent of the "Deltic" diesels thirteen years later did it become possible once again to span the 268¼ miles between London and Newcastle in 4 hours and the 393 miles between the English and Scottish capitals in the "Coronation's" 6 hours.   The year 1966 has seen the London-Edinburgh allowance of the "Flying Scotsman" cut to an all-time record of 5 hours 50 minutes, while the up "Tees-Tyne" has introduced the first 80 m.p.h. run over former L.N.E.R. metals and over the same course as the one-time "Fastest Train in the British Empire"—from Darlington to York, 44.1 miles, in 33 minutes, 10 minutes less than the 1901 time.

XXV

Maritime Interests

THE FORMATION in 1923 of the London & North Eastern Railway brought under a single control the largest aggregation of docks and harbours owned by any single British company, and in addition a considerable tonnage of shipping. These ranged up the whole length of the East Coast from Harwich in the south to Burntisland and Methil in Scotland, with the greatest concentrations those of the North Eastern Railway on the Humber, Tees and Tyne. Many notable battles had been waged by the N.E.R. in acquiring their harbour rights, especially on the Humber, where the Hull Corporation steadfastly opposed every effort of the North Eastern to develop its dock interests; and after the Hull & Barnsley Railway in 1885 had invaded N.E.R. territory, with Hull Corporation support, as described in Chapter II, the only way in which the North Eastern in later years had been able to build the great King George V dock, opened in 1914, was by doing so jointly with the Hull & Barnsley.

It had been in 1893 that the North Eastern Railway secured its first major footing on the Humber by taking over from the Hull Dock Company the Town Docks, with a water space of 140 acres and a quay space of 280 acres. These actually comprised eight individual docks and various basins, three of them tidal, with a sufficient depth of water for ships of moderate draught at all states of the tide; included among them was St. Andrew's Dock, where an extensive fish trade was conducted. Most subsequent improvements planned by the N.E.R. were blocked by the Hull Corporation, but at last powers were obtained jointly by the North Eastern and Hull & Barnsley Railways, as just mentioned, for the construction of the magnificent deep water dock opened in person by King George V in June, 1914. This included two spacious graving docks, electric belt conveyors, coaling appliances and hydraulic hoists, warehouses and a grain silo. The two companies also constructed a deepwater oil jetty, 1,500 ft. long, at Salt End, and in 1928 the North Eastern had added a similar jetty 1,900 ft. in length, to enable the largest vessels to discharge oil in bulk. Just before the end of independent N.E.R. history, in April, 1922, the North Eastern and Hull & Barnsley Companies had amalgamated, and the N.E.R. therefore came into the L.N.E.R. Group in exclusive possession at Hull of docks with a total water area of 220 acres and of 7 miles of water frontage.

On the south side of the Humber there had been closely comparable energy in dock development by the Great Central Railway. Grimsby has always regarded itself as the premier fishing port in the world, and its trade had been largely fostered by the original Manchester, Sheffield & Lincolnshire Railway, which early in its history acquired the Old Dock. Then followed the building of the Royal, Alexandra and Union Docks and further extensions, completely equipped for dealing with fish in bulk, and in the later years for the export of coal and the import of pit props, at wharves totalling 28,160 ft. in length. But the greatest Grimsby dock enterprise, after the Manchester, Sheffield & Lincolnshire had become the Great Central Railway, had been the opening in 1912 of the great Immingham Dock, to the west of Grimsby, with a central basin 1,000 ft. square in area, and two lengthy parallel jetties enclosing a total water area of 45 acres, with a large graving dock. Coal had been the principal export, and imports had ranged from pit props and mining timber to iron ore and many other commodities. One jetty was used by ocean-going steamers.

Further north the North Eastern Railway was in possession of the Middlesbrough Dock, with a water area of 25½ acres, whence there were regular services to all parts of the world; this was used mainly for the export of iron and steel products from the many works on Tees-side. Another large group of docks was at Hartlepool, with a water area of 138 acres, including the 45 acres of the West Harbour and 45 acres of timber ponds, for the main commodity dealt with here has always been pit props and mining timber for the Durham coalfields. Further north still was Tyne Dock, with a water area of 50 acres, a tidal basin of 10 acres and 21 acres of timber ponds; here the chief industry has been the export of coal and the import of iron ore and pit props. Mention also must be made of the extensive coal-shipping staiths at Dunston-on-Tyne and at Blyth in Northumberland.

Of great importance to the London & North Eastern Railway, but in this case more from the passenger than the freight or mineral point of view, was the acquisition of the Great Eastern Railway port and shipping activities at Harwich. All over Northern Europe the G.E.R. steamer services between Parkeston Quay and both the Hook of Holland and Antwerp had earned a very high reputation. As early as 1836 Harwich had become a mail packet station of note, and by 1863, in face of much opposition, the G.E.R. had begun its own steamship services to the Continent. By 1883 the traffic had expanded to such an extent as to justify the building and opening of the new up-river Parkeston Quay, which by the end of Great Eastern history had attracted other services, in particular that of the United Shipping Company of Denmark to and from Esbjerg. With the Parkeston Quay port facilities the London & North Eastern Railway also acquired the small docks at Felixstowe, on the opposite side of the river.

While Grimsby, as we have seen already, was Britain's principal fishing port, with Hull not far behind, the Great Eastern Railway's Lowestoft Harbour ranked but little inferior in importance; it included 74 acres of tidal basins, and over 11,000 ft. of quayage, with a dry dock and other equipment for dealing with the trawlers. The G.E.R. also owned the South Pier, much used as a promenade by holiday makers, and was responsible for providing band performances and other entertainments not usually associated with a railway.

Scotland also made its contribution to the docks ownership of the London & North Eastern Railway. The North British Railway had an extensive docks installation at Methil, on the Fifeshire coast, for shipping the products of the Fife coalfield, with three docks having a water area of 27½ acres and capable of shipping 7,000,000 tons annually. Further up the Firth of Forth was Burntisland, terminus of the train ferry from Granton (Leith) before the Forth Bridge was opened, and also engaged mainly in the shipment of coal. Further still up the Firth, and in this case on the south shore well inside the Forth Bridge, were the smaller docks at Bo'ness, at which the principal activity was the import of pit props for the Lanarkshire coalfield. Then the North British owned the only harbour and docks to come into L.N.E.R. ownership on the west side of the country, at Silloth in Cumberland. Traffic which used this tidal harbour on the Solway Firth was mainly to and from the Isle of Man and Ireland, particularly the import of Irish cattle.

There was also the fleet of steamers which came into the possession of the London & North Eastern Railway on the formation of the Company; with the harbours and docks this was of no inconsiderable size, as Table 30 reveals. Here the most notable contribution was that made by the Great Eastern Railway. We have seen already that the G.E.R., notwithstanding its limited financial resources, had established an enviable reputation for the excellence of its steamer services from and to Parkeston Quay, Harwich, maintained by vessels which despite their modest tonnage were like miniature liners in their equipment. By 1922 the losses during the First World War had been made good, partly by the entry into service between 1919 and 1921 of three fine new ships— the *Antwerp*, *Bruges* and *Malines*, and also by the acquisition from the Canadian Pacific Ocean Services of the *St. George*, which made it possible to provide daily service to and from the Hook of Holland in April of that year, and to and from Antwerp a year later. This made a total of six passenger ships, the *St. Denis*, the *Archangel* and the old *Vienna* having survived the war hazards while in Government service; in addition there were the *Cromer* and the *Felixstowe* still engaged on cargo service to and from Rotterdam.

The Great Central owned a much larger fleet, but of smaller vessels. From 1891 this company maintained a daily Royal Mail service between Grimsby and Hamburg, and various other services to and from Northern Continental ports. Five of the vessels had passenger accommodation; two carried passengers in the summer season only; while the remaining four were almost exclusively cargo vessels, accommodating no more than 12 passengers apiece. As compared with the 20 to 22½ knots speed of the Great Eastern passenger fleet, the Great Central ships were far less powerful, maintaining no more than a uniform 13 knots. A curious feature of the Great Central steamers was that five of the eleven of them were named after cities or towns not actually on the Great Central system.

The remainder of the London & North Eastern fleet was made up of river or ferry steamers. On the Clyde the North British Railway, from its pier at Craigendoran, on the north side of the river, was engaged in competition with the steamers of the Caledonian and Glasgow & South Western Railways and one or two private companies operating from Gourock, Wemyss Bay and Fairlie on the opposite shore. The former were all paddle steamers, the most powerful being the *Waverley*, 235 ft. long, with a gross tonnage of 405, engines developing 2,200 i.h.p. and a speed of 19 knots. The *Marmion*, *Kenilworth* and *Talisman* were 210 to 215 ft. long, of 393 to 409 gross tons, and with an i.h.p. rating of 1,500 to 1,700. The *Lucy Ashton* was a smaller ship of 1,000 gross tons only.

In addition, the *William Muir* still continued from pre-Forth Bridge days the ferry service across the Firth of Forth between Granton and Burntisland, and the *Dundee* that further up the Firth between North and South Queensferry. On Loch Lomond the North British was joint owner with the Caledonian of five paddle steamers, which from 1923 became joint London Midland & Scottish and London & North Eastern property. The list was completed by the four Great Central paddle steamers *Brocklesby*, *Killingholme*, *Cleethorpes* and *Frodingham*, which plied across the Humber between Hull and New Holland, the small G.C. tenders *Barton* and *Marple*, used in the Grimsby Docks, and the Great Eastern motorboats *Epping*, *Hainault* and *Brightlingsea*, which maintained a service up and down the River Orwell between Harwich, Felixstowe and Shotley.

Apart from its extensive docks ownership, the North Eastern Railway had not developed much maritime activity. As far back as 1905 it had obtained Parliamentary powers to run steamer services between Hull and various Continental ports, and in 1906 it had acquired a half-share with Thomas Wilson & Company in a cargo service between Hull and Hamburg, Antwerp, Ghent and Dunkerque. The year 1907 also saw the introduction of a passenger and cargo service jointly with the Lancashire & Yorkshire Railway between Hull and Zeebrugge, using for the purpose two L. & Y. steamers, the *Colleen Bawn* and the larger *Duke of Clarence*. In the summer efforts were made to popularise the *Duke of Clarence* passenger business, with the help of a connecting boat train to and from Hull Riverside Quay, which included through coaches between the Quay and Liverpool, Manchester, Glasgow and Newcastle. But this service never found much favour with the travelling public, and though resumed after the 1914-1918 war it was mainly for cargo purposes. With the Grouping it became a joint London & North Eastern and London Midland & Scottish activity.

After the formation of the L.N.E.R. the first development of note on the water was one of considerable importance; it was the establishment of a train ferry between Harwich and the Belgian port of Zeebrugge. In July, 1921, the Great Eastern Railway had begun a tri-weekly steamer service between Parkeston Quay and Zeebrugge with the 27-year-old *Vienna*, but in summer only and chiefly for passengers; this did not attract the passenger patronage sought and did not last for long. Not so, however, with the Harwich-Zeebrugge train-ferry, designed for freight; this has not only become permanent, but apart from the setback of the 1939-1945 war has steadily proved more popular and has required more and more sailings each week. Two new companies were formed: Great Eastern Train Ferries, Ltd., on this side, and La Société Belgo-Anglaise des Ferry Boats on the other side of the North Sea. Terminals suitable for the transfer of the railway wagons from shore to ship and *vice versa* had to be built at Harwich and Zeebrugge, and a stock of large white wagons, bearing the legend "Anglo-Belge", soon became a familiar sight in this country.

The service was begun with three train-ferry steamers which during the war had carried munitions between Richborough in Kent and Dunkerque; each had four railway tracks and could accommodate 54 of the large ferry wagons. Prince George, later the Duke of Kent, formally inaugurated the service on April 24th, 1924, and before very long this means of communication was used to transport a much more distinguished cargo, of Pullman and sleeping cars which had been built in this country for the Continental services of the International Sleeping Car Company. In 1933 the L.N.E.R. bought up Great Eastern Train Ferries Ltd., including the three steamers, and came to a new agreement with the Belgian company.

The next happy event affecting Harwich was in 1927. Since 1876 the Zeeland Shipping Company of Holland had run a passenger service between Queenborough Pier near Sheerness in the Thames estuary (formerly owned by the London Chatham & Dover Railway and from 1899 by the South Eastern & Chatham) and the Dutch port of Flushing. Owing to the inadequate facilities at Queenborough and delay to the steamers through Thames fogs, in 1911 it was decided to transfer the service to Folkestone. But Folkestone was considerably further from Flushing than Queenborough, and in 1926 a further transfer was decided on, and this time to Parkeston Quay, effective from January 1st, 1927. Not until after the 1939-1945 war did the Zeeland Shipping Company come to its final decision, to change its port on the Dutch side from Flushing to the Hook of Holland; from then on the London & North Eastern Railway could advertise both day and night services between Parkeston Quay and the Hook of Holland, with the Dutch steamers by day and the L.N.E.R. steamers by night.

By now the use of Parkeston Quay was so much more intensive that increased accommodation was becoming urgently necessary. In 1928 the number of passengers by the Hook route alone showed an increase of 8 per cent. over those in the preceding year. An extension of the quay was therefore put in hand, and brought into use in 1934, with an additional and well-equipped passenger station called Parkeston Quay West. The latter from now on accommodated the steamers of the Zeeland Shipping Company, and those of the United Shipping Company of Denmark to and from Esbjerg; the L.N.E.R. Hook and Antwerp steamers still used the original quay, which in the interim had been completely rebuilt in reinforced concrete and thoroughly modernised in its equipment.

Encouraged by the steadily increasing traffic, the London & North Eastern Railway now placed contracts for three more steamers, identical in design, all taking the names of older vessels which had been scrapped or had been war casualties. Each was 366 ft. long, 50 ft. in the beam, of 4,220 gross tons and capable of 21 knots; and it was significant of greatly increased internal comfort and cabin spaciousness that whereas the *Antwerp*, *Bruges* and *Malines* of 1919-1921 had accommodated 758 to 776 passengers in ships 332 to 337 ft. long and of 2,949 to 2,969 tons, the much larger new ships had accommodation for 716 passengers only. They were the *Vienna*, delivered in 1929, and the *Amsterdam* and *Prague*, which followed in 1930. The previous *Vienna*, which had been renamed *Roulers* in 1920, and as previously mentioned had been used on the thrice-weekly Harwich-Zeebrugge service, was sold for scrap in the same year, 1930, and the ex-Canadian *St. George* had gone to scrap in 1929.

In the summer of 1932 the L.N.E.R. tried a new experiment by inaugurating week-end pleasure cruises, using the new *Vienna* for the purpose, and the venture proved so successful that in later years a number of Continental ports additional to the original Antwerp and Zeebrugge were included in the itineraries. In 1936 structural alterations were made to the *Vienna* specially to increase her adaptability to cruising, particularly in the matter of greater protection and comfort in bad weather.

Another shipping enterprise during this period was the building of a fine new paddle-steamer for the Clyde services, the *Jeanie Deans*, larger and more powerful than any of her North British predecessors. She was 250 ft. long and 30 ft. in the beam, was capable of 18½ knots and entered service in 1932. Three years later another and much more original type of vessel joined the *Jeanie Deans*; it was the *Talisman*, 215 ft. long and 27 ft. 6 in. in the beam, which was unique in that her paddles were driven by diesel-electric power. She proved a most economical ship to run, and for the first time on the Clyde it became possible for a captain to regulate the speed of his motors direct from the bridge. The only other steamer development up to the outbreak of war in 1939 was the introduction to the cross-Humber service between Hull and New Holland of two new paddle-steamers, the *Wingfield Castle* and *Tattershall Castle*, both with ample accommodation for motorcars and cargo as well as for passengers.

Meantime there had been other happenings at Hull. That coming events were casting their shadows before was seen in the bringing into use of another jetty, 1,900 ft. long, for unloading oil at Salt End, Hull. Some costly improvements to the Fish Stage at St. Andrew's Dock, Hull, begun in 1928, had an unhappy sequel. After making the stage half as wide again as formerly—a by no means easy task without interference with the work of the trawlers and fish merchants—the work had only just been completed in 1928 when the entire structure was destroyed by fire and a fresh start had to be made. In the end the St. Andrews Dock was extended to a total length of 1,250 ft., making this the largest fish dock in Britain, with a water area of 23½ acres; the scheme also included a quay on the north side 1,000 ft. long and five new slipways for hauling the largest trawlers out of the water.

A further change in Hull involved the sale to the Corporation of the old Queen's Dock, which took place in 1930. This dock, of which the brick-lined sloping walls provided one of the few remaining examples of the form of dock construction used in the days of the clipper-bowed sailing ships, dated back to the Eighteenth Century; it had long been outmoded and latterly had been used only for the laying up of small craft. The Corporation had it filled in, and used the site to form part of their handsome new city centre. Another L.N.E.R. dock disposal, which took place in 1936 and was due in part to diminishing coal exports, was of Tyne Dock, sold to the Tyne Improvement Commissioners in 1936 for £600,000.

Across the Humber there had been developments at Grimsby also. Here the London & North Eastern Railway had joined hands with the Grimsby Corporation in building another fish dock, at a total cost of nearly £1,700,000. This had been planned originally by the Great Central Railway as far back as 1912, when Parliamentary sanction had been obtained, and a contract was about to be let when the 1914-1918 war broke out. Not until 1934 did the plan materialise, the formal opening taking place on October 4th of that year. By its completion the total fish dock area at Grimsby was increased to 66 acres, with a main quay 2,000 ft. long and a south quay 690 ft. long.

In 1939 the outbreak of war once again laid its heavy hand on all the railway steamer fleets, that of the London & North Eastern included, and this time the toll was far heavier than in the 1914-1918 war. The *St. Denis*, which had served as a hospital ship, was scuttled at Rotterdam in May, 1940; a month later the *Bruges* was lost off Le Havre; an enemy bomber sank the *Archangel* in May, 1941; while the *Malines* was the victim of a torpedo off Port Said in July, 1942. The last of five fine ships to be lost was the 1930 *Amsterdam*, which was serving as a hospital ship when sunk by a torpedo off the Normandy coast in August, 1944. The War Office retained the *Vienna* to use her for troop transport between Parkeston Quay and the Hook of Holland, and the only passenger ship returned to the L.N.E.R. was the *Prague*; the *Essex Ferry* also had survived to take up the Harwich-Zeebrugge train-ferry service once again.

War damage at the ports had to be made good, and the North Sea cleared of mines, before any regular sailings from Parkeston Quay could be resumed.   The first trips began in November, 1945, three times weekly; early in 1946 the Danish sailings to and from Esbjerg recommenced; and in the summer of the same year an attempt was made to revive the Parkeston Quay-Antwerp service, but the only vessels available were the relatively small Great Central *Dewsbury* and *Accrington,* which were both much slower and offered less comfort than formerly. It was a great relief when the first post-war ship made its appearance, the *Arnhem,* delivered in the summer of 1947.   She was faster and more commodious than any previous ship plying between Parkeston Quay and the Hook of Holland; 375 ft. in length, 52 ft. in the beam, and of 4,490 gross tons, the *Arnhem* had a speed of 22 knots, and provided cabin accommodation for 416 passengers and berths for 96 more, as well as 23,000 cub. ft. of storage in the holds and special space for motorcars. Initially the experiment was tried of making her a one-class ship, but this did not find favour with a section of the travelling public, and conversion to the usual two classes followed at a later date.

Table 30
Ocean-going Steamers brought into L.N.E.R. Stock in 1923
and acquired by L.N.E.R. 1926–1947

Owning Railway	Name of Steamer	Gross Tonnage	Length Feet	Speed Knots	Passenger Accommodation	Date of Bldg.
Great Eastern	Vienna‖	1,753	314	18	320	1894
,,	Cromer	812	254	13	*0	1902
,,	St. Denis¶	2,435	343	20	696	1908
,,	Archangel¶	2,448	343	20	650	1910
,,	Felixstowe	892	225	14½	*0	1919
,,	Antwerp	2,957	332	21	758	1920
,,	St. George‖	2,676	352	22½	700	1920
,,	Bruges¶	2,949	332	21	776	1920
,,	Malines¶	2,969	337	21½	776	1922
Great Central	Staveley	1,047	240	13	†12	1891
,,	Nottingham	1,051	240	13	†12	1891
,,	Lutterworth	1,007	240	13	†12	1891
,,	City of Leeds	1,361	257	13	‡199	1903
,,	City of Bradford	1,360	257	13	‡182	1903
,,	Marylebone	2,082	270	13	425	1906
,,	Dewsbury	1,678	265	13	422	1910
,	Bury	1 683	265	13	420	1910
,,	Accrington	1,678	265	13	416	1910
,,	Stockport	1,681	265	13	418	1911
,,	Macclesfield	1,018	250	13	†12	1914
London & North Eastern	Sheringham	1,088	265	14	*0	1926
,,	Vienna§	4,220	366	21	716	1929
,,	Amsterdam¶	4,220	366	21	716	1930
,,	Prague	4,220	366	21	716	1930
,,	Arnhem	4,490	375	22	422	1947

*Cargo only; †Mainly cargo; ‡In summer only; in winter cargo only.
§Second ship of this name; taken over by War Ministry and not returned to L.N.E.R.
‖Disposed of in 1929 and 1930; ¶Lost by enemy action in 1939–1945 war.

Not until the summer of 1948, the first year of nationalisation, was it possible once more to provide a nightly service throughout the week between Parkeston Quay and the Hook of Holland, with the help of the *Duke of York*, which had been transferred from the London, Midland & Scottish Heysham-Belfast route. By this time also the Parkeston-Antwerp service was running three nights a week, with the *ex*-G.C.R. steamers, but with diminishing patronage; air competition was now beginning to have its effect, as well as the relatively poor accommodation, and in 1956 this service was withdrawn. Further, the new *Suffolk Ferry* had joined the *Essex Ferry* on the Harwich-Zeebrugge run, where traffic was now booming. And here the maritime story ends. Table 30 records the changes in the L.N.E.R. seagoing fleet during the 25 years of the Company's history. The magnificent new *Amsterdam* of 1950, and the even finer *Avalon* of 1963, belong to the British Railways era.

XXVI

The Chief Officers—1923-1947

BEFORE WE review the changes in the highest administrative posts during London & North Eastern history, it is pertinent to recall a development which took place within the largest of the four railway groups, the London Midland & Scottish Railway, in May, 1925, two and a half years after the grouping. This was the appointment of an economist, Sir Josiah Stamp, to occupy the newly created post of "President of the Executive". Whereas the London & North Eastern group had been formed by a number of railways of which the principal constituents had been accustomed to work in harmony, and the remainder had had reasonably harmonious relations, the two largest constituent companies in the L.M.S.R. group had been rather less friendly competitors, with very different organisation and methods, and, it must be admitted, the leadership at Euston from the time of amalgamation had been distinctly shaky. The interest of the radical change which was now taking place lay principally in the creation of a form of organisation at the top and a title, culled from American practice, both of which were new to British railway circles.

The bringing in from outside of a distinguished personality to a high administrative post was not new, of course, in British railway history. The Great Eastern Railway had done the same in 1914, when Henry W. Thornton had been appointed as its General Manager, in this case himself an American; but though Thornton in course of time introduced certain American methods on the G.E.R., he did not go as far as to follow the American practice of a President and a number of Vice-Presidents, the latter each representing one section of the organisation and the whole forming a kind of administrative council. This, however, is what Stamp did. After the retirement in succession of Sir Arthur Watson and Rt. Hon. H. G. Burgess, who for short periods from the amalgamation onwards had been General Managers of the L.M.S.R., in 1926 the position of General Manager was abolished, and four Vice-Presidents were appointed, two to represent the operating and commercial sections, one in charge of works and ancillary undertakings, and the fourth to represent the accounting side, all responsible to the President.

But this was not all. In the following year, 1926, Sir Guy Granet gave up the L.M.S.R. Chairmanship, and there was a certain lifting of eyebrows at King's Cross and Marylebone when it became known that he was to be succeeded by Stamp, who from then on had the unique distinction in British railway history of being both Chairman and President of the Executive of his Company. There was some concern in L.N.E.R. circles as to what this might mean in inter-railway relations, but in the event the arrangement caused little or no embarrassment to harmonious working between the two Companies' headquarters. While this history of Sir Josiah Stamp has no immediate connection with that of the London & North Eastern Railway, it has been included as recalling an organisational development in the early years of the four grouped railways that might have influenced the L.N.E.R. organisation, but actually did not, nor for that matter those of the Great Western and Southern Railways.

It is not without interest to note, from the biography by Professor J. Harry Jones entitled *Josiah Stamp—Public Servant*, how this author appreciated the special difficulties of the L.N.E.R. during these developing years. In his own words, "None of the problems confronting the railways were common to all four groups, while others varied in character between the four companies. Thus, for example, the most unfortunate was the L.N.E.R. group. It inherited in certain districts some of the most inefficient and antiquated systems and methods of operation; there was more leeway to be made up. Moreover it depended more than any of the others upon coal traffic between the North East and London, and bore the brunt both of the coal depression and that in the shipuilding industry.

"I travelled between Yorkshire and London at least twice a month throughout the inter-war period, and was able to bear witness to the tremendous improvement that took place, year by year, after the railways had been restored to private enterprise. In some ways the L.N.E.R. had the hardest struggle of any, and without fuss or bother achieved a degree of success that won the respect of experienced travellers on the system." Truly it might be said that "E'en the ranks of Tuscany could scarce forbear to cheer"!

We come now to the changes which took place during London & North Eastern history in its higher administrative personnel.

The Company had been in existence for no more than a year when S. A. Parnwell, who had been General Manager of the Great Eastern Railway at the time of the amalgamation and from then on Divisional Manager of the Southern Area, L.N.E.R., elected to withdraw from railway service and to return to professional practice as a land surveyor. He was succeeded in 1924 by Alexander Wilson, who had been the first North Eastern Area Divisional General Manager at York. This opened the way for George Davidson, former General Manager of the Great North of Scotland Railway, who since amalgamation had been acting as Solicitor to the Scottish Area, to resume managerial status at York. But not for long, however, as he died in harness in 1928.

The office of Divisional General Manager, North Eastern Area, was now assumed by Thomas Hornsby, the same Area's Goods Manager. A solicitor by profession, Hornsby for many years had been very closely in the confidence of the North Eastern Railway management while engaged in their Legal Department, and was well known to the trading community and public authorities of North Eastern England, with whom he was a popular figure.   Always sartorially immaculate, he was an extremely able negotiator and an impressive figure in the witness box.   His elevation had the result of bringing the historic name of Gibb once more into prominence in York railway circles, for his successor as Goods Manager was Paul Gibb, son of Sir George Stegmann Gibb, best known of all former General Managers of the North Eastern Railway. Until then Paul Gibb had been District Goods Manager at Newcastle.

In considerable contrast to what had happened at Euston, as already related, few organisational changes were found by experience to be needed from the scheme originally laid down for the L.N.E.R.   One important development took place, however, in 1927.   The first Southern Area Superintendent had been W. M. Clow, and on his retirement it was decided, for operating purposes, to divide the Area into two parts. The former Great Eastern lines came under the direction of Col. H. H. Mauldin, a thoroughgoing Great Eastern man, who became Superintendent, Eastern Section; while the Great Northern and Great Central lines were entrusted to V. M. Barrington-Ward, who had had a wide experience on the Midland and North Eastern Railways, and whose title from now on was Superintendent, Western Section.

The year 1928 saw the death of C. L. Edwards, Chief Accountant of the L.N.E.R., and his place was taken by C. H. Newton, who had graduated in the Great Eastern Railway, and who was destined ultimately to succeed Sir Ralph Wedgwood as Chief General Manager. At the end of the same year Sir Francis Dunnell retired from the post of Chief Legal Adviser; he had long been at the centre of things, both as regards the railways and also during the First World War in Government service; the latter in 1919 earned him a K.C.B.   Two years later he was created a baronet.   A former North Eastern man, Dunnell had added considerable lustre to every office that he had filled.   His successor, I. Buchanan Pritchard, came from the Metropolitan Railway, whose Solicitor he had been; later he was to achieve the unique distinction of acting as Legal Adviser to two railways simultaneously—the London & North Eastern and the Great Western—during the unsettled years between the end of the 1939-1945 war and nationalisation.   His accumulated experience of negotiations with the Government was of particular value to the four railway groups collectively in those days when they were facing all the uncertainties of the future.

At midsummer, 1929, there was a change in the direction of Southern Area affairs at Liverpool Street.   Alexander Wilson, who had occupied the post of Divisional General Manager, Southern Area, since 1924, now was succeeded by G. F. Thurston, a Great Eastern man whose first experience had been in the Goods Manager's Department, then from 1919 as Secretary of the G.E.R., and finally, from 1925, as Chief Stores Superintendent of the L.N.E.R.

A serious loss to the Company was the death early in 1930, at the age of only 48 years, of J. A. Wickham, the Chief Engineer for Docks—a post that he had held for no more than two years.   He was a civil engineer who had had world-wide experience before joining the Chief General Manager's staff at King's Cross in 1924, with special responsibility for overseeing important new works proposals.   In the following year he became Assistant General Manager (Parliamentary) and Industrial Agent, and it was from the beginning of 1928 that he went to Hull as Chief Engineer for Docks.   There he brought a breath of the wide open spaces to bear on the dock engineering, with his use both of novel methods and also of pungent expression.   His tall, imposing figure created an impression in Hull, and not in railway circles alone; he was greatly missed.

His successor as Assistant General Manager at King's Cross was W. M. Teasdale, who had brilliantly directed the London & North Eastern Advertising Department since its formation.   But after holding his new position for between three and four years, Teasdale gave up his railway career to become a director of Allied Newspapers Limited. The newspaper world was the richer by having gained the services of this able officer, who had he remained with the L.N.E.R. might well in the course of time become their chief executive.   This was not the only occasion during these years on which the business world had enriched its personnel at the expense of the L.N.E.R., for in 1927 Bolsover Colliery had attracted to its service as General Manager C. A. Lambert, up till then Passenger Manager of the North Eastern Area.

In the years 1933 and 1934 death laid its hand on the London & North Eastern directorate.   In September of the former year one of the best-known of all the directors and a past Chairman of the North Eastern Railway, Viscount Grey of Fallodon, passed away.   He had played a notable part in railway development and politics for nearly 30 years, and his death removed a revered figure from the L.N.E.R. Board.   An equally severe blow fell in March, 1934, with the passing of Lord Faringdon, who had been Chairman of the Great Central Railway throughout from the opening of the London Extension until the end of its independent history, when he became Deputy Chairman of the London & North Eastern Railway.   As Chairman of the Finance Committee his genius and skill had done very much to bring the Company through its difficult financial troubles, and then in influencing a wise expenditure of capital to pave the way for the service given by the L.N.E.R. to the public and to industry.   He was succeeded as Deputy Chairman by Sir Murrough John Wilson, who had been a member of the Board of the former North Eastern Railway.

At midsummer, 1934, a change of note took place in Scotland.   James Calder, who from 1918 up to the time of the Grouping had served the North British Railway faithfully as General Manager, and from 1923 had become General Manager, Scotland, decided to retire.   His place in the managerial chair at Waterloo Place, Edinburgh, was taken by George Mills, another Scotsman, whose experience up till 1927 had been in N.B.R. accountancy, after which he had become Assistant to the Chief General Manager for Rates and Statistics, and later, from 1929, Assistant Goods Manager and finally Goods Manager in the Southern Scottish Area. The title of the highest administrative post in Scotland now became Divisional General Manager, Scottish Area. In 1936 a similar change took place at York, on the retirement of Thomas Hornsby from the post of Divisional General Manager, North Eastern Area. His place was taken by C. M. Jenkin Jones, already referred to in Chapter IX as having first set in motion the L.N.E.R. Central Wagon Control. His translation to the Divisional General Managership was from the office of Superintendent, North Eastern Area, and Freight Rolling Stock Controller.

Nothing has been said in this chapter as yet concerning the Civil Engineering Departments of the London & North Eastern Railway. Unlike the Mechanical Engineering, which was under the supreme direction of H. N. Gresley as Chief Mechanical Engineer, with a Chief Assistant, Mechanical Engineers in charge of the works at Darlington, Doncaster, Stratford and in Scotland, and also an Electrical Engineer, there was no Chief Civil Engineer as yet for the whole of the L.N.E.R. Each Area therefore had its own independent Engineer, and not until during the 1939-1945 war was a Chief Civil Engineer appointed for the entire system.

When the American Henry W. Thornton came to the Great Eastern Railway as General Manager in 1914, he brought with him from the Long Island Rail Road an engineer of Ulster origin, John Miller, who had been serving under him in the U.S.A. At first Thornton combined the post of Civil Engineer with that of General Manager, while his *protégé* was finding his feet, but soon Miller became Engineer in his own right. Various American methods were introduced by him, especially in the matter of programming future work, and certain of these methods in the end found country-wide acceptance. Towards the end of 1924, when C. F. Bengough was retiring from the position of Engineer at York which he had held from North Eastern days, John Miller was appointed to succeed him. An individualist indeed, Miller left his mark on the North Eastern Area in many different ways. An able engineer, he was also an advocate of physical fitness, as the large gymnasium which he created at York for the use of railwaymen still bears witness. He was also keen on making the railway presentable to the public eye, and many were the untidy waste stretches of ground alongside the main lines that he beautified by grass plots, with neat concrete verges.

On the vacation of the Engineer's chair at Liverpool Street, Charles J. Brown, previously Engineer of the Great Northern Railway, to which the Great Central had been added since the grouping, now took over the Great Eastern also, and became Engineer, Southern Area. This particular post was destined to become the stepping stone to considerably greater responsibilities, and it is of interest that it was occupied by an unbroken succession of engineers who had graduated on the former North British Railway. Whispers used to go the round of the Engineer's Office about the influence of the "old school tie"; be that so or not, from Charles J. Brown onwards, himself a former North British man, five successive occupants of the Engineer's chair at King's Cross all were Scotsmen. When Brown retired in January, 1937, he was succeeded by R. J. M. Inglis, who at the beginning of 1941 was to become Divisional General Manager of the Scottish Area. His successor was J. C. L. Train, who ultimately became a member of the Railway Executive and subsequently of the British Transport Commission also.

By 1938 the old order was definitely changing. It came as a great shock to many when in the autumn of 1938 William Whitelaw announced that, owing to the increased pressure of private affairs, he proposed to resign from both the Chairmanship and the Board of the London & North Eastern Railway. It seemed almost impossible to think of the Company without Whitelaw who, with his splendid presence, his courtesy, and the tenacity with which he had grappled with the Company's many problems from its beginning onwards, had inspired profound respect among proprietors and staff alike. His selfless service was widely recognised, and his going was regretted by all.

The election by the Board of Sir Ronald Wilfred Matthews to succeed William Whitelaw, from September 30th, 1938, gave general satisfaction, especially in his native city of Sheffield, where Sir Ronald had important business interests and had occupied the honourable office of Master Cutler. In speaking of his successor, Whitelaw described him as one of the ablest business men in the country. Matthews had little opportunity of displaying this ability, however, for the days of war once again were near at hand. His tenure of office lasted until the end of independent London & North Eastern history, but from September 1st, 1939, when the Government took over the control of the railways, that control was never relaxed, and the conduct of L.N.E.R. affairs, as those of the other four groups, was fraught with the complexities and acute difficulties that are inescapable at a time of war and its aftermath. Otherwise Sir Ronald might have been able to inspire and guide the L.N.E.R. to even greater achievements than the previous fifteen years had seen.

Just over five months later, the London & North Eastern Railway was to suffer another great loss; it was the retirement, on March 3rd, 1939, on reaching the age limit, of Sir Ralph Wedgwood, Chief General Manager. Characteristically he slipped out of his office quietly at the end of a Saturday morning's work, and the L.N.E.R. officially knew him no more, although a little later in the year his officers from the length and breadth of the line showed their respect and affection for him at a farewell gathering held in the Liverpool Street Station Hotel. Sir Ralph had been intimately associated with the former North Eastern Railway, in its final year as General Manager, and for the 17 years since the grouping had occupied the supreme office of Chief General Manager of the London & North Eastern Railway. His task had been an uphill fight throughout, with little or no relaxation, but with the loyal co-operation of his officers he had brought the Company up to a high level of efficiency, and left behind him an organisation imbued with a fine spirit of keenness. As evidence that Wedgwood's reputation extended well beyond the confines of the L.N.E.R., almost immediately after his retirement he was nominated by the Minister of Transport to serve as Chairman of the shadow Railway Executive Committee which already, behind the scenes, was preparing plans for running the railways of Britain in the event of war.

To succeed Sir Ralph the directors appointed C. H. Newton, up till then Divisional General Manager of the Southern Area. Although an accountant by training and for most of his railway career, Newton in his outlook was far from being the typical financier. He had strong views on matters of general railway interest, and needless to say his financial upbringing and experience were of great value to him in forming his judgments. But for him as with Sir Ronald Matthews the sands of time were running out rapidly; six months later, on September 3rd, 1939, the outbreak of the Second World War put an end, for a number of years, to any hopes of further progress. Meantime Newton was succeeded as Divisional General Manager at Liverpool Street by Col. H. H. Mauldin, Superintendent, Eastern Section, Southern Area. He too, however, had little opportunity to settle down in his new sphere before having to uproot his Liverpool Street office and transfer it to a safer emergency location in the wilds of Hertfordshire, near Hitchin. With the Great Eastern staff in particular the appointment of "The Colonel", as he was affectionately known, was popular, but he was destined to hold the office for no more than two years before death claimed him, at the relatively early age of 59, at the end of March, 1941. His successor was George Mills, coming south from his position as Divisional General Manager, Scotland; he in his turn was succeeded by R. J. M. Inglis—later Sir Robert Inglis—who up till then, as previously mentioned, had been Engineer, Southern Area.

A far more serious loss by death, on April 5th, 1941, had been that of Sir Nigel Gresley, Chief Mechanical Engineer, one of the most able and renowned locomotive engineers that the country had ever known. Chapters XVI to XVIII have described in detail his work for the London & North Eastern Railway, on which his "big engine" policy had equipped the Company more than adequately for the rigours of war operation. As already mentioned, his successor was Edward Thompson, whose final post, before this appointment, had been Mechanical Engineer, Southern Area (Western Section) combining the posts formerly known as Mechanical Engineer, Doncaster, and Mechanical Engineer, Gorton.

Another popular figure removed by death shortly afterwards, in December, 1943, was that of Archibald Leslie Gibson, Continental Traffic Manager. His rise from a clerkship in the Great Eastern General Manager's Office at Liverpool Street had been due to his coming under the notice of Henry W. Thornton, the American, who was always interested in anyone with original ideas, which Gibson certainly had. During the 1914-1918 war and on into 1920 he was stationed at the G.E.R. General Agency in Paris, from which, after the war, his travels took him to various parts of Europe, and fitted him in 1924 to be appointed Continental Traffic Manager (South), that is, in charge of the L.N.E.R. services based on Harwich. By 1930 he had become Continental Traffic Manager for the entire system.

As an old Great Eastern man, naturally his major affection was for the services which that company had developed with such conspicuous success, and the reputation of which had increased still further under his inspiring direction. From 1940 onwards he had assumed also the responsibility of Passenger Manager, Southern Area, and with little doubt it was this burden, added to such maritime preoccupations as the requisitioning of ships and wartime relations with the Admiralty, that hastened his death.

In 1942 a considerable change was made in the civil engineering administration of the L.N.E.R. Until this time, as previously mentioned, each Area had its independent Engineer and staff, but it was now decided that, as with the Chief Mechanical Engineer over the whole line, there should similarly be a Chief Civil Engineer. This important responsibility fell on the shoulders of J. C. L. Train, up till that time Engineer, Southern Area. Shortly after the end of the war, in September 1945, George Mills retired from the office of Divisional General Manager, Southern Area, to be succeeded by V. M. Barrington-Ward, who, it will be remembered, had been appointed Superintendent, Western Section, Southern Area in 1927; in 1939, on the promotion of Col. Mauldin from Superintendent, Eastern Section, to the Southern Area General Managership, Barrington-Ward had added the Eastern Section to his supervision, becoming Assistant General Manager (Operating) in 1942. Meantime he had been, from 1938, Chairman of the Operating Committee of the "shadow" Railway Executive, which, as previously mentioned, had been brought into being by the Ministry of Transport to prepare for the eventuality of war. The year 1946 saw the death of Sir Murrough John Wilson, Deputy Chairman of the Company, and the election as his successor of Walter K. Whigham, who had been a member of the Board of the former North Eastern Railway and a Director of the Bank of England.

To complete the record of personalities, it only remains to be added that Sir Charles Newton, who had been knighted in 1943, retired from the position of Chief General Manager in June, 1947, and Miles Beevor, the Company's Chief Legal Adviser, assumed this post in a temporary capacity until the Railway Executive took over the country's newly nationalised system. On this body the L.N.E.R. was well represented, for under the British Transport Commission both J. C. L. Train and V. M. Barrington Ward became members. The former proceeded even further, for in a later reorganisation of British Railways, as previously mentioned, he became a member of the British Transport Commission. And, to complete the story, both these gentlemen eventually received the accolade, to become Sir Landale Train and Sir Michael Barrington Ward. It is difficult not to contrast these past honours conferred on distinguished railwaymen with the almost complete absence of any such recognition in the days in which we now live.

During all these years there had been no difficulty in finding suitable officers to fill the less senior positions which became vacant as the result of changes in top management. This availability of trained men was largely due to the Traffic Apprenticeship scheme which Sir George Stegmann Gibb had introduced during his time as General Manager of the North Eastern Railway. On becoming Chief General Manager of the L.N.E.R. Sir Ralph Wedgwood had been quick to extend this scheme, together with the staff educational arrangements which had been in operation on his former railway.

He was fortunate in being able to delegate the oversight and administration of the extended scheme to his Assistant General Manager, Robert Bell, under whose guiding hand it flourished and produced a never-failing supply of men well trained for responsible posts. It is a remarkable testimony to the intrinsic value of the training given by the London & North Eastern Railway Traffic Apprenticeship scheme that when, in the autumn of 1964, Robert Bell reached his 90th birthday, an album was presented to him containing the signatures of all former L.N.E.R. Traffic Apprentices still in the service. No fewer than 111 of them were found to be occupying positions of responsibility at all levels on British Railways and the associated undertakings of the British Transport Commission, from district officers even up to members of the British Railways Board. Others of the trainees had found their way into important posts in the outside world.

This is but one of the valuable contributions made by the L.N.E.R. to the nationalised railways—a generation of highly trained and experienced railwaymen whose heart has been in their work and who have laboured through the years since nationalisation to keep alive the traditions of service that they learned in the days when their loyalty was given unreservedly to the London & North Eastern Railway.

Index

Aberdeen–Penzance Service, 196
Admiralty, 11, 87
Agreement, Anglo-Scottish Time, 36, 199
Air Services, Railway, 84
Airways, Imperial, 84
Amalgamation, G.N., G.C. & G.E. Proposal, 38, 44
Area Board, 67
Association, Railway Companies, 13

B

Balmoral Castle, 28
"Beer Trains," London–Cambridge, 185
Board, L.N.E.R., Members, 1923, 47
Brakevans, Freight Train, 193
Bridges and Viaducts:
  Belah & Deepdale, N.E.R., 94
  Dinting Vale, G.C.R., 94
  Forth, 25, 93
  High Level, Newcastle, 34, 93
  King Edward, Newcastle, 93
  Queen Alexandra, Sunderland, 94
  Royal Border, Berwick, 34, 93
  Staithes, N.E.R., 94
  Tay, 25, 93
  Welwyn, Herts, G.N.R., 94
Bridges, Swing, Selby & Naburn, 95
British Empire Exhibition, Wembley, 72, 119
British Transport Commission, 92
Buffet Cars, 185, 187
Bus Companies, 84

C

Cartage Equipment, 84
Cathedral Route, 19
Centenary, Railway, 73
Chairmen:
  Banbury, Sir Frederick, G.N.R., 13, 17, 43, 45, 48, 62
  Duffus, Alexander, G.N.S.R., 27, 47
  Faringdon, Lord, G.C.R., 18, 44, 47, 49, 51, 57, 62, 217
  Granet, Sir Guy, Midland R., 50, 51, 214
  Hamilton, Lord Claud, G.E.R., 19, 48
  Knaresborough, Lord, N.E.R., 11, 23, 40, 43, 48, 63, 68
  Matthews, Sir Ronald, L.N.E.R., 85, 91, 219
  Meysey-Thompson, Sir Harry, N.E.R. 23
  Stamp, Sir Josiah, L.M.S.R., 50, 60, 214
  Watkin, Sir Edward, M.S.&L.R., 17, 25
  Whitelaw, William, L.N.E.R., 26, 40, 44, 48, 49, 60, 62, 66, 69, 74, 76, 79, 219
Clyde Steamers, 26, 208, 210

Coaches:
  Articulation, Gresley, 179, 182, 187
  Bogies, Compound Bolster, Gresley, 178
  Colours, 182
  "Coronation" Train-sets, 186
  "East Anglian" Train-set, 187
  "Flying Scotsman" Train-sets, 182, 184, 187
  "Hook Continental" Train-set, 182, 187
  "Silver Jubilee" Train-set, 185
  Six-a-side Suburban, 20, 180
  Sleeping Cars, First Class, 184
  Sleeping Cars, Third Class, 78, 183
  Stockton & Darlington "Experiment" 73
  With Bucket Seats, 185
  With Coupé Compartments, 182
  With Hairdressing Compartment, 184
  With Radio Receivers, 184
Coal Strike and Supplies, 75
Coal Traffic, 20, 24, 26, 30, 70, 78, 85, 91, 98, 190
Coal Trains, Express, 83
Coat of Arms, L.N.E.R., 72
Commercial Agency, N.E.R., 22
Committees:
  Railway Executive, 9, 59, 60
  Select, on Transport, 9
  Weir, Railway Electrification, 59
Commission, Railway and Canal, 35
Compensation, Railways Post-War, 13, 26, 39, 70
Conciliation Board, N.E.R., 22
Containers, Freight Train, 193
Corporation, Hull, 24
Court of Enquiry, Wages, 92

D

Defence Regulations, 1939, 87
Derailment, Prevention of, 179
Derailment, Strike, in 1926, 75
Directors:
  Bell, Sir Hugh, N.E.R., 40, 45, 51, 54, 65
  Grey, Viscount, N.E.R., 22, 41, 45, 49, 51, 74, 217
  Hope, Sir Harry, N.E.R., 41
  Joicey, Lord, N.E.R., 41, 47, 51
  Noble, John Henry, N.E.R., 45, 51
  Pease, Sir Arthur, N.E.R., 41, 45, 51
  Whigham, Walter K., N.E.R., 41, 47, 221
  Wilson, Murrough, J., N.E.R., 41, 217, 221
Dividends, 31, 76, 79, 80, 85, 88, 92
Docks and Harbours:
  Blyth, 190, 206
  Burntisland, 207
  Dunston-on-Tyne, 206
  Felixstowe, 206
  Grimsby, 17, 38, 63, 82, 205, 211

Docks and Harbours, *continued*
  Hartlepool, 206
  Harwich, Parkeston Quay, 19, 79, 82, 206
  Hull, 24, 38, 205, 208, 211
  Immingham, 17, 18, 38, 63, 206
  Lowestoft, 206
  Methil, 207
  Middlesbrough, 206
  Tyne Dock, 190, 206
Drivers, Locomotive:
  Cage, Arthur, G.E.R., 152
  Chapman, Harry, G.E.R., 153
  Duddington, L.N.E.R., 161
  Hoole, W., 168
  Pibworth, A., L.N.E.R., 121
  Sparshatt, W., L.N.E.R., 161, 163
  Young, W., G.W.R., 121

E

East Coast Trains Department, 35
East Coast Joint Stock, 25, 35, 178
East Coast Route, 16, 34
Economy Measures, 79, 80, 82, 91
Eight-hour Day, 69
Electrification:
  G.E. Suburban, 84, 100, 175, 176
  G.N. Suburban, 176
  Manchester, South Junction & Altrincham, 138, 175
  Shildon–Newport, 175
  Tyneside, 22, 175
  Wath–Manchester, 87, 90, 102, 138, 176
  Weir Committee, 59
Euston Square Confederacy, 34

F

Fastest Train in British Empire, 22, 151
Five-year Plan, Post-war, 90
Freight Traffic, 81, 85
Freight Trains, Express, 83

G

General Managers:
  Beevor, Miles, L.N.E.R., 221
  Burgess, Rt. Hon. H.G., L.M.S.R., 214
  Butterworth, Sir Alex, N.E.R., 10, 23, 40, 41, 43–45, 49, 52, 55–59, 62–66
  Calder, James, N.B.R., 26, 54, 68, 217
  Dent, Charles Hastings, G.N.R., 17, 54
  Fay, Sir Sam, G.C.R., 18, 54
  Gibb, Sir George, N.E.R., 21, 23, 40, 41, 52, 58, 65, 216, 222
  Hyde, Walter Henry, G.E.R., 20
  Newton, Sir Chas., L.N.E.R., 64, 216, 220
  Parnwell, S. A., G.E.R., 68, 215
  Pole, Sir Felix, G.W.R., 120

General Managers, *continued*
  Thornton, Sir Henry, G.E.R., 20, 54, 180, 196, 214, 218
  Walker, Sir Herbert, L.S.W.R., 9
  Watkin, Edward, H. & B. R., 25
  Watson, Arthur, L.N.W.R., 214
  Wedgwood, Sir Ralph Lewis, L.N.E.R., 23, 51, 55–60, 65, 66, 82, 120, 216, 219
General Managers, Divisional:
  Barrington-Ward, Sir Michael, 216, 221
  Davidson, George, 215
  Hornsby, Thomas, 215
  Inglis, Sir Robert, 219
  Jenkin Jones, C.M., 23, 72, 218
  Mauldin, H. H., 216, 220, 221
  Mills, George, 217, 220
  Thurston, G. F., 67, 216
  Wilson, Alex, 68, 121, 215, 216
General Strike, 1926, 70, 75, *et seq.*
Gold Standard, 79
Government, Labour, 1945, 90
Government Loans, 84
Great North Road, 62

I

Interim Joint Board, Proposed, 41
International Railway Congress, 73

J

Joint Railways, 28

K

King Edward VII, 93
King George V, 134, 200, 205
King George VI, 73, 186, 200

L

Locomotive, Details:
  Blast-pipe, Double, 135, 145, 165, 167
  Boiler, Water-tube, 128
  Boosters, 123, 129
  Brakes, 118, 119
  Colours, 111
  Compound, 108
  Cylinder Arrangements, 108
  Exchange Trials, 116, 119, 120, 129, 135
  Feed-water Heaters, 126
  Fireboxes, 110, 122
  Lettering, 118
  Numbering, 117, 143
  Roller Bearings, 146
  Streamlining, 134, 136
  Tenders, Corridor, 127, 199
  Thermic Syphons, 131, 138
  Valve-motions, 105, 109, 123, 125, 126, 132, 140, 141
  Working, Newcastle–Edinburgh, 35
Locomotives, Famous:
  G.E.R. *Decapod* 0-10-0 tank, 106,108

Locomotives, Famous, *continued*
L.B.S.C.R. *Gladstone* 0–4–2, 74
L.N.E.R. *Flying Scotsman* 4–6–2, 72, 119, 133, 142, 149, 161
L.N.E.R. *Great Northern* 4–6–2, 109, 142
L.N.E.R. *Mallard* 4–6–2, 74, 83, 134, 149, 165
L.N.E.R. *Silver Fox* 4–6–2, 165, 203
L.N.E.R. *Silver Link* 4–6–2, 133, 134, 165, 167
L.N.E.R. *Sir Nigel Gresley* 4–6–2, 168
Stockton & Darlington *Locomotion No. 1*, 73
Locomotives, Types:
G.C.R. Tender, 78, 104, 105, 107, 115, 125, 144, 154
G.C.R. Tank, 107, 108, 115, 129
G.E.R. Tender, 104, 106, 107, 115, 125, 127, 129, 130, 152, 153
G.E.R. Tank, 106–108, 115
G.N.R. Tender, 77, 103, 105, 106, 158
G.N.R. Tank, 107, 115, 117
G.N.S.R. Tender, 104, 106
N.B.R. Tender, 104, 131, 156
N.B.R. Tank, 107
N.E.R. Tender, 103, 105, 107, 116, 126, 129, 131, 144, 151, 156
N.E.R. Tank, 105
Locomotive Classes, L.N.E.R.:
A1, Gresley 4–6–2, 72, 119, 133, 142, 149, 161
A1, Peppercorn 4–6–2, 146, 173
A2, Raven 4–6–2, 105
A2/1, Peppercorn 4–6–2, 146, 172
A2/2, Thompson 4–6–2, 143, 145, 170
A3, Gresley 4–6–2, 123, 142, 163
A4, Gresley 4–6–2, 132, 140, 142, 147, 164, 168, 200
B1, Thompson 4–6–0, 140, 143, 171
B12, Holden 4–6–0, 104, 125, 127, 129, 153
B17, Gresley 4–6–0, 127, 130, 136, 143, 169
C1, Ivatt 4–4–2, 103, 158, 159
C4, Robinson 4–4–2, 104, 154
C7, Raven 4–4–2, 103, 129, 158
D11, Robinson 4–4–0, 104, 115, 155
D16, Holden 4–4–0, 104, 152
D49, Gresley 4–4–0, 125, 131, 143, 170
Garratt 2–8–8–2, No. 2395, 73, 124, 192
Gresley High Pressure, 4–6–4, No. 10000, 128
Gresley Projected 4–8–2, 136
J38, Gresley 0–6–0, 125
J39, Gresley 0–6–0, 125
K1, Thompson 2–6–0, 144
K3, Gresley 2–6–0, 106, 109, 125, 132, 143
K4, Gresley 2–6–0, 137, 144
L1, Thompson 2–6–4 Tank, 144
O2, Gresley 2–8–0, 106, 125

Locomotive Classes, L.N.E.R., *continued*
O4, Robinson 2–8–0, 105, 125, 143, 144
P1, Gresley 2–8–2, 73, 124, 132
P2, Gresley 2–8–2, 132, 137, 141, 170, 202
V1, Gresley 2–6–2 Tank, 129, 143
V2, Gresley 2–6–2, 129, 143
V3, Gresley 2–6–2 Tank, 137, 143
V4, Gresley 2–6–2, 137
London Passenger Transport Board, 83, 90

M

Marshalling Yards:
Hull, 83, 101
Mottram, 78, 83, 101
Whitemoor, March, 71, 98
Mechanical Engineers:
Bulleid, O. V. S., 114, 128, 139
Chalmers, W., 114
Chapelon, Andre, 131, 134
Churchward, G. J., 105
Collett, C. B., 121
Glaze, C. W. L., 114, 139
Gresley, Sir Nigel, 60, 68, 113, Chapters XV–XIX & XXII, 220
Harrison, J. F., 146
Heywood, T. E., 114
Hill, A. J., 106
Holden, James, 104, 151, 180
Holden, Stephen, 104
Ivatt, H. A., 105, 158
Maunsell, R. E. L., 109
Peppercorn, Arthur H., 145
Raven, Sir Vincent, 68, 113, 139
Reid, W. P., 104
Robinson, John G., 104–108, 114, 179
Stamer, A. C., 114, 120, 139
Stanier, Sir William, 109
Thom, R. A., 114, 139
Thompson, Edward, 90, 114, 129, 139, 153, 220
Webb, F. W., 17
Worsdell, Wilson, 103, 106, 108, 151
Ministry of Munitions, 58
Ministry of Transport, 10, 26, 50, 78, 81, 85
Museums, Railway, Clapham & York, 74

N

National Union of Railwaymen, 54
Nationalisation, 69, 91
Newton Plan, 80, 91
Non-stop Runs, London–Edinburgh, 126, 128, 199

O

Officers, Railway:
Bell, Robert, 67, 222
Brown, Charles, J., 218

Officers, Railway, *continued*
  Burtt, Philip, 58
  Clow, W. M., 216
  Dunnell, Sir Francis, 68, 216
  Edwards, C. L., 68, 216
  Gibb, Paul, 216
  Gibson, A. L., 79, 220
  Gracie, W. M., 192
  Kerr, Kenelm, 67
  Lambert, C. A., 217
  Maclure, W. G. P., 121
  Marriott, William, 29
  Miller, John, 218
  Paget, Sir Cecil, 72
  Pearson, A. J., 60
  Petrie, John J., 29
  Pritchard, I. Buchanan, 216
  Spencer, B., 120, 137, 145
  Stemp, C. H., 26
  Teasdale, W. M., 68, 217
  Train, Sir Landale, 219, 221
  Trask, E. D., 121
  Watson, H. A., 156
  Watson, James, 41
  Weeks, W. T., 68
  Wickham, J. A., 217

P

Paris Exhibition, 1900, 117
Passenger Duty, 78
Personalities:
  Acworth, Sir William, 13
  Allom, Sir Charles, 184
  Brabazon, Lord, 60
  Darwin, Charles, 58
  Geddes, Sir Eric, 10, 27, 48, 50, 58,
    69, 82
  George, Prince, Duke of Kent, 209
  Haig, Sir Douglas, 11
  Hudson, George, 22, 23, 34
  Salter, Sir Arthur, 81, 86
  Stephenson, George, 73
  Stephenson, Robert, 93
  Thomas, J. H., 54
  Wedgwood, Josiah, 58
  York, Duke & Duchess of, 73
Prime Ministers:
  Law, Bonar, 71
  Lloyd George, David, 10, 11, 69
Pullman Cars, 180, 187, 195
Pullman Trains:
  Clacton Belle, 198
  Eastern Belle Limited, 198
  Queen of Scots, 159, 198
  Harrogate Pullman, 195, 196, 198
  Sheffield Pullman, 197
  Tees–Tyne Pullman, 204
  West Riding Pullman, 136, 197
  Yorkshire Pullman, 198, 201, 203
Punctual Expresses, C.L.C., 28
Punctuality, G.E.R. Suburban, 19

Q

Quaker Tradition, N.E.R., 21

Queen Elizabeth, 73
Queen Mary, 134
Queen Victoria, 28, 93

R

Race to Aberdeen, 36, 198
Rail-brakes, Fröhlich, 98
Railcars, Steam, 78, 130
Rail-Road Conference, 1931, 81
Railway Clerks Association, 71
Railway Companies Association, 71, 81
Railway Executive Committee, 9, 59, 60,
  61
Railway Rates Tribunal, 60
Railways Absorbed by L.N.E.R., 14
Railways Act, 1921, 9, 13, 38, 39, 48, 70
Railways L.N.E.R. Constituent:
  Great Central, 17
  Great Eastern, 19
  Great North of Scotland,
    27
  Great Northern, 16
  Hull & Barnsley, 23
  North British, 25
  North Eastern, 21
    } With many
      other
      references
      throughout
      the book
Railways, Other:
  Border Counties, 25
  Caledonian, 16, 25, 98, 181
  Canadian National, 55
  Cheshire Lines Committee, 14, 28
  Eastern Counties, 30
  Great Northern & Great Eastern
    Joint, 20, 30, 78
  Great Northern & London & North
    Western Joint, 30
  Great Southern & Western, 17
  Great Western, 18, 22, 23, 72, 73,
    82, 88, 119, 184, 216
  Highland, 25, 103
  Lancashire & Yorkshire, 16, 22, 34,
    38, 208
  London & Birmingham, 34
  London & North Western, 16, 22, 38,
    95, 97
  London & South Western, 9, 22
  London, Brighton & South Coast, 74,
    196
  London, Midland & Scottish, 14, 28,
    38, 52, 60, 71, 73, 82, 85, 88, 109,
    170, 181, 184, 198, 201, 214
  London Tilbury & Southend, 20, 97
  Long Island, U.S.A., 20
  Manchester, Sheffield & Lincolnshire,
    17, 97, 206
  Metropolitan, 97, 99
  Midland, 16, 22, 24, 25, 28, 29, 35,
    50, 52, 72, 97
  Midland & Great Northern Joint, 14,
    20, 29
  Midland Counties, 34
  Newcastle & Berwick, 34
  Newcastle & Darlington, 34
  Paris–Orleans, 131, 132
  Pennsylvania, U.S.A., 105

Railway, Other, *continued*
  South Eastern & Chatham, 39, 196
  Southern, 73, 88, 109, 194
  Stockton & Darlington, 21, 73
  West Highland, 25, 137, 181
  York & North Midland, 34
Record Speeds, 134, 161, 165
Restaurant Cars, 17, 20, 179, 184, 188
Road & Rail Traffic Bill, 81
Road Competition, 79, 80, 84, 85
Road Services, 28, 77
Royal Trains, 19, 28, 73
Running Powers, 21, 24, 25, 30, 97, 98

S

Ships:
  Great Central, 207
  Great Eastern, 207
  L.N.E.R. Fleet (Table 30), 212
  Lost in 1939–1945 War, 211
  New Post-War Ships, 213
  North British, 208
Shipping Services:
  Associated Humber Lines, 85
  Clyde Steamers, 208, 210
  Harwich–Zeebrugge Train-Ferry, 209
  Hull–New Holland Ferry, 208, 210
  Hull–Zeebrugge, 208
  Parkeston Quay–Antwerp, 206, 212
  Parkeston Quay–Esbjerg, 206, 209, 212
  Parkeston Quay–Hook of Holland, 206, 207, 209, 212
Signalling:
  All-electric signal boxes, 100, 101
  Automatic, 100, 101
  Electro-pneumatic, Newcastle, 101
  Entrance-exit Panel, Thirsk, 100
  Hall Electro-pneumatic, 100
  Low-pressure Pneumatic, 101
  "Somersault" Signal Arms, 17
Staff National Tribunal, Railway, 87
Standardisation, 90, 143
Stations:
  Aberdeen General, 27, 98
  Berwick, 99
  Cambridge, 97
  Clacton-on-Sea, 99
  Colchester, 102
  Darlington Bank Top, 96
  Edinburgh Waverley, 25, 36, 95
  Euston, 34
  Fenchurch Street, 97
  Gidea Park, 99
  Glasgow Queen Street, 98
  Hull Paragon, 22, 95
  King's Cross, 16, 17, 34, 96, 99, 101
  Leeds New, 96
  Liverpool Street, 19, 60, 96
  Manchester Central, 97
  Manchester London Road, 97
  Marylebone, 17, 97
  Newcastle Central, 96, 101
  Norwich Thorpe, 97

Stations, *continued*
  Nottingham Victoria, 17, 97
  Perth General, 97
  Romford, 99
  St. Pancras, 96
  Sheffield Victoria, 97
  Southend Victoria, 102
  York, 22, 95, 102
Statistical Scrap-Book, Butterworth, 43
Stockholders' Association, 79
Strike, General, 1926, 70, 75 *et seq.*
Suburban Traffic, G.E.R., 20, 84, 90, 180
Sugar Beet Traffic, 71, 78, 98
Superannuation Fund, 71
Suspension of New Works, Pre-war, 87

T

Through Coach Working, 36
Tickets, First Class, 1,000-Mile, 22
Tourist Trains, 185
Trains:
  Aberdonian, 132, 203
  Caledonian, 37
  Cambridge Buffet Expresses, 185, 202
  Cheltenham Flyer, 150
  Clacton Belle, 198
  Cornish Riviera Express, 121, 203
  Coronation, 36, 60, 83, 134, 150, 163, 165, 173, 189, 200, 203
  Coronation Scot, 36
  East Anglian, 136, 187, 189, 201, 203
  Eastern Belle, 198
  Fastest in British Empire, 22, 151
  Fife Coast Express, 189
  Flying Hamburger, 133
  Flying Scotsman, 35, 36, 127, 128, 162, 173, 189, 200, 203
  Harrogate Pullman, 195, 196, 198
  Hook Continental, 153, 180, 182, 187, 189, 195
  Master Cutler, 188, 203
  Norfolk Coast Express, 152, 180
  North Briton, 180
  Queen of Scots, 159, 198
  Royal Scot, 37, 198
  Sheffield Pullman, 197
  Scarborough Flyer, 161, 201
  Silver Jubilee, 60, 83, 134, 150, 165, 185, 200
  Talisman, 36, 173, 188
  Tees–Tyne Pullman, 204
  West Riding Limited, 60, 83, 134, 136, 187, 189, 200
  West Riding Pullman, 136, 197
Trades Unions, 27, 54, 70, 75
Traffic Apprenticeship Scheme, 21, 89, 222
Transport Act, 1947, 91
Transport Advisory Council, 86, 87
Transport, Ministry of, 10, 26, 50, 78, 81, 85
Transportation, Director-General of, 58
Transportation, Inspector-General of, 20

W

Wage Reduction, Voluntary, 77
Wagon Control, Central, 71
Wagons:
All-steel, 191
Bolster, 191
Brick, 191
Cantilever (Outsize Loads), 192, 193
Coal, 190, 191
Hopper, 190

Wagons, *continued*
Refrigerator, 192
Steel Plate, 191
War Office, 11, 18
Waverley Route, 25, 26
West Coast Route, 16, 36
Widenings of Line, 78, 83, 99, 102

Z

Zeeland Shipping Company, 79, 209